ALL-NIGHT PARTY

Actress Aileen Dresser and two revelers. Photo by Jessie Tarbox Beals.

ALL-NIGHT PARTY

THE WOMEN OF BOHEMIAN
GREENWICH VILLAGE AND HARLEM
1913–1930

Andrea Barnet

Algonquin Books of Chapel Hill   2004

Published by
Algonquin Books of Chapel Hill
Post Office Box 2225
Chapel Hill, North Carolina 27515-2225

a division of
Workman Publishing
708 Broadway
New York, New York 10003

First published in German translation under the title *Crazy New York:
Die Frauen von Harlem und Greenwich Village*, edition ebersbach, Berlin, 2001.
Printed in the United States of America.
Published simultaneously in Canada by Thomas Allen & Son Limited.

Library of Congress Cataloging-in-Publication Data
Barnet, Andrea.
    [Crazy New York. English]
    All-night party : the women of bohemian Greenwich Village and
Harlem, 1913–1930 / by Andrea Barnet.—1st ed.
      p. cm.
    Originally published: Crazy New York. Berlin : Edition Ebersbach, 2001.
    Includes bibliographical references and index.
    ISBN 1-56512-381-6
    1. New York (N.Y.)—History—1898–1951. 2. Women—New York (State)—
New York—History—20th century. 3. Bohemianism—New York (State)—New
York—History—20th century. 4. Greenwich Village (New York, N.Y.)—
Intellectual life—20th century. 5. Harlem (New York, N.Y.)—Intellectual life—
20th century. 6. New York (N.Y.)—Intellectual life—20th century. I. Title.

F128.5.B26513 2004
305.4'09747'1—dc22   2003066444

10 9 8 7 6 5 4 3 2 1
First Edition

Jacket design: Anne Winslow
Front cover photographs (clockwise from top left): Mina Loy (Stephen Haweis, courtesy of Rare Book and Manuscript Library, Columbia University [Stephen Haweis Papers]); Jane Heap (Berenice Abbott, © Commerce Graphics Ltd., Inc.); Bessie Smith (Frank Driggs, courtesy of Schomburg Center for Research in Black Culture, Photographs and Print Division, the New York Public Library); Alberta Hunter (Frank Driggs, Schomburg); Mabel Dodge (Berenice Abbott, © Commerce Graphics, Ltd., Inc.); Ethel Waters (Frank Driggs, Schomburg); Edna St. Vincent Millay (Special Collections, Vassar College Libraries); Fania Marinoff (Nicholas Muray, *Vanity Fair*, July 1922); Mina Loy and Djuna Barnes (Man Ray, © Man Ray Trust, Paris/VG BildKunst, Bonn [Princeton])

For Kit, who makes everything possible,
and Philippa, who keeps me smiling,
And to Lily Brett, for the gift of this book.

Beauty for the eye, satire for the mind, depravity for the senses! Of such is the new kingdom of art. Amen.
—Dame Rogue (Louise Norton), 1915

CONTENTS

Partygoers dressed for a Greenwich Village artist's ball. Photo by Jessie Tarbox Beals.

ACKNOWLEDGMENTS

No book is a solo endeavor. I owe enormous thanks to a great many people for their contributions to this one. I am deeply indebted to my writer friends Barbara Wright and Sheran James, who each provided close readings and sensitive editorial advice at crucial junctures, and to my original German publisher, Brigitte Ebersbach, whose enthusiasm and belief in the project spurred me on, as well as to her hard-working assistants Anett Schwarz and Ilka Litzke.

Thanks also to Kurt Andersen and Jonathan Galassi for their generous readings of the manuscript and publishing advice; to my agent Jennifer Lyons, who gave up far too many hours during her pregnancy leave to complete the contract; and to Maria Campbell, for her wise counsel in leading me to Jennifer.

Special thanks are due to Elisabeth Scharlatt, my publisher, for her savvy, her enthusiasm, and her in-depth knowledge of the period; my editor, Andra Olenik, for her perceptive reading and smart editorial suggestions; to Constance Sayre, for her unforgettable help at the Frankfurt book fair; and to Paul Chaleff, for introducing me to Constance. Grateful thanks also to Roger L. Conover for permission to use photographs from his private collection and to quote from Mina Loy's published work and to Carolyn Burke and Francis M. Naumann for permission to use photographs from their private collections. I am indebted to Bonnie Yochelson for invaluable help in securing permissions for Berenice Abbott photographs; to Deb Futter and Bill Cohan for their generosity in giving me a summer writing space when I had none; to Steven Hoffman and Howard Watler for their time and expertise in helping me with photographs; to Kim Sloane, Michael Anderson, and Geoff Young for sharing several difficult-to-find, out-of-print books from their libraries; to Adam Van Doren for an article by his great-uncle Carl Van Doren, which I hadn't known existed; and to John Coston for an article by Ethel Waters.

Thanks are also due to Barbara Ensor, Lili Francklyn, Kim Springer, Barbara Fey, James Barnet, and my daughter, Pippa White, for sympathetic readings of individual chapters; Bill Strong for copyright advice; Heidi Cunnick for generously arranging my first reading; Bill Pangburn for expert German translation skills, Jill Choder for wise coaching, Caroline Stewart for flowers at a critical moment; and Eliza Hicks for her time and generosity in taking photographs. Finally, I remain forever grateful to my husband, Kit White, for his extraordinary patience and unflagging emotional support, for readings far beyond the call of duty, and for gourmet cooking that never stopped.

I would also like to acknowledge the many generous museum and library curators who shared their time and expertise during my search for photographs, and provided inestimable help with photographic reproductions and permissions. Special thanks to Margarite Lavin at the Museum of the City of New York; Marie-Helene Gold, Schlesinger Library, Radcliffe Institute; Dean Rogers, Special Collections, Vassar College; Margaret M. Sherry and Annalee Pauls, Rare Books and Special Collections, Princeton University Library; Ben Primer, Harvey S. Firestone Library, Princeton University; Matt Wiegle, Yale Collection of American Literature, Beinecke Rare Book and Manuscript Library; Geraldine Aramanda, The Menil Collection, Houston; Christine Maass, Special Collections, Golda Meir Library, University of Wisconsin, Milwaukee; Bruce Kellner, trustee to the Estate of Carl Van Vechten; Evanne Gargiulo, Commerce Graphics; Jane Siegel and Dr. Jean Ashton, Rare Book and Manuscript Library, Columbia University; Beth Alverez, Special Collections, University of Maryland Libraries; Stacey Bomento, Philadelphia Museum of Art; Julie Zeptel, Metropolitan Museum of Art.

Though I have made every effort to trace copyright holders, I would be most grateful to hear from any who have been missed.

CAST OF CHARACTERS

Berenice Abbott (1898–1991) A photographer who took portraits of many of the female modernists and who began her career as Man Ray's studio assistant. In the 1930s, she made her name taking pictures of a now vanished New York.

Margaret Anderson (1886–1973) Founder and editor of the avant-garde magazine the *Little Review*. The companion of Jane Heap and a resident of Greenwich Village from 1916 to 1922.

Louise Arensberg (1879–1953) Salon hostess. Patron of modern art and the wife of Walter Arensberg.

Djuna Barnes (1892–1984) A journalist known for her arch cultural commentary. She also wrote sardonic poetry, dreamlike plays, short stories, and several novels with lesbian themes. Her experimental novel *Nightwood* is an underground classic.

Mabel Dodge (1879–1962) Fabulously wealthy, her fabled salon on lower Fifth Avenue was the social hub of early Greenwich Village. She was an early convert to psychoanalysis, a pioneer in free love, one of the impresarios of the scandalous 1913 Armory Show, the first international exhibition of modern art in America, and a generous patron of the arts.

Isadora Duncan (1878–1927) A pioneer of modern dance, a member of the Arensberg circle, and an outspoken champion of women's emancipation. She lived most of her life in Paris.

Left: Alberta Hunter. Photo by Frank Driggs, 1934.

Baroness Elsa von Freytag-Loringhoven (1874–1927) German-born artist, poet, artist's model, and eccentric, she personified the essence of New York Dada. She was a member of the Arensberg circle and a cohort of Marcel Duchamp, Mina Loy, and Djuna Barnes.

Emma Goldman (1869–1940) An anarchist, women's rights activist, writer, and the symbol of working-class militancy. She lectured on free speech, birth control, free love, and radical politics, and edited the anarchist magazine *Mother Earth.* She was arrested and incarcerated countless times.

Jane Heap (1884–1964) Writer, legendary conversationalist, and co-editor, with her companion, Margaret Anderson, of the avant-garde literary magazine the *Little Review.*

Alberta Hunter (1897–1984) Songwriter and blues singer known for her glamorous style and sophistication. She performed both in Broadway revues and at A'Lelia Walker's legendary Harlem Renaissance salons.

Mina Loy (1882–1966) English-born painter and modernist poet, she experimented in free verse, designed her own clothes, acted, created stage sets, and was widely published in Greenwich Village literary magazines between the wars.

Edna St. Vincent Millay (1892–1950) A poet, playwright, and much-sought-after figure in Greenwich Village in the 1920s, she was the first woman ever to be awarded the Pulitzer Prize for Poetry.

Marianne Moore (1887–1972) Modernist poet and editor of *The Dial* magazine, she was intensely private and lived with her mother all her life.

Ma Rainey (1886–1939) Known as the Mother of the Blues, she was one of the greatest blues singers ever, second only to Bessie Smith. A brassy, tough-talking diva, she was openly lesbian.

Margaret Sanger (1897–1966) Led the birth control movement in America and published a feminist newspaper, *The Woman Rebel*. In 1914–15, she fled to Europe to avoid arrest for publishing birth control information, returning to New York in 1916.

Bessie Smith (1894–1937) Earthy and famously hot-tempered, a wild, violent, hard-drinking woman who indulged her appetite for alcohol and sex to extremes. Dubbed the "Empress of the Blues," she was an immensely talented singer and an electrifying performer.

Gertrude Stein (1874–1946) A modernist writer and one of the foremost collectors of Postimpressionist art, she presided over a legendary salon in Paris. Her radical literary experiments influenced countless others, including Mina Loy.

Clara Tice (1888–1973) An artist and illustrator known for her stylish line drawings of female nudes, butterflies, and dogs. She designed posters and invitations for the Greenwich Village artists' balls, and from 1915–1921 was a regular illustrator for *Vanity Fair* as well as underground magazines such as *Rogue*.

A'Lelia Walker (1885–1931) Harlem's premier social hostess, she was the richest black woman in America, heiress to a mighty beauty empire built from a secret patented hair treatment that "dekinked" black women's hair. The guest lists for her glittering interracial parties of the 1920s were a veritable who's who of the arts.

Ethel Waters (1896–1977) One of the first black vocalists to take her blues-based jazz into the cultural mainstream, she broke down barriers for black entertainers in music, theater, nightclubs, and film. She was a sex symbol and recording star in the 1920s, a Broadway actress in the 1930s, and a Hollywood film star in the 1940s.

Beatrice Wood (1893–1998) An artist and ceramicist, she was part of the irreverent modernist circle that included Marcel Duchamp, Man Ray, Francis Picabia, the Arensbergs, Edgard Varèse, and Mina Loy. A co-founder of *The Blind Man* magazine, one of the earliest manifestations of the Dada art movement, she lived in New York until 1928.

Elinor Wylie (1886–1928) A poet and creature of scandal, she was born into a socially prominent family and moved to New York in 1922, where she quickly became part of Manhattan literary society. She was a close friend of Edna St. Vincent Millay and married the poet Bill Benet in 1924.

ALL-NIGHT PARTY

INTRODUCTION

WILD IN PURSUIT

When the exquisitely impulsive Louise Brooks, a teenage Ziegfeld Follies girl, stepped off the train from her native Kansas and glanced up at the soaring Manhattan skyline, she "fell in love with New York forever."

"No one who has not lived in New York has lived in the Modern World," pronounced the artist and writer Mina Loy in 1916.

"How do I like New York?" wrote the twenty-year-old poet Edna St. Vincent Millay to her mother in 1913: "Oh inexpressibly!"

In the flamboyant and irreverent years of the 1910s and 1920s, bohemian New York, like Paris and Berlin, acquired "mythic status." It was the apotheosis of the new, a flashpoint of artistic and intellectual energy. There was an improvident, risk-taking spirit in the air, a celebration of spontaneity, experiment, creativity, and spectacle.

In Greenwich Village, cradle to the avant-garde, the dream of a cultural revolution was ubiquitous. Creative dissent, whether expressed as artistic innovation or as liberating lifestyle, was the revolutionary cri de coeur; sparkling talk and racy innuendo were the fashion. Sexual relations between men and women were lusty and unbinding. In bars and crowded basement restaurants, literary salons and former stables turned into ateliers; the talk was of Freud, free love, feminism, homosexuality, modern art, birth control, personal fulfillment, and radical politics.

Victorian morality was the oppressor, a code worthy of ridicule if not outright subversion. "Going public with one's animal nature" was the vogue, as were jazz and its companion the blues, both creations of a much-neglected black America, both perfect expressions of the stepped-up, sexually charged rhythms of the era. White bohemians not only embraced the music; they borrowed the frankly libidinous dances it spawned—steps with suggestive names like Scratchin' the Gravel and Ballin' the Jack, the Lovers' Walk and the Shiver.

Revelers migrated nightly to Harlem's hot spots to bump and grind in crowded speakeasies or sumptuous clubs with shimmering floor shows. They flocked to cabarets and raucous honky-tonk joints, awash in "bathtub" gin;

Greenwich Village, Christopher and Bleecker Streets. Photo by Berenice Abbott.

thronged dance halls and late-night eateries like Tillie's Chicken Shack or Pod's & Jerry's, wrapping up their revels at "rent parties," where couples gyrated until dawn and celebrity musicians like Fats Waller and Duke Ellington tuned up at 4 A.M.

Harlem was an ongoing after-hours extravaganza, a place where the rebellious rich and the bohemian poor rubbed shoulders. There was elegance and exotic low life—the glamorous Cotton Club and seedy dives like "buffet flats," where "varied and often perverse sexual pleasures were offered cafeteria style." Harlem's sizzling nightlife drew everyone from Charlie Chaplin to the Rothschilds, gangsters to the moneyed Park Avenue set, Village bohemians to European royalty.

THE ENACTMENT IN 1919 of Prohibition, a nationwide ban on the sale and consumption of alcohol, not only intensified the lawlessness in the air; it also gave the forbidden an aura of glamour. Overnight, from one end of Manhattan to another, a vast underground network of speakeasies appeared, making heroes of mobsters, fools of the police. As bootleg liquor bloomed into big business and illegal bars and nightclubs multiplied, café society rubbed shoulders with gangsters, black artists with white bohemians and the well-heeled. In the shared desire for transgression, all lines invited crossing: racial, sexual, artistic, and, of course, social.

Liquor was easing the way to a new informality of manners. "Nice girls" were swigging from hip flasks, going out joyriding with men at 4 A.M., petting and necking in parked cars. Along Harlem's Lenox Avenue, alcohol could be bought almost anywhere: in shoe shops, at newsstands, in delicatessens, stationery shops, and soda fountains. In Greenwich Village it was much the same. A rough count of the illegal speakeasies in Manhattan alone was estimated at between "a monstrous 32,000 and an unbelievable 100,000."

IT WAS AGAINST this backdrop of gaiety mixed with social subversion that the women of Harlem and Greenwich Village began to plot their own parallel insurgent stories. In fashion as well as art and politics, disdain for the stifling pieties of bourgeois morality was palpable. The stout, full-figured Victorian matron was out, replaced by her emancipated sister, the angular, scantily clad flapper with her bobbed hair and slash of red lipstick, her brazen sexuality and outspoken views. The new paradigm was petite Irene Castle. She and her husband, Vernon, were successfully turning the mania for dancing into a permanent fixture of the 1920s: As the historian Lloyd Morris writes:

Cheese Store, 276 Bleecker Street.
Photo by Berenice Abbott.

The Castles were not only national idols, but national arbiters of etiquette . . . dainty Irene Castle was setting sartorial fashion. Because Castle dances were mildly acrobatic, she had bobbed her hair, replaced unyielding corsets by an elastic girdle, substituted silk bloomers and a slip for petticoats, adopted short, light, flowing frocks . . . these radical innovations soon produced a nationwide revolution in feminine attire. The final collapse of a whaleboned morality was signalized by "the new lingerie, in which everything is combined in one garment, easily slipped on." And—as the wild younger generation soon discovered— just as easily slipped off.

It wasn't only white women who were discarding their corsets. By 1914, black society women were doing the tango and other "modern" Castle dances. Moral watchdogs in Harlem warned that "the Negro race [was] dancing itself to death." *The Age,* one of the oldest and largest black newspapers in the city, admonished women entertainers for being "extremely careless about their attitudes and actions in dancing"—Ethel Waters being one of the most forthright.

Self-confident and hungry for adventure, the new modern woman not only drank, smoked, and talked like men; she insisted—whether white or black—on living with the same liberties and sexual license, rejecting the demands of motherhood and family. Rebellion was brewing in every corner, from the anarchist Emma Goldman's fiery lectures on free love to Margaret Sanger's controversial birth control pamphlets to the modernist poet Mina Loy's "lewd," sexually explicit poetry to the virtuoso black dancer Ethel Williams's salacious dance steps.

The desire to overturn a repressive, moribund culture was making unlikely allies among distinctly different political and artistic camps. For a brief but exhilarating moment, New York bohemia experienced a cultural commingling of blacks and whites, poets and painters, Americans and Europeans, anarchists and modernists, men and women, with Greenwich Village and Harlem as its twin centers.

FOR WOMEN, THE revolutionary years in Greenwich Village began not in the 1920s, in fact, but in the early teens. A small band of artists and intellectuals, regulars at Mabel Dodge's fabled Fifth Avenue salon or the newly formed feminist group the Heterodoxy Club, began filling the little magazines and newspapers with their poetry, pictures, and radical convictions. They lived impecuniously and informally, often cooperatively, eating together, criticizing one another's work, gathering with their lovers and male cohorts in the tearooms and inexpensive restaurants that filled the neighborhood.

They were a wide-ranging and disparate circle, loosely joined by a network of intersecting friendships and artistic patronage. Not all were poets, artists, and writers. Some were salon hostesses, some editors and publishers, some simply provocateurs. Mina Loy, the English avant-garde poet and painter, was an expatriate, as was the German-born Dadaist eccentric, Baroness Elsa von Freytag-Loringhoven. Others were escapees from the American provinces.

The poet Edna St. Vincent Millay came from rural Maine; the journalist Djuna Barnes from upstate New York; the infamous wit Jane Heap, co-publisher with Margaret Anderson of the *Little Review*, from Chicago.

Their passions, artistic ambitions, and private lives were equally various. Mina Loy was self-consciously, willfully modern; determined to live and speak in the emancipated voice of the "new woman." Marianne Moore, prim and schoolmarmish, desired neither travel nor the bohemian life, choosing to live sedately with her mother. Mina appeared at poetry readings in a leopard-skin coat. Marianne dressed in sober Victorian tailored suits and her trademark black tricorne hat. The flamboyant Baroness wore fantastical clothes made from found objects—a bra fashioned from tin cans; a birdcage necklace, complete with a live canary—turning her person into a work of art.

The disparities in their economic circumstances were similarly extreme. Some, like Mabel Dodge, had money and used it to help others to live or publish. Others were poor. There were weeks when Margaret Anderson and Jane Heap lived solely on a diet of potatoes. The Baroness worked for pennies as an artist's model. Mina Loy designed lampshades and made her own clothes. Edna Millay wrote commercial potboilers under a pseudonym when funds were low.

What they all had in common was that none lived conventional "feminine" lives. Some were lesbian, some bisexual; some promiscuous, some seemingly asexual. Djuna Barnes was gay and childless. Edna St. Vincent Millay, also childless, was bisexual, although she married. Elinor Wylie had a son whom she abandoned to live incognito with a lover. Beatrice Wood "loved seven men she didn't marry, and married two men she didn't love." Marianne Moore chose celibacy.

What connected these women, even the black blues divas from Harlem like Bessie Smith, Ethel Waters, and Alberta Hunter, who faced down different taboos and lived in a different part of town, was the way in which they dealt with the anomaly of being women *and* artists. How they contrived to ensure the necessary space for creative work; how they negotiated the bonds of monogamy, marriage, childbearing, and economic dependence; how they

Herald Square, West 34th Street and Broadway. Photo by Berenice Abbott.

expressed their feminism in their lives and their work—these were the common threads of their collective insurgency.

IN THE MOST literal sense, the degree to which white and black women formed a conscious "community" was negligible. Yet despite all that separated their respective worlds, there were surprising overlaps in their social lives and in their friendships. Bessie Smith and Ethel Waters were often guests at the same Carl Van Vechten parties as Edna St. Vincent Millay and Elinor Wylie. Mabel Dodge entertained black performers at her Greenwich Village soirees, while her black counterpart in Harlem, A'Lelia Walker, was hosting white high society and bohemians in *her* salon in Harlem. The commingling of class and race was both an expression of freedom from a separated society and a gleeful transgression against it. However, for women there was added

significance: The social fluidity of the age not only fed but linked their shared drive for emancipation. If the encounters between black and white females didn't always lead to friendships, the fact that their lives crossed so continuously prophesied the new world that awaited women who embraced them as models.

WHEREAS THE VILLAGE was a magnet for white bohemians, it was to Harlem that black women were drawn. The promise of Harlem was personal freedom—not only the anonymity to allow a black woman to live as she wanted but real alternatives to the heterosexual imperative and to occupational choices beyond those historically open to her sex: domestic work or prostitution. Harlem signified opportunity: recording contracts, places to publish or perform, and, for rising stars like Bessie Smith and Ethel Waters, the chance to play before white audiences—something not only new but culture-altering.

It was not so much what the neighborhood north of 125th Street gave but what it didn't take away that was important. Harlem was a quarter that left its newcomers alone, and in Harlem, at that novel moment, everyone seemed to be a recent arrival fleeing the bigotry of another place.

By 1918, the mass migration of southern blacks moving north to urban cities had peaked, doubling Harlem's population in less than a decade and seeding an explosion in the arts, a flowering in the music, entertainment, and literary worlds that would be later dubbed the Harlem Renaissance.

"It was a period when every season there was at least one hit play on Broadway acted by a Negro cast," recalled the black poet Langston Hughes. "Books by Negro authors were being published with . . . greater frequency than ever before." The music industry was recording black music by black vocalists for the first time.

For black America, the timing couldn't have been more propitious. Progressive white thinkers—in revolt against intolerant, philistine America, disillusioned with war and searching for authenticity—greeted the onslaught of

Left: **Manhattan Skyline II. Photo by Berenice Abbott.**

Map of pleasure: Nightclubs in Harlem, 1932.

black talent and ambition as the answer to their prayers. As Carl Van Doren, editor of *Century Magazine,* declared in 1924, "What American literature decidedly needs at this moment is color, music, gusto, the free expression of gay or desperate moods. If the Negroes are not in a position to contribute these items, I do not know what Americans are."

According to the 1926 *Vanity Fair,* the Negro was "in the ascendancy." And so, paradoxically, was the black woman, who previously had always occupied the lowest rung of the social ladder, a victim of discrimination from the broader society and suppression within her own community. As the writer Julia Cooper pointed out as early as 1904, the "colored" woman "is confronted by both a woman question and a race problem." Yet in the transgressive, racially mixed Harlem of the Jazz Age, the lowly black woman was suddenly, improbably, being given a leg up.

Though female writers of color were making modest inroads into the mainstream literary world—Zora Neale Hurston wrote two of the era's most celebrated novels; Jessie Fauset was the literary editor of the movement's most influential journal—it was the blues women, the singers, who most embodied the possibilities of power and personal freedom that a black woman might attain. Even before the jazzmen stepped onstage, the blues queens, as the best paid and most popular of all black performers, were reinventing the possibilities for black women—and black entertainers—in every field.

Bold and brassy singers like Bessie Smith, Ma Rainey, Alberta Hunter, even the more polished Ethel Waters, strutted and shimmied, singing their hearts out, accruing power and respect by openly defying old stereotypes. Offstage they lived as they liked, flaunting their raucous ways, gleefully indifferent to social rules. Like their bohemian counterparts downtown, few had traditional marriages; most were either bisexual or lesbian. Almost none had children.

The truth of their lyrics was cathartic for the singers, as well as their female audiences, who identified with their tales of two-timing husbands and no-good men. If most sang first to explore their own feelings, they also gave voice and affirmation to the collective emotions of the black community. Regal as queens in their sequined gowns and shimmering satins, their furs and feather boas, the blues women proved that a black female could be outspoken and sexually savvy, financially independent and physically attractive. They projected a bold, new paradigm of what a black woman could be: assertive, complex, sensuous, and indomitable.

HARLEM AND GREENWICH Village were places where women of energy and spirit, free of the encumbrances of the outside world, could invent their way. Those who came—Mina Loy, Margaret Anderson, Jane Heap, Djuna Barnes, Mabel Dodge, Edna St. Vincent Millay, Alberta Hunter, Bessie Smith, Ethel Waters—possessed a new self-consciousness about themselves as women, as well as what Carole Marks has called an "anarchy of spirit." The contrasts between them were often dramatic: Bessie Smith was a barroom brawler; Mina Loy a worldly sophisticate. Ethel Waters grew up in a slum shanty; Beatrice Wood was raised with a ladies' maid. Margaret Anderson

The chorus line from the Broadway show *Dixie,* 1924.

was eternally optimistic; Edna Millay was a depressive. And yet, even with all that divided them, there were striking similarities—both in the parallel impulses that drove them and in the common problems they faced. For they grappled with so many of the same conflicts and quandaries: the confusions that came with sexual freedom; the destructive aspects of romantic love; the sacrifices attendant to creating an identity independent of men, versus the need for emotional ballast; the powerful, sometimes undermining influence of mothers—or the absence of mothers; and the difficulties of balancing emotional satisfaction with artistic need, that is, love with work.

"I have come to know by experience that work is the nearest thing to happiness I can find," wrote the black novelist Zora Neale Hurston, who made her way through life mostly alone.

Yet even work came with few guarantees. When it faltered, as it sometimes did for these women, the emotional costs could be devastating. Loneliness, breakdown, alcoholism, and retreat were common. Even so, the capacity of these women to reinvent themselves, often against tremendous odds, was seemingly endless. However severe their setbacks, these were women who lived and created against the grain, subverting the expected; women who moved bravely forward without aid of map or model. For all their uncertainties, none backed down or gave in; none stopped believing that their lives as women were theirs to shape.

CHAPTER 1

MINA LOY

A MODERN SELF-EXPERIMENT

In the summer of 1916, in Florence, Italy, a strikingly beautiful young woman waited with her small towheaded daughter at the passport office. The woman would soon be moving to New York, leaving both her daughter and son behind in Florence. Having placed them in the care of their Italian nurse and in the able hands, she hoped, of the English school where she had enrolled them, she promised herself that she wouldn't abandon them for long.

She was not an unfeeling mother; she believed what she was doing was the right thing. She saw herself as someone setting out on a crucial journey, a kind of pilgrim's progress of the soul, an adventure that she defined for herself—no doubt to justify her decision to leave the children—in nothing less than heroic terms. She had come to believe that there was a new way to live as a woman in the world; not because she'd seen it done but because she could no longer imagine enduring the confinements of the old way, a life such as her mother had lived, engulfed by an unappeasable rage, hobbled by the shackles of the familial and the domestic.

If she was guilty of benign neglect of her children, in her own mind she had cast it as something quite different: not hardheartedness but an act of responsibility. She realized that in order for her life to change, she must script her own story. It was no longer permissible to be a victim of circumstances, which is what, up until now, she had been.

Left: Mina Loy

The line inched forward slowly. The woman thought of the children. They wouldn't miss her terribly, she told herself. Her daughter, Joella, was nine now; her son, Giles, was seven. They were old enough to stand on their own. She would send for them once she earned some money.

She glanced down at her daughter now, saw the flicker of adoration that crossed her face as she tended the doll nestled in her arms, and felt her throat tighten. "I must run away from this [feeling]," the woman remembered thinking, recording it later in her journal. Swallowing hard, she beat back the swell of maternal longing. Anxious feelings about motherhood crowded in now, "that gripping panic," as she would later describe it, "that so long had worn on me" choking off the other, more vulnerable, sensation. She steeled herself, determined not to be overwhelmed by her doubts.

Mina's children, Joella and Giles, in Florence, 1911

AS THE ENGLISH-BORN artist and poet Mina Loy later elaborated in her fragmented memoirs, it had been hard to scrape together even the money for a single passage. Unbeknownst to her estranged husband, Stephen Haweis, she had sold his antiques to raise the funds: the Jacobean chests and Queen Anne tables, the china and silver. A penniless philanderer from one of England's oldest families, Haweis had all but abandoned her anyway. He had left Florence the year before with a mistress and that was the last she'd heard.

Mina had also been desperate to leave Florence. Despite its seductive charms, it was immured in the past, a cultural backwater. But then the war had broken out in 1914, and it had become impossible to travel. It was only now, with the kaiser's alleged promise not to attack neutral ships, that it seemed safe enough to make the trip.

All that summer Mina had been dreaming up fabulous schemes to support herself once she arrived in New York: creating hat designs and fashion covers she would sell to *Vogue,* drawing up blueprints for a line of couture clothing she would use to attract backers. "I have only one idea in my mind," she gamely wrote to her new American friend Carl Van Vechten. *"Make money."*

She had been sending a steady stream of new poems to Van Vechten too, hoping that American readers would be more open-minded than the English. "I don't believe men in England have got any of the new consciousness about things. . . .," she wrote him in a letter. "I believe we'll get more 'wholesome sex' in American art." Van Vechten had already placed several dissonant poems from the thirty-four-piece sequence she had titled *Love Songs* in a new avant-garde literary magazine called *Others,* edited by Alfred Kreymborg.

Mina had been surprised to hear that the poems had created a minor literary scandal. Detractors had "shuddered" at the sexual explicitness of her subject matter and "derided her elimination of punctuation marks and the audacious spacing of her lines," Kreymborg reported. Parodists compared her to Isadora Duncan, the unfettered high priestess of modern dance, satirizing "the Isadora-like abandon" of her verse. Some had called the work "eroticism gone to seed," others "pure pornography," Van Vechten wrote with contemptuous amusement.

Still, when Van Vechten wrote back, asking if she might send "something without a sex undercurrent," Mina's response had been playfully arch. She saw no choice but to stay the course, she told him. She knew "nothing about anything but life—& that is generally reducible to sex!" she quipped. After all she had suffered, she explained, she felt sure "that life can only evolve something more ample for us—if we help it by getting right into our emotions. . . . We moderns have hardly a proscribed psychic area."

Several weeks later, Mina Loy, alone, boarded the early-morning train bound for Naples. It was the first link of her trip to America. The children and their nurse were there to see her off. Standing inside the train compartment, she pressed her face to the window, fixing in her mind's eye the last image of her children as the train pulled away: "the coiled wisps" of her daughter's "corn-colored hair blowing about the unbelievable blue . . . of her eyes . . . the sun-baked muscles of my boy's sturdy legs stamping out a dance of excited farewell." She watched as if through a telescope as their forms grew smaller and smaller, receding as the train gained speed. It would be three years before she saw them again. What she didn't know yet, what she couldn't know, was that in the "modern self-experiment" of a life she had begun, loneliness would be one of the prices she had to pay for the seductions of her imagination.

Modern dance pioneer Isadora Duncan

TALL AND WILLOWY, a glamorous creature with chiseled features and a razor-sharp wit that masked her many despairs, Mina would never fail to be noticed. Though she would travel in pivotal international circles, befriending everyone from Gertrude Stein to Djuna Barnes, James Joyce to Constantin Brancusi; though in the 1920s she would become as well

Mina Loy: painter, poet, actress, playwright, designer, and conceptual artist

known as her poet-rival Marianne Moore, her verse printed in every avant-garde journal of the day, Mina's pilgrim's progress would never be easy. An exile everywhere, she would move from Victorian London to fin-de-siècle Paris to Futurist Florence to bohemian Greenwich Village to revolutionary Mexico and back to America, in the process having four children, two husbands, and several heartbreaking love affairs. Thereafter, having found love to be all-engulfing, she would try to destroy her need for it.

Impeccably modern, in her eighty-four years she would wear many hats: painter, poet, actress, playwright, designer, conceptual artist, ambivalent mother; her polyglot identity would echo the "self-constructing strategies" of a new kind of woman, the experimental shapes of a life invented as it went along. Like her poetry, Mina's life would be filled with ironic swerves and ceaseless change, sexual dissonance and sly evasions—neither predictable nor safe. Though Mina would find an alternative to the smothering confinement of marriage and domesticity, just as she intended, she would also find that freedom was difficult to sustain, that entanglements were inevitable. To escape them it would be necessary to keep moving, plowing under her old life.

BORN IN LONDON in 1882, Mina Gertrude Lowy was the eldest of three daughters in a loveless family. Her father was a second-generation Hungarian Jew, her mother English and Protestant. Seven months pregnant at her own wedding, her mother was a malcontent, bitter and filled with rage, blindsided by self-hatred for what she perceived to be the stigma of her own mixed marriage. To compensate, she was unfailing in her attentions to outward appearances, convinced that the family's social shortcomings could be masked by genteel affectation. It was Mina, as the unwelcome disaster of this unholy union, who experienced the brunt of her mother's corrosive fury. Mina learned early to escape into her imagination, taking comfort in her own solitude.

She was drawn to art and design, despite all efforts to dissuade her. In the monocular, class-conscious milieu of Victorian London, it was still considered unladylike for a woman to work. Mina was not permitted to attend design school, as it might be inferred either that her father couldn't provide for her, or that she was unmarriageable. Grudgingly, her parents agreed to let her study painting in Munich.

Two years later she returned to London and became involved with a fellow art student, Stephen Haweis. A mediocre painter, Haweis was a duplicitous character, opportunistic and perpetually in debt. Later, Mina would deny having had any complicity in their affair, claiming that Haweis had tricked her into marriage. As she described the seduction scene, reconfiguring the story throughout her life, the sordid events had taken place outside the scope of her free will: she had been drugged, only to find herself half dressed the next morning with Stephen naked beside her. A month later, horrified to discover she was pregnant, she had yielded to Stephen's proposal of a platonic union to evade her parents' censure.

It was a repeat of her mother's story. At twenty-one, Mina was four months pregnant and unhappily married, though, unlike her mother, she refused to take her husband's name, the one small flag of defiance she managed to raise.

The couple moved to Paris and, despite Mina's faltering spirits, she continued to paint, exhibiting six watercolors in the Salon d'Automne of 1903. After the baby was born, Mina was surprised by the love she felt. When the baby died of meningitis a year later, she was inconsolable.

Shattered, the couple moved on to Florence, where no one would know

**Mina Loy's first husband,
Stephen Haweis**

their history. The marriage had gone from bad to worse. Most of the time she and Stephen lived apart, he with a mistress, she alone, though she occasionally took lovers. Mina had two more children nonetheless, Joella (fathered by a lover) in 1907 and Giles (fathered by Stephen) in 1909.

Nearly buried beneath the twin burdens of motherhood and her artistic ambitions, Mina oscillated between exuberance and despair, defiance and listless passivity. On good days, she whistled and brazenly smoked cigarettes on the street, designed new dresses and painted. On bad days, she shuttered herself inside her villa, taking to her bed, though she continued to work. "My conceptions of life evolved while . . . stirring baby food on spirit lamps—and my best drawings behind a stove to the accompaniment of a line of children's cloths hanging round it to dry," she wrote.

IT WASN'T UNTIL she met the beguilingly seductive Mabel Dodge, who was living in a grand hilltop villa nearby, that life began to brighten. Mabel,

Mina Loy and Stephen Haweis in Paris, 1905

observed Mina, had a way of giving "the latest philosophy, no matter how
. . . austere—a ribald flavor of lubriciousness." Mabel fed her books on
Freud and Henri Bergson, Buddhism and Madame Blavatsky, telepathy and
tarot. She introduced her to Gertrude Stein and, later, after Mabel moved to
America, the bohemian New Yorkers who made up her entourage whenever she briefly took up residence again in Florence: John Reed, Mabel's
lover for a time; the critic and dandy Carl Van Vechten; the writer Hutchins
Hapgood; and many others. For all her airs and affectations, her duplicity
and deceptions, Mabel was "a great salvation," Mina said. Mina nick-
named her Moose, and Mabel became Giles's godmother.

But it was Mina's involvement with the Futurists and their abrasive, out-
sized leader Filippo Marinetti, the self-proclaimed "caffeine of Europe,"
that would finally move her from the fin de siècle to the modern. Futurism,
which was dedicated to the overthrow of the classical art tradition, had
been spreading through Italy like a brushfire. Marinetti had been staging
theatrical "happenings" and exhibitions in every major city. "Burn the

museums" was his war cry. "Let's murder the moonlight!" What was needed, he preached, was a new, dynamic art that would embody the "steel" and "fever" and "speed" of modernity. It was only by "revolutionizing all forms" he cried, that art could be saved!

To illustrate his points, Marinetti had already begun to set down his revolutionary proclamations in a new aphoristic form he called "vers libre—prose set free."

For Mina, such inflammatory words touched the spark of her own discontent. If she was perplexed by her "susceptibility to

Mina's drawing of
Carl Van Vechten, 1913

this bombastic superman," as she called him, she was also intrigued by his colossal theatricality. Watching the glorious spectacle of Marinetti in performance one night, as he mesmerized an angry, egg-pelting crowd of Florentines into silence, she observed that "she felt as if she had benefited by a fortnight at the seashore." For all his posturing, his infuriating hubris, there was an energy in Marinetti she found magnetizing.

Marinetti's prose experiments caught Mina's attention as well. Intrigued by the notion that traditional sentence structure might be replaced by the "bizarre rhythms of free imagination," as Marinetti put it, Mina began composing a set of aphoristic statements of her own. It was her first attempt at writing. The result, which she titled "Aphorisms on Futurism," was a list of fifty-one precepts, which she was now trying to live by, her head spinning with Marinettiesque polemics.

LOVE the hideous in order to find the sublime core of it.

OPEN your arms to the dilapidated, to rehabilitate them.

YOU prefer to observe the past on which your eyes are already opened.

BUT the future is only dark from outside.
Leap into it—and it EXPLODES with *Light.*

FORGET that you live in houses, that you may live in yourself—

FOR the smallest people live in the greatest houses.

BUT the smallest person, potentially, is as great as the Universe.

WHAT can you know of expansion, who limit yourselves to compromise?

HITHERTO the great man has achieved greatness by keeping the people small.

BUT in the Future, by inspiring the people to expand to their fullest capacity, the great man proportionately must be tremendous—a God.

LOVE of others is the appreciation of one's self.

Mina was by now having an affair with Marinetti, though when she wrote to Mabel, who had recently moved to New York, she didn't share the details. "I am in the throes of conversion to Futurism," she told Mabel. "But I shall never convince myself. There is no hope in any system that [combats the bad against the bad,] & that is really Marinetti's philosophy—though he is one of the most satisfying personalities I ever came in contact with."

Later Mina would credit the charismatic Marinetti with having added "twenty years . . . to my life from sheer contact with his exuberant vitality." Marinetti had encouraged her to take her life and her work more seriously. The "destination did not matter," he repeatedly told her. "What counted was to go."

Mina had decided to go to New York, where she hoped it would be easier to live as she imagined, and to obtain a divorce.

"Everyone I know at present is trying to forget what a complicated affair life has been mistaken for," she wrote Mabel. "We are all busy re-simplifying ourselves—I am 29—next year I shall be 28."

In fact Mina was thirty-two and her life was not getting simpler but more complicated. The affair with Marinetti was beginning to unravel. She had

The futurist Filippo Tommaso Marinetti, 1910

initially viewed the relationship as an amusement, but now she wasn't sure she trusted this egoistic showman, who seemed to view her as yet another conquest. In a letter to Mabel she alluded to the awkwardness of the situation: "I cannot tell you anything about myself—without telling you *all*—which is impossible—for I don't know—at present—anyway Life can be interesting, even if the old values are gone—& my roots are being tugged out . . . in exquisite and terrific anguish." Still, she wondered, where were they all going?

That June, Mina saw her writing appear in print for the first time, when "Aphorisms on Futurism," which Mabel had sent to Alfred Stieglitz, was published in his vanguard New York quarterly *Camera Works.* Though Gertrude Stein was also excerpted in the issue, it was Mina's aphorisms that drew the most attention. Readers gaped at the daring futurist topography, with ellipses and white spaces, the absence of punctuation and isolated words printed in bold capitals, as if the writer was shouting.

MARINETTI'S ATTENTIONS, meanwhile, had all but ceased. The possibility that Italy would enter the war completely absorbed him. Mina went through some sort of breakdown, writing to Mabel that she was "dreadfully ill—in bed 7 weeks & nervous collapse afterwards." I want to see you, she continued, "& am so afraid of America—I've got the latins in my blood—and the only latin's got me in his spleen."

She had begun to accept that the cat and mouse game she was playing with Marinetti was hopeless. "I don't describe to you my utter defeat in the sex war," she wrote. "You will put it down to feminine pride of which I haven't a jot—anyhow [Marinetti's] interest in me only weathered two months of war fever."

Something positive *had* come of the affair, however: their sparring over the "woman question" had radically realigned her thinking about feminism. Though publicly Marinetti defended the suffragette movement, in private he claimed that women's appetite for the vote was ridiculous. Women were inferior in character and intellect, he said. They were either femme fatales or madonnas. Like animals, they embodied the *amore* to which male attention was drawn, luring men away from technological innovation.

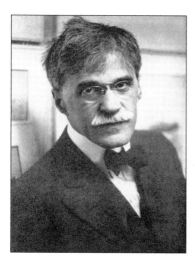

Alfred Stieglitz, 1915.
Photo by Edward Steichen.

Though Marinetti denied that his ideas applied to Mina's "advanced nature," as he called it, Mina was appalled by the misogyny of his views. As a rebuke to their ongoing verbal parries, she began to write a feminist manifesto, which she referred to as "an absolute resystemization of the feminist question."

The goal of equality between the sexes was a spurious one, she argued:

"Leave off looking to men to find out what you are *not*. Seek within yourselves to find out what you *are*. As conditions are at present . . . you have the choice between Parasitism, Prostitution, or Negation."

The fictitious value of woman "as identified with her physical purity," she continued, was too easy a standby. It rendered women lethargic in the acquisition of character.

The remedies Mina went on to offer included the surgical destruction of virginity at puberty, the right to sexual experience and motherhood regardless of marital status, and collective resistance to the misleading bargain of marriage.

"Woman must destroy in herself the desire to be loved," Mina declared. Sex or so-called love would have to be separated from "honor, grief, sentimentality, pride & consequently jealousy." Only then would women be prepared to exert "intelligent curiosity" in meeting life.

Mina immediately posted the manifesto to Mabel in New York and wrote, "Do tell me what you are making of Feminism? I heard you were interested. Have you any idea in what direct[ion] the sex must be shoved—psychologically I mean?"

Writing to Van Vechten, she also alluded to a shift in her priorities: "What I feel now are feminine politics." She went on to describe her new optimism, claiming she was too full of "Marinettian vitality" to be despondent. This self-transformation sounded easy, she added, but "it *meant* years of hard work—& Marinetti blithe fellow—was sent from heaven to put the finishing touch—& they say he is a brute to women!"

Despite the fact that the manifesto sounded confident and her letters upbeat, Mina was finding it harder to detach pride and jealousy from sex and love than to speak of it. In Marinetti's absence, she had begun an awkward flirtation with Marinetti's archrival, Giovanni Papini, the other significant leader of the Futurists. Now the three were involved in a complicated romantic triangle, with Mina taking turns in bed with the two feuding men. Papini, married and a Catholic, had meanwhile been sending Mina mixed signals, despite his initial overtures.

"I am rather blue," she wrote Mabel. "I've seen Papini again and I'm frightfully in love—& he hates me with a voluptuous and erotic frigidity. I want to run away and come to New York." She was struggling to gain some perspective, worried that Papini was only using her to get back at his rival.

"I can just hang on to my sanity—by a thread there's not a soul here to *talk* to," she added. "Giovanni [Papini] came within an ace of really smashing me for good." Demoralized, Mina wondered now "if hatred is the truth and love the lie—or whether even hatred is only jealousy."

"Don't ever live to see the day when the man you love sobs out the other one's name in the ultimate embrace," she added. "Philosophy is inadequate."

MINA'S WRITING continued, despite her ricocheting moods. Mabel had been urging her to come to New York as soon as possible. But there was no one, Mina wrote back, to take her children. "I want to design for a business," she added. "I do hope that family arrangements will work themselves out so that I can go to New York."

Finally, in late 1916, the nanny grudgingly agreed to stay on with the children. At last she was on her way.

NEW YORK WAS more startling than Mina had imagined. What she saw, as the ship entered the harbor, was an "architecture conceived in a child's dream." Manhattan's soaring skyline shone "with the glittering clamor of a myriad of windows set like colored diamonds." No one who has not lived in New York, she would later write, has lived in the Modern world.

Her reputation as a free-verse radical had preceded her, Mina soon learned. She was already associated with a slew of vanguard magazines with peculiar names like *Trend* and *Rogue,* an arch little journal that advertised itself as the "cigarette of literature—a 'necessary evil.'"

Though Van Vechten had teasingly written about the critics' shock at her "nonchalance in revealing the secrets of sex" after her sardonic love poem "Pig Cupid" had appeared in the inaugural issue of *Others,* what he hadn't told her was that its visceral evocation of carnal love had also earned her a hallowed place in the bohemian underground. Alfred Kreymborg immediately welcomed her into his circle, which included Man Ray, William Carlos Williams, Marianne Moore, and the wealthy art patrons Walter and Louise Arensberg, the financial backers of *Others.*

Within a few weeks, Kreymborg had recruited Mina for the Provincetown Players, enlisting her to play the lead in his experimental one-act *Lima Beans.* A send-up of traditional marriage, the play seemed the perfect mouthpiece for expressing Mina's antimatrimonial sentiments. Wildly eccentric, it featured a bizarrely clad husband and wife, who moved with mechanical puppetlike gestures, bowing in comical unison throughout the drama. Mina, cast as the wife, played opposite the doctor-poet William Carlos Williams, who with each rehearsal became more infatuated with his leading lady. The set, designed by Greenwich Village sculptor William Zorach, was painted like a checkerboard. On opening night, Mina appeared in gold slippers and a green taffeta décolleté gown of her own creation. Despite the play's challenge to naturalistic theater, it was a wild success. The applause finally stopped after sixteen curtain calls.

Drawing by Mina Loy of Man Ray

Mina became even better known four months later, when a reporter from the *New York Sun* profiled her as the embodiment of the New Woman. With a caption below her picture that read "Her poems would have puzzled Grandma," the article described Mina as that "rare and exotic species" called the New Woman. "No natural history contains her habitat," the reporter mockingly observed. "If she isn't the modern woman, who is, pray?"

The piece went on to enumerate Mina's modernist credentials, mentioning that she wrote free verse, designed lampshades,

William Carlos Williams

made her own clothes, acted, illustrated magazines, and drew up stage designs. "This woman is half-way through the door into tomorrow," the writer said.

Yet how exactly did one live as a "Modern?" Mina was asked. The "modern way meant not caring if you transgressed familiar categories," Mina declared, living "not as your grandmother thought you ought to . . . according to the rules." The "modern flings herself at life and lets herself feel as she feels."

BY NOW MINA was spending nearly every evening at the home of Walter and Louise Arensberg, the couple Mina would later describe as the "most civilized people she had ever known."

Almost overnight, the Arensbergs' salon had become the epicenter of the new, the unofficial clubhouse to a tightly knit circle of writers and artists, a cosmopolitan mix of European and American modernists who nightly congregated to gossip and flirt, play chess and analyze each others dreams. Bookishly tweedy, Walter Arensberg seemed an improbable figure to play impresario to the avant-garde. With his tailored suits and intellectual mien, his glasses perpetually slipping down his nose, he had the air of a "distracted academic." A poet as well as a literary patron, he composed symbolist verse, parsed obscure literary texts, and, like Mabel Dodge, bankrolled several vanguard magazines, among them *Rogue* and the short-lived *Others.*

Arensberg collected art as well as artists. By the time Mina met him he had already assembled one of the earliest and most adventuresome collections of modern painting and sculpture in New York. The seventeen-foot walls of his elegant duplex apartment on West 67th Street were hung with canvases, works by Cézanne and Matisse, Braque and Picasso. For several

Soirée (Evening Party), drawing by Beatrice Wood, 1917

years now he had been Marcel Duchamp's sole support, paying his rent, buying every piece of work he made, and showering him with hospitality.

Evenings at the Arensbergs' were more selective than Dodge's soirees. Those who gathered dressed more formally. Hors d'oeuvres and whiskey flowed, as did witty repartee laced with bilingual puns and sexual innuendo. It was considered sport to venture into outré subject matter and to partake of all manner of racy parlor games. Guests were habitually well liquored. "No sooner had we arrived," recalled Gabrielle Buffet-Picabia, "than we became part of a motley international band which turned night into day, conscientious objectors of all nationalities . . . living in an inconceivable orgy of sexuality, jazz and alcohol."

To some of the Americans, among them the reticent William Carlos Williams, the sexual precocity of the Arensbergs' evenings could be intimidating. One evening, recalled Williams, he walked into a scene that stunned him. At the end of the room, an attractive young Frenchwoman lay

New York apartment of Louise and Walter Arensberg.
Photo by Charles Sheeler.

reclining on a divan, surrounded by young men, each of whom was kissing and caressing a different part of her body: her shins, her knees, her thighs, her elbows. She was wearing a black lace gown and seemed "fully at ease," he reported. "As far as I could tell, there was a gentlemen's agreement that she not be undressed there."

To Mina, such risqué amusements seemed harmless beside the bombast and macho swagger she had witnessed in the company of the Futurists. She felt at ease amidst the Arensbergs' urbane and iconoclastic company, drawn not only to their circle of French friends: Marcel Duchamp; Francis and Gabriella Picabia; Albert Gleizes and his wife, Juliette, but to the Americans she now met: the poet Wallace Stevens; the artists Beatrice Wood, Man Ray, and Clara Tice; the satirist Louise Norton, who wrote under the pseudonym Dame Rogue. The most outlandish and intriguing of Mina's new cohorts, however, was Baroness Elsa von Freytag-Loringhoven, a certified eccentric.

The Baroness was considered the Mama of Dada. She had been living in aristocratic splendor at the uptown Ritz when the war broke out. Her husband, a wealthy German businessman, had decided it best to return to his homeland, though upon setting foot on German soil, he took his own life in protest of the war's "organized fratricide." Strenuously avant-garde, the Baroness pronounced his suicide noble, despite the fact that his death left her widowed and penniless. She immediately migrated downtown to Greenwich Village, where she earned a meager living posing in the nude as an artist's model and working part-time in a cigarette factory, before abandoning commerce altogether to write Dadaist poetry and construct Cubist assemblages.

Tall and androgynous, the Baroness, though not beautiful by conventional standards, was impressively statuesque. Well over forty, her masculine body was sinewy and taut, her skin mottled, her hair (when she had hair) hennaed a beguiling eggplant purple. Square-jawed and straight-backed, she had an overbite that lent her face an air of haughty finality, a decisiveness that few could miss.

Every evening at the same hour, it was the Baronesses's habit to parade through Washington Square, five leashed dogs in tow, her head half shaved and lacquered a bright vermilion, her face smeared with yellow powder, her lips inky with black lipstick. Often she wore a bolero jacket, a Scottish kilt, and a moth-eaten fur coat, to which she affixed kewpie dolls, stuffed birds, canceled postage stamps, bottle caps—what lesser souls might have

Baroness Elsa von Freytag-Loringhoven. Photo by Man Ray.

33

considered detritus. Not so with the Baroness. She was an ardent garbage collector.

Daringly inventive with her accessories, sometimes she wore a lit birthday cake atop her head, or a halo of dangling spoons. In summer she donned a birdcage necklace, complete with a live canary; in more inclement weather, she preferred the lid of a coal scuttle, strapped under her chin like a helmet. She turned celluloid curtain rings pilfered from a store in passing into an arm's length of clattering bracelets, tea balls into earrings. On the bustle of a certain black dress she liked, she attached a blinking taillight. Once, offering her modeling services to a male painter, she threw open her scarlet raincoat, revealing herself to be quite naked. Or almost so. Covering her nipples was a makeshift bra made of two tomato cans fastened with a green string around her back. Insistent in her lack of shame, she liked to carry a certain life-size plaster-cast penis she'd made, which at opportune moments she would brandish to "shock old maids."

There were times, according to legend, when the Baroness ran afoul of the law. She was arrested several times for public nudity. In fact, Williams Carlos Williams first met her at the Women's House of Detention, where she was briefly residing, having been caught shoplifting an umbrella.

One evening in April 1918, Williams was visiting the apartment of Margaret Anderson and Jane Heap, the irreverent editors of the *Little Review,* when his eye fixed itself on an odd piece of sculpture. It was housed under a glass dome and looked, as he described it, something like "chicken guts" cast in wax. Moved by the quirky spirit of the piece, he inquired as to its creator, who was none other than the Baroness. She was a fabulous creature, he was told, a working artist and a Dadaist poet. Would he care to meet her?

Several days later, Williams found himself seated across from the Baroness at a Greenwich Village coffee shop, sharing a celebratory breakfast in honor of her release from prison. In a moment of impetuousness, Williams told her that her lack of inhibition excited him. He promised to call again and sent her a basket of peaches. On a later occasion, visiting her dismal

Baroness von Freytag-Loringhoven. Drawing by George Biddle, 1921.

flat, he made the further mistake of gently kissing her. Encouraged, she grabbed him. What he needed to free his mind for serious art, she told him, was to contract syphilis from her. "She reminded me of my 'gypsy' grandmother, old Emily," Williams later wrote, "and I was foolish enough to say I loved her. That all but finished me!"

The Baroness became obsessed with Williams and, to his dismay, began to stalk him. The more he pulled away, the more vehemently she pursued. One night, as he was getting into his car, she ambushed him. "You must come with me." she purred, grabbing his arm. When he refused, she punched him in the face.

He bought a punching bag to practice boxing at home in order to be better prepared in the future. The next time she jumped him, Williams retaliated with a stiff punch to her mouth and then called for the police, demanding that she be arrested.

Marcel Duchamp

Later, Williams would confide, "She revolted me, frightened me, beat me finally . . . I was really crazy about the woman."

The Baroness was a protégée of Marcel Duchamp, whose spirit of nihilistic whimsy she more than shared. Though obsessed with Williams, she considered Duchamp her greatest passion. Once, while posing nude, she is said to have rubbed a newspaper reproduction of Duchamp's *Nude Descending a Staircase* over every inch of her anatomy. She made numerous portraits and poems for him and, despite his disavowals, was convinced that Duchamp was also infatuated with her. "Marcel, Marcel I love you like hell," she would chant to the amusement of her friends.

Since the scandalous Armory Show of 1913, the first international exhibition of modern art in America, Duchamp had become the emblematic avant-gardist, the standard for New York attitudes toward modernism. At the Arensbergs', as Mina soon observed, he was also the measure by which one judged worldliness. Uncommonly charming, with chiseled features and penetrating blue eyes, Duchamp was an immensely seductive character. A master of elusiveness, he kept his emotions coolly reined in, deflecting others with his wit. Mina was drawn to his enigmatic reserve, but she was also circumspect about what she saw as a certain disingenuousness in the way he conducted his sexual affairs. He was "slick as a prestidigitator," she later reflected, "he could insinuate his hand under a woman's bodice and hug her very body without it being at all apparent." Privately she was uncomfortable with his tendency to diminish women to the sum of their sexual parts by continuously insinuating slang and sexual puns into the conversation.

FOR MINA, APART from the revolving love affairs she watched that winter at the Arensbergs', which she wryly made note of in her journal, there were other, deeper distractions. The year 1917 would be forever marked by the arrival of an enigmatic newcomer to the Arensberg circle, the poet-boxer and Dadaist icon Arthur Cravan.

Born Fabien Lloyd in 1887, Cravan was a provocateur of legendary proportions, a "fugitive, forger and master of disguise," who had evaded military conscription for years. Tall and ruggedly handsome, with an appetite for scandal almost as insatiable as his taste for drink, he claimed, among his various personae, to be Oscar Wilde's nephew. He was already a notorious figure in European circles by the time he reached New York. In Paris he'd been a fixture of the avant-garde, sighted at balls with the painter Robert Delaunay, dancing the tango in wildly colored costumes, or in a black shirt with cutouts through which one could see obscenities penned in red on his chest. In Berlin he had paraded through the streets carrying four prostitutes on his shoulders.

Cravan's true métier was self-dramatization. He never missed an opportunity to grandstand. When his name was announced before a boxing match, he would leap from his chair by the rails and boastfully introduce himself as a "hotel thief, muleteer, snake-charmer, chauffeur . . . sailor, gold prospector and the poet with the shortest hair in the world."

A belligerent in print as well as in the boxing ring, he published a journal called *Maintenant* devoted solely to his own writing, which he distributed from a wheelbarrow. Here he harangued peers and proffered antisocial advice, extolling the superiority of the physical whenever he could. "Do a lot of fucking or go into rigorous training," he wrote. "When you have nineteen inches around the arm, you'll be gifted." Once he publicized a lecture, which, for "the ladies' benefit," he said he'd deliver "in a jock strap and put his balls on the table." He also promised to commit suicide at the finale of the speech. Sold out, the lecture hall was packed. But instead of killing himself, he gave a talk on Victor Hugo.

Marcel Duchamp, Francis Picabia, and
Beatrice Wood at Coney Island, 1917

Not everyone was taken in. The first time Cravan appeared at the Arensbergs', Juliette Gleizes pronounced his blond, Anglo-Saxon beauty "the sort common among lifeguards" and judged him extremely brutish under the influence of alcohol. Mina felt much the same. He looked like a "half-imbecile savage," she wrote.

Their second meeting, a few months later, did little to change her negative impressions. It was May of 1917, and the Arensberg circle had begun to plan their last diversion of the season, the Blind-man's Ball. It was to be a party in celebration of a new little magazine co-published by Duchamp, the French writer Henri-Pierre Roché, and Beatrice Wood, which Mina, among others, had been writing for. The twenty-third and final "Pagan Romp" of the year, the ball was to be held in Greenwich Village's Webster Hall, the run-down community center fondly known as the Devil's Playhouse. Beatrice had drawn the poster, an insolent, high-stepping stick figure thumbing its nose at the world. All were invited to stay until dawn. "The Blind Man must see the sun," the invitation read. "Romantic rags are requested."

Guests were told to dress as schools of modern art. Most invented their own schools. Clara Tice came as a steam radiator, a friend as a hard-boiled egg. Duchamp dressed in drag, Mina came as a cross between a Pierrot and a lampshade. Beatrice Wood was clad as a Russian peasant.

The Arensbergs and friends gathered on the balcony that evening. Mina sat next to Duchamp, at his insistence. Drinking champagne, they joked and flirted, watching the revelries below. From their perch they spotted Arthur Cravan, who had just arrived, sheathed in a bedsheet. A towel was wrapped like a turban about his head. Mina watched as Cravan moved through the crowd, then after a moment saw him stagger up the stairs toward their table. With a lurch, he slumped down beside her, threw off the bedsheet—revealing himself in all his naked manliness—and slung a sweaty arm around her bare shoulder.

"Slouched in his chair, the sneering muscles of his mouth and chin sunk into his chest," she later recalled in *Colossus,* her thinly veiled roman à clef about her life with Cravan. His "unspoken obscenities . . . chilled my powdered skin."

Repelled by the coarseness of Cravan's advances, Mina rose and moved away. Later, passing him again as she was leaving, she noted he was "completely drunk" and "lurching among the mob," asking women for their telephone numbers.

Toward morning, Mina and a few friends taxied uptown to the Arensbergs', where they breakfasted

THE

BLINDMAN'S
BALL

For the BLINDMAN
A Magazine of *Vers Art*

Friday May 25th

at Ultra Bohemian, Pre-Historic, Post Alcoholic

WEBSTER HALL 119 East 11th Street

DANCING EIGHT-THIRTY

Tickets $1.50 each in advance—$2.00 at the gate. Boxes not requiring Costume, but requiring Admission tickets $10.00

Everything sold by the BLINDMAN

7 East 39th Street   Telephone Vanderbilt 3280

Poster for the Blindman's Ball, 1917, by Beatrice Wood

on scrambled eggs and wine at 3 A.M., after which she and four others—Beatrice Wood, the actress Aileen Dresser, Charles Demuth, and Duchamp—repaired to Duchamp's quarters, where the "ménage à cinq" sprawled across the crowded bed and went to sleep. When Mina's notes on the evening later appeared in their magazine *The Blind Man,* they elicited "a bewildering uproar as to the base immorality of the modernists," she remembered with amusement.

LATER, SOMEWHAT defensively, Mina would write that Cravan was "a giant who carried the circus within him." An outsider herself, Mina had always had a weakness for others of her ilk—in the case of men, difficult, larger-than-life characters. Cravan would prove no exception. As spring progressed, she found herself drifting toward this peculiar, belligerent man, despite her initial hostility. Often she and Cravan buried themselves in the same deep armchair at the Arensbergs, sharing a book. One night, as they were leaving, he said, "You had better come and live with me in a taxicab. . . . We can keep a cat."

Rootless, nomadic by nature, Cravan was a drifter, a perpetual tramp. He lived, said Mina, in a state of "semi-destitute ease," his pleasures those of the open air, sleeping on park benches, in empty boxcars, on the roof of Pennsylvania Railway Station. That spring, as the weather warmed, they

Louise Arensberg, Henri-Pierre Roché, and Francis Picabia

began to wander the city together, exploring his secret haunts: abandoned railroad yards, the overgrown edges of the Hudson River, the desolate parks at night. What she admired, Mina wrote, was his ability to "push his entire consciousness into a wisp of grass, . . . a dish of frost in a wheel rut." As the weeks passed, she began to feel the poetry of these forlorn places, to share in his rapture. A tentative courtship began, which she struggled to resist. His companionship sometimes felt antagonistic, she wrote. She tried to feign indifference, taking refuge in her humor.

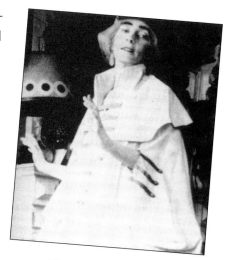

Mina Loy dressed for the Blindman's Ball, 1917

"All your irony is assumed," Cravan said to her one night. "My one desire is to be so very tender with you that you will smile without irony."

To her dismay, Mina realized she was falling in love. She wondered if he was simply trying to get the upper hand. "It occurred to me," she wrote, "that were I on every occasion to say exactly the opposite of what I thought, Colossus would be in as great a psychological fix as any woman."

Yet the more they parried, the more their defenses fell away. Cravan thought Mina the first woman who was not trying to "put something across" on him. As for Mina, for the first time in her life, she felt protected. If she also sensed that this need he'd touched inside her, this feeling of refuge that had so eluded her, went back to her earliest, inchoate yearnings as a child, she wasn't able to say it. Instead she chalked up her feelings to emotions that were "primitive inversely to the sophistication of her brain."

She had tamed Cravan, her friends claimed. He had become courteous, "almost bourgeois," observed Gabi Picabia. "No longer did he invade drawing rooms with a sodden, insolent sulk," Mina noted in her journal. "In public he was civilized—in private, sublime."

They talked endlessly now, and hungrily. "I had found the one man with whom my mind could go the whole way," Mina wrote. By the end of the summer, she and Cravan had two fantasy children: a paper lion and tiger from Chinatown they named Gaga and Moche.

Their bliss came abruptly to an end in September, when, in order to elude military conscription, Cravan fled the country. In a few short months, war fever had entered the air. The government was suppressing radical journals, and it was rumored that a blacklist of antiwar activists had been compiled. Federal agents were watching Isadora Duncan because she had danced the "Marseillaise" wrapped in a red flag. Even former leftists were showing patriotism. "It is a great thing to be living when an age passes," remarked Jane Heap sardonically. *The Masses* magazine, the political mouthpiece of bohemia, was shut down for displaying antiwar sentiments.

Mina, meanwhile, hadn't seen her children for more than a year. She'd recently learned that her divorce had come through and that she had won custody of the children, though, apart from this, she was oddly silent on the subject of her irregular motherhood, hardly mentioning her children in her writing. She was still unable to contemplate their needs amidst the clamor of her own.

By December, Cravan was in Mexico City and had begun to bury her with letters, imploring her to join him. He was lost without her, he wrote. "Tell me that you will come right away and that we will spend the rest of our lives together."

He begged her to send a lock of hair. "Better yet, come with all of your hair," he urged. He wanted to marry her, he said.

"Tenderness in a strong man is always a deluge," Mina observed, "because it is a luxury which the weak can not afford." She bought a ticket for Mexico and by January was at his side.

They spent their first days in Mexico City wandering the streets, "making love or respectfully eyeing canned foods in groceries," she wrote, "eating our tomatoes at street corners or walking among the weeds." They had tapped "the source of enchantment," she said, "and it suffused the world."

Impetuously, they married. "Now that I have caught you," Cravan told her, "I am at ease."

He had been earning a meager income as a boxing teacher when, to their dismay, he lost a critical match and with it, his job. Itinerants now, they wandered the provinces of Oaxaca and Veracruz, their money dwindling. Still, they were blissfully happy. They subsisted on a diet of oatmeal and reboiled coffee grounds, leavened with talk. Drifting around the docks of Salina Cruz, they decided to spend their last savings on a decrepit sailboat, which they now began to transform into a trim sailing vessel. Mina dressed in sailor's pants and cooked their meals on the beach. Sitting under a shade tree, she sewed the sail. She was pregnant now, and they began to worry about how they would survive. One night Cravan rashly suggested joint suicide. "How can we die when we haven't finished talking?" Mina asked.

They began to make new plans. There was a Japanese hospital ship bound for Chile docked in Salina Cruz, which still had one berth open. They decided Mina should sail alone, because her papers were in order. Cravan would come independently, sailing their refurbished boat. Once the baby was born, they would return to Europe and pick up the other children. Life would be easier soon.

Arthur Cravan

Cravan decided to give the boat a try. Standing on the shore, Mina saw the breeze catch the sail, watched it luff and fill, then balloon with air. Her eye followed Cravan as he gave the little craft its second test run. She watched the taut white sail move steadily away, tacking back and forth, trailing stitches of sea foam. She watched it shrinking into the distance, a toy boat now, a speck of white against blue. The sail touched the horizon, then dipped out of sight.

MINA STOOD FOR hours on the beach, waiting, certain he would re-appear. When he hadn't by nightfall, she grew frantic, her mind spinning in futile circles. Perhaps there had been a problem; under duress, he had had to land somewhere beyond the beach. He was delayed, perhaps, making minor repairs.

Day after day Mina waited on the beach, wrapped in Cravan's coat as she scanned the horizon. After a week passed and he still hadn't appeared, Mina felt she might go mad. The boat for South America was leaving; there were no more scheduled for weeks to come, and she was out of money. Racked with uncertainty and barely suppressed fear, Mina waited until the last minute before boarding, comforting herself with the thought that Cravan would soon be following, making his way down the jagged coast-line to join her, just as they'd planned. Mina arrived in Buenos Aires four weeks later and waited. She waited for months. But Cravan never came; nor was he ever seen again.

MINA FINALLY SAILED alone to England in March. To her humiliation, she'd had to wire her family for funds. There she spent the remainder of the winter with her mother, whom she still despised, waiting for her unborn child. The English class system still appalled her: its anti-Semitism, xeno-phobia, suspicion of artists. In April she gave birth to a daughter, Fabienne. By summer she'd returned to Florence to be reunited with the two older children, now ten and twelve.

She was shocked by how much they had changed. Though she tried to resume her old life, it was useless. Her friends were gone, her spirit bro-ken. And she was still obsessed with Cravan.

Though more than a year had passed, Mina refused to believe he was dead. She pictured him trapped somewhere: stranded on some rocky, windswept island in the middle of the sea or starving in a dank Mexico prison. His body still hadn't been found. Unable to move forward, Mina made plans to leave Florence to resume her search. The nanny tried to dissuade her, arguing that it would be damaging to the children if she left again. But after Mina smashed all the dishes in anger, the nanny realized she couldn't be deterred. This time Mina left all three children behind in Florence, sailing for New York in March of 1920.

THE CITY WAS much changed. With Prohibition in effect, bar after bar was boarded up, the windows of old haunts covered, like a ghost town. Downtown bohemia gathered in teashops now, or in illegal speakeasies, where bootleg liquor was served in prim coffee cups. The Arensbergs' evenings were different too. Walter and Louise were drinking too much. Many of the French had repatriated. Though Duchamp tried to rekindle the old spirit of antic play, the mood had shifted.

Mina headed downtown to Greenwich Village, settling into a small apartment on Bedford Street. Within days, she had renewed her ties with the Provincetown Playhouse, which was still active, and rekindled her friendship with William Carlos Williams. And she found her way back to the Brevoort, the one night-spot that, to everyone's relief, hadn't changed.

After the demise of Kreymborg's *Others,* two new literary magazines had arisen in its stead, *The Dial* and the *Little Review,* Margaret Anderson's audacious little brainchild, which she published with her lover Jane Heap.

Anderson and Heap had moved to the village in 1917 from Chicago, where the *Little Review* had quickly become the hub of Chicago's bohemian fringe. In New York, one of the magazine's first issues had been suppressed on charges of pornography, though the real offense, many suspected, was its antiwar stance. Famously obstinate, Margaret was immovable. In an endearingly fiery announcement heralding the magazine's first anniversary, she wrote: "As 'sanity' increases in the world the *Little Review* will strive more and more to be splendidly insane: as editors . . . continue to compromise in order to get their public, as book makers continue to print rot . . . the *Little Review* will continue to rebel, to tell the truth as we see it."

Now in its sixth year, the *Little Review* was publishing more and more new writing by women: Djuna Barnes, Mary Butts, Dorothy Richardson, Marianne Moore, Gertrude Stein, and the Baroness among them. As Mina hoped, the editors were highly receptive to her work as well.

Soon Mina found herself gravitating toward this new circle of women associated with the *Little Review,* many of whom gathered at Anderson and Heap's Eighth Street apartment in the evenings.

If Mabel Dodge's temple to art and titillating talk had been assiduously white and pristine, Anderson and Heap had set their sights by a different star. Theirs was a more comedic and subversive vision, the stygian splendor of a smoky cabaret rather than the sanctity of a shrine. The walls of their living room were lacquered black, the floors magenta, "the color of the inside of a stomach," as one friend remembered. To cap the nocturnal aura, an enormous divan hung from heavy black chains suspended from the ceiling.

It was, by all accounts, the unofficial center of Village bohemia now, "an oasis for creative minds," as one friend recollected. Even the foppish Van Vechten, always the first to nose out a new scene, had quickly caught scent of this gathering demimonde, installing himself as a regular guest.

EXCEPT FOR MABEL, Mina had experienced few intimate friendships with women. Perhaps her bitter relations with her mother had made her reticent. Perhaps the unrelenting turbulence of her love life, combined with the pull of her writing, had simply left her no time. But the pattern was changing. Since Mina had returned, she found herself drawing closer to an old acquaintance, the wry poet and reporter Djuna Barnes.

Djuna and Mina had known each other before the war, when both had been members of the Provincetown Players, part of the crowd gathered

Right: **Mina Loy in 1905. Photo by Stephen Haweis.**

Mina Loy and Djuna Barnes. Photo by Man Ray.

around Kreymborg's short-lived *Others.* Each had admired the other from afar. Long-legged Mina appeared at literary gatherings in a leopardskin coat, Djuna in her signature black cape. Both had kept to themselves, however, safely self-contained, though they shared a similar sense of social isolation and personal oddity. Now that reserve had finally been breached.

DJUNA WAS THE emblematic Greenwich Village bohemian. Tall and busty, with auburn hair and angular features, she was a regular at the Brevoort Hotel. She always wrote in bed, kept a pet parrot who once almost bit off her first husband's nose, and made a decent living as a reporter for several big New York dailies, illustrating her own articles with stylish, Beardsley-like drawings. Though widely celebrated for her arch cultural commentary, which appeared in a weekly column in the *Brooklyn Daily Eagle,* her heart was in the writing she did on the side: reams of sardonic poetry, dreamlike plays, short stories, and several edgy novels with lesbian themes, all of which earned her enormous underground notoriety, though little money.

Djuna's fraught love life was equally divided. By her own account, she went through nineteen male lovers before giving up on men altogether. After that she took female lovers, though she didn't fare much better. At thirty-eight, Djuna found herself brokenhearted and betrayed, painfully abandoned by the beautiful but alcoholic artist Thelma Wood, who'd left her for another woman after a torturous ten-year affair. At that point Djuna swore off women as well.

In his autobiographical novel about avant-garde New York, *Post-Adolescence,* Robert McAlmon includes a telling vignette recalling how Djuna and Mina reconnected after the war. The two women, who appear under pseudonyms, immediately fall into conversation, commiserating over each other's travails: for the Djuna character, multiple abortions and the burden of having had to support three brothers, a husband, and all her lovers; for the Mina character, her bereavement over the disappearance of her husband.

Man Ray, also noting the affinity, asked if he might photograph the two women together. "They were stunning subjects," he remembered of the session. Dressed as each other's foil—Mina in beige and Djuna in black—the contrast between them "made a fine picture; they posed as if the camera wasn't there."

Years later, Djuna would write to Mina: "I often think of the jolly times we had, do you remember, when there was a fire & I read aloud and you did cross-word puzzles?" Mina, for her part, would note in her diaries Djuna's loyalty as a friend, recalling also her "supreme elegance of clothing."

Drawing by Djuna Barnes of Mina Loy

Blossom Restaurant, 103 Bowery. Photo by Berenice Abbott.

BY NOW IT had become commonplace to compare Mina with Marianne Moore. Ezra Pound had grouped the two poets together in a critical article for the *Little Review* in 1918, describing their work as "a mind cry, more than a heart cry." Theirs was a "poetry of ideas," he said, a "dance of the intelligence among words." Loy, Moore, and Williams, he added, were the only poets in America who were writing anything of interest in verse.

Williams, by contrast, saw rivalry between the two women rather than conjunction. Both had accomplished "novelty, freedom, [and a] break with banality," he argued, but had done so with "divergent virtues." Nonetheless, when he and Robert McAlmon began publishing their new magazine *Contact,* Williams included verse by both women.

Marianne Moore couldn't have been more different from her glamorous

rival. Mina exuded worldliness and charm, she was a seductress and a social butterfly. Marianne was girlish and reserved, a great intellect, according to friends, though intensely private. She lived with her mother all her
life, neither traveling nor partaking much of Village nightlife. She wore her
carrot-colored hair in a crown of braided coils atop her head and dressed
like a spinster, often sporting an odd tricorne hat. Four years earlier, meeting Mina for the first time, Marianne had confided to a poet friend afterward that she thought Mina "rakish" and "clever," admitting also that she'd
felt intimidated by her rival's beauty and sophistication. Still, she had liked
Mina and pronounced her a "sound philosopher." They'd had a short but
satisfying exchange "about George Moore, and the hollowness of the fashionable life," she said.

In truth Marianne's feelings were more complex. Some years later,
presenting new work at one of Lola Ridge's poetry evenings, Marianne,
now managing editor of *The Dial* magazine, read a poem that many have
said is a thinly disguised portrait of her unofficial rival. The poem, called
"Those Various Scalpels," questions the purpose of Mina's acerbic tone, describing her as hard and too analytical. Marianne viewed Mina's poetry in
the context of the "vers libre" movement, of which Walter Arensberg and
Gertrude Stein were a part. She saw Mina as an "internationalist," which
she herself didn't wish to be.

For her part, Mina's impression of Marianne was summed up in a drawing that captures Marianne's sartorial oddness while also insinuating an
edge of emotional frigidity. Mina likened Marianne's writing to the "soliloquies of a library clock."

MINA CONTINUED TO write, though the effort was harder now. She was
working on a long poem about crossing the continent with Cravan, as well
as several prose pieces—the beginnings, perhaps, of a novel, also autobiographical. All were laced with despair, all difficult to push to completion.
She was thirty-nine now, still unable to let Cravan go and ashamed by her
inability to do so. A man had an easier time than a woman, she noted in her

journal. In the end a woman is defeated by life, "whether she cares about others' opinions or not."

"My health is very smashed up & I don't know what will be next," she wrote Mabel in Taos, New Mexico, where she was now living with her new husband, Tony Luhan. Too miserable to continue work on her novel and worried now that she was beginning to crack, Mina left for a "rest cure" at the Rose Valley sanatorium in Pennsylvania, where she remained for the next two months.

Her life was coming apart. Cravan's mother had recently sent a letter accusing her of maternal neglect. Her friends were increasingly critical as well. She needed to bring the children to New York, though she didn't have the funds. Joella was almost fourteen now, Fabienne no longer an infant. Adding to her worries, she had heard that Stephen had come through Florence and taken twelve-year-old Giles back with him to the Caribbean. Mina felt things closing in. Desperate, she wrote Mabel asking for help. She wanted to start a little restaurant in Paris, she said. She felt that there she could make enough to support the children.

> I suppose this is a ridiculous thing to ask after all these years—but I was so wondering what to do next. . . . I want to be free of worry—& work. . . . I have so much accumulated that is bursting for expression—it is getting unbearable. Would you lend me a thousand dollars to be paid back in two years—to help me start a Restaurant? When once I have got it going, I shall have some time and peace. . . . I've had a hell of a time off and on—the last few years—& it has fired my imagination—must vent it or break. Do let me know if you will do this for me.

Mina's pleading letter to Mabel requesting money seemed to have been met, at least in part. A few months later, sometime in 1921, Mina was en route to Paris and soon after to Florence, where she finally joined her two daughters, Joella, now fifteen, and Fabienne, her daughter by Cravan, now three.

Right: **Marianne Moore**

Over the next several years, Mina and the children wandered, moving to Berlin and then Paris. There Mina hooked up with an old friend, the writer-playboy Lawrence Vail (also one of Djuna's former lovers) and Vail's wealthy new wife, Peggy Guggenheim. Peggy agreed to fund Mina in a lampshade business, which for a time thrived, gradually expanding to include glass novelties, paper cut-outs, and painted flower arrangements. But by 1928, the two women had quarreled, bringing the business to a close. Djuna, who lived in Mina's building in Paris and was now her closest friend, decided to return to New York soon after, leaving Mina feeling increasingly stranded.

Djuna and Mina exchanged a flurry of letters over the next several years, with Djuna doing whatever she could to place Mina's work in America.

Djuna, having barely survived her failed affair with Thelma Wood, had decided that living alone with *no* companionship was preferable to being hurt again. Writing to Mina from New York in 1930, she observed,

> I've messed my life up all right—but we all do I presume—by thinking that life the way it seems in 1920 is going to come to a logical 1930—only it never does—
>
> I don't think I can live with *anyone* again—I've gotten cranky & old-maid like—I don't even like to have an animal looking at me, & when I lay a thing down I want to find it exactly where I put it—its [sic] as bad as that!

Mina had come to a similar conclusion. Having been defeated by love, she now tried to obliterate her need for it, reasoning that whenever she had found it, it had diminished her capacity to maintain the emotional authority and independence she needed as an artist. "Looking for love with all its catastrophes is a less risky experience than finding it," Mina wrote.

IN 1936, MINA finally moved back to New York, this time with few illusions. Initially she stayed with her daughter Fabienne, who lived in lower Manhattan. But she was restless there, increasingly ill at ease among people. She had never completely accepted Cravan's disappearance, nor the

Mina Loy and Peggy Guggenheim in Mina's lampshade shop, rue du Colisee, 1927

death of her son, Giles, who had succumbed to cancer in the Caribbean at the age of fourteen. Mina's losses had begun to catch up with her, her daughter Joella thought. She was becoming more introverted, detached.

After a few years, Mina insisted on taking a solitary room in the Bowery, a destitute neighborhood of addicts, lowlifes, and alley dwellers. There she lived for the next seventeen years alone, moving every few months to a new communal rooming house. At first Mina saw a few old friends, but as the years went on, she became progressively more antisocial. And money became a problem. Finally, she refused to see anyone. "Mina is in the last stages of depression and won't let me come see her," Djuna wrote to McAlmon in 1940.

Mina *was* writing, however. And she had begun making art again. Her sole preoccupation was now the drunks and vagrants of the neighborhood. She wrote poems about them; made elaborate sculptural portraits, using rags, clothespins, and egg crates, trash and found objects scavenged from the street. She sketched their stubbled faces, their gap-toothed smiles and battered shoes.

In 1959, Mina's old friend Duchamp would organize an exhibition of her Bowery bum constructions. Though gratified, Mina declined to attend the opening. A recluse now, she felt a crowd would be too much.

THROUGHOUT HER LIFE, Mina had adopted identities as readily as she adopted countries. An outsider everywhere, she had cultivated her own rootlessness, finding continuity in a life riddled with change,

Mina Loy with a thermometer earring. Photo by Man Ray, 1920.

familiarity in displacement. Having started out life as an "Anglo Mongrel," as she called herself, a child of mixed ancestry and uncertain class, Mina had made the most of her fractured identity. Christian and Jew, painter and poet, wife and lover, Dadaist and romantic—she had used her multiple and contradictory selves as she liked, and when she wanted, seeing her mutability for what it was: an elaborate masquerade, a feint behind which there was freedom. In her mongrel status had lain the possibility of remaining a work in progress, a modern, self-invented soul.

Once Mina had been a modernist icon: louche seductress and playmate of the Futurists, the prototypical New Woman making the rounds of Village parties, author of radical verse and nervy feminist polemics, "the most beautiful of a beautiful generation of poets," as Van Vechten called her. Now she was matron saint of the Bowery sidewalks, a ghostly presence in chalked face powder who held séances with the street people, dispensing cures for hangovers and pennies for wine, a curbside mystic who communed with the dispossessed. In some ways, Mina's pilgrim's progress had come full circle. Living in the Bowery, she was finally home, as Roger Conover writes: "an insider" among a world of outsiders.

The street vagrants called her Mama Mina. It was an ironic twist that even she, at some earlier moment, might have appreciated. Having spent her life fleeing the maternal—first her own mother, then the care of her own children—Mina had now become the beatific, white-nightgowned surrogate mother to a world of outcasts, *über*-mother of the streets.

CHAPTER 2

MARGARET ANDERSON AND JANE HEAP

LIFE FOR ART'S SAKE

"I have never felt much like a human being. It's a splendid feeling," Margaret Anderson scrawled, as she sat down, sometime in the mid 1920s, to begin her memoirs. "I am no man's wife, no man's delightful mistress, and I will never, never, never be a mother. . . . I have always held myself quite definitely aloof from natural laws."

Margaret also insisted she was not a writer. That she wrote and published scores of editorials, an extraordinary three-volume memoir, a book on the Russian mystic George Gurdjieff, and several unpublished novellas, including one on lesbian love, was, in her opinion, beside the point.

What she was, by her own description, was a person who loved to think about ideas, a "dilettante" from Chicago determined to start a literary magazine that would publish the best and most daring work of her time.

Blond and chic, Margaret Anderson appeared demure in her unprepossessing robin's egg blue suit and stylish hat. Yet, as with the magazine she founded in 1914, its plain tan covers concealing what were undeniably provocative contents inside, appearances can be deceptive. Margaret's brainchild the *Little Review*, which she eventually brought to Greenwich Village, was the most audacious arts magazine America had ever seen.

Left: **Margaret Anderson**

Margaret Anderson.
Photo by Man Ray.

"It was Art," said Ben Hecht. "The *Little Review* was nakedly and innocently, Art."

Ezra Pound called it "an insouciant little pagan paper." Margaret Anderson was the only editor in America, he said, who "ever felt need of, or responsibility for, getting the best writers concentrated" in a single periodical.

By all logic, Margaret's dream venture shouldn't have succeeded. It had no advertising, no money to pay contributors, and the material she printed was so advanced that no one else would publish it. But Margaret was not a woman to be deterred by practicalities. She was too obstinate, too self-confident, too certain in her ability to will miracles to worry much about how things happened.

"My greatest enemy is reality," she famously claimed in the first volume of her memoir, *My Thirty Years' War*. "I have fought it successfully for thirty years."

"HYSTERIC" WAS THE word Gertrude Stein used to describe Margaret Anderson when they met in Paris in the 1920s. "Wild" was the label given her by friends from the midwestern city of Indianapolis, where she was born in 1886. Lawless by nature, Margaret spent her childhood scheming to subvert her sedate bourgeois upbringing. Though she agreed to go to college, she flatly refused to take any required courses. By her fourth year, she had informed her father that paying her tuition would no longer be necessary. She was moving to Chicago. Her parents protested: It was improper for a single woman to live on her own. She was too young, too irresponsible, far too extravagant.

Margaret, however, was not to be dissuaded. In her view, the first and most important rule of life was always to do what one wanted to do. Margaret always did. She promptly wrote to the Chicago journalist Clara Laughlin. How, she inquired, could a "perfectly nice but revolting girl leave home?" Clara suggested she come in for an interview and was so entranced, after an afternoon in Margaret's company, that she offered her a job on the spot, interviewing stage celebrities. Outflanked and outmaneuvered, her parents were forced to surrender.

Gloriously free of her family, Margaret was ecstatic from the moment she set foot in Chicago. She resolved to make her life beautiful from that moment on. Her first gesture was to rent a fine and expensive piano from Steinway and Company. Her father had given her a minuscule allowance to spend on necessities. This Margaret tore through in no time. Fresh roses, preferably yellow, were at the top on her list of necessities, as were books, fine chocolates, and tickets to the Chicago symphony. As for the delicate matter of her dwindling funds, this could be easily solved by opening a charge account at Chicago's leading department store, she reasoned.

Within weeks her irate parents were pounding at the door, having learned from an informer that their daughter was "going to the dogs": not only smoking in public and spending money wildly but also consorting with literary radicals of the most rakish and unattractive sort.

Margaret was ordered home immediately, her meager allowance suspended and the matter, her parents assumed, closed. But Margaret, who visibly quickened at such shows of opposition, was not to be denied. She would go it alone, she said. And from that moment forward she did.

A series of provisional jobs followed: Margaret proofread; worked as a bookstore clerk; set type for a progressive poetry journal; and wrote highly opinionated book reviews by the hundreds. In no time, these had earned her such notoriety that she was offered the position of literary editor at one of Chicago's leading newspapers.

Preternaturally opinionated, it was one of Margaret's cardinal rules that one must never dissemble. Life, as she saw it, was a question of either yes or no. Indecision was unthinkable, the mark of a dreary and undiscerning mind. In Margaret's view, it was imperative that one pronounce on every topic that swam into one's ken, even those subjects about which one knew little—or nothing. Sometimes, by her own accounting, Margaret reviewed a hundred books in a single afternoon. A quick glance at the cover notes, another at the style, and she was off, her arch pronouncements searingly sure, her inventiveness absolute.

But Margaret was bored, despite such fiendish opinion making. One night in 1913, seized by a vague sense that her life had drifted off course, Margaret awoke to a stunning revelation. As she later described it in her memoirs: "First precise thought: I know why I'm depressed—nothing inspired is going on. Second: I demand that life be inspired every moment. Third: the only way to guarantee this is to have inspired conversation every moment. Fourth: most people never get so far as conversation; they haven't the stamina. . . . Fifth: if I had a magazine I could spend my time filling it with the best conversation the world has to offer. Sixth: marvelous idea . . . Seventh: decision to do it."

With that, she dropped off to sleep.

By morning, epiphany had become accomplished fact. Though Margaret's idea seemed unreality of the highest order, bohemian Chicago was ready to rally to her cause. One enthusiast gave $100. The novelist and editor Floyd Dell hosted a small soiree where she collected another $450, along with a pledge from an impressionable supporter, Dewitt Wing. He was so seduced by Margaret's idea, or perhaps by svelte Margaret herself, that he promised to foot every month's rent and printing bill. It was more than Margaret could have hoped for. The magazine was all but launched.

The *Little Review* would make no compromises with public taste: this was Margaret's foremost commitment. It would be a magazine of Art and Revolution, a forum for fresh opinion, ideas that were "intelligent from the artist's point of view."

The first issue came out in March of 1914. True to Margaret's effervescent character, it contained a riotous mix of writings, pieces on everything from Nietzsche to birth control; Bergson to Cubism; free love to the Little Theatre movement and Gertrude Stein. Despite countless typographical errors—Margaret refused to proofread galleys before printing—and claims by a few that it seemed rather "amateurish" (the "triumph of wide-eyed and high-hearted ineptitude," as Eunice Tietjens put it), the magazine received rave notices.

Off to a rollicking start, Margaret immediately began planning a second issue, which featured an impressive list of contributors including William Butler Yeats and Sherwood Anderson. As the third issue was about to go to press, Margaret met the anarchist Emma Goldman, "just in time to turn anarchist before the presses closed," as she remembered. Enthralled by Emma's flaming oratory, Margaret fired off a passionate editorial lauding Red Emma's anarchist views. Why, she asked, did people feel the need to own private property? Art and anarchy, she concluded, were in the world for the same reason. They shared the same drive for liberation.

Despite the satisfying furor that arose in the wake of Margaret's piece, Chicago wasn't entirely ready, it seemed, to endorse free love and beneficent bomb throwing. Dewitt announced that he could no longer continue his association with a magazine that was "going anarchist." Margaret assured her beleaguered-looking backer that she would manage fine without him. She would simply have to will a few more miracles.

TRUE TO MARGARET'S claims, the magazine continued unabated, despite what could only be described as an abrupt crimp in her fortunes. It was a tribute to Margaret's resilience that somehow she managed to adapt to her poverty with cheerful goodwill. Her housing arrangements were perpetually in flux. She lived for a while in a huge, drafty apartment with no furniture.

Next she moved to a house north of the city, overlooking the shores of Lake Michigan, which was even cheaper. When spring came, she realized she couldn't afford even that. The solution, she decided, was to move to the beach, where she could camp at the water's edge, rent free. At this point her small entourage—which consisted of two staff members, her sister Lois, and Lois's two children—understandably balked.

Margaret coaxed and cajoled. Life, she assured them, was "beneficent if [one] insisted upon it." They would live the "pristine life of nomads," she promised. "Roast corn over the campfire, bake potatoes in the ashes . . . swim in early morning, by moonlight, have great campfires, coffee and bacon for breakfast."

By May it was done. Margaret's ménage had built wooden tent platforms, pitched canvas tents, and moved in their few possessions, including manuscripts and galley proofs.

The days came and went, passing, said Margaret, in a dream. Every morning began with a plunge in the lake, followed by a run on the beach, coffee, breakfast cooked over a brushwood fire, and finally, Margaret's first morning cigarette. Though her work wardrobe consisted of a single blouse—crepe georgette, which she washed out by moonlight—a hat, and her one blue-tailored suit, she gamely climbed into them each morning and marched off to the *Little Review* offices in Chicago, making a point of returning every evening in time to watch the sunset. "So this is nature!" she would sigh, leaning back in her deck chair as the sun slipped behind the horizon.

Contributors trooped out to the lakeshore and pinned their submissions to the tent flaps. "She was always exquisite," one friend remembered, "as if emerging from a scented boudoir, not from a mildewed tent . . . valiant, always."

EVERYONE HELPED WHEN they could. The poet Eunice Tietjens pawned a diamond wedding ring to subsidize one *Little Review* issue. Frank Lloyd Wright contributed $100 toward another. Vachel Lindsay pledged the money he'd won in a poetry prize. She was "so unbelievably beautiful," as

Tietjens put it, "so vital, and so absurd," that people adored her. They were mesmerized by her spirit, her irreverent daring.

Sometimes Emma Goldman came out to visit on weekends, appearing, as one onlooker recalled, "like a disgruntled tragedy queen dispossessed by her rightly throne." Emma, always garbed in heavy clothing, would sit on a stool, unable to focus on anything but swatting mosquitoes. Margaret's answer to the bugs was action: stripping off her clothes, she would leap into the icy lake. "You see, [Emma's] a city Anarchist," Margaret would coyly observe. "She's not used to real freedom."

Occasionally a solitary policeman showed up, looking grim and purposeful as he trudged awkwardly through the sand, but Margaret's persuasive charm always won the day. They were never evicted. Reporters appeared too, which led to a spate of feature stories, including one especially unfortunate one that described them as a band of "Nietzchean revolutionaries." This, to Margaret's horror, caused them to lose the house she had just secured for the upcoming winter.

Margaret's summer residence at Lake Michigan, 1915

Then "the most interesting thing" that ever befell the *Little Review* occurred: Jane Heap joined the staff.

Jane defied all categories. Her hair was shorn like a man's and she made no secret of her fondness for cross-dressing, favoring sober men's suits and bow ties. In winter, she wore a Russian fur hat and an oversized greatcoat. High-cheekboned and darkly poised, with chiseled features and deep, thoughtful eyes, Jane bore a striking resemblance to Oscar Wilde, and she had the wit to match.

There were times when Margaret, who was normally oblivious to what people thought or with whom she was seen, refused to go out with Jane until Jane changed into something less conspicuous.

Margaret also had her moments of conspicuous dress, however. Sometimes she wore only one glove—always on the right hand. This was the hand she hated, she explained to anyone who asked. The left one she loved.

In truth, it was easy to overlook Jane's sartorial peculiarities; Margaret was so smitten by Jane's talk that nothing else mattered. It wasn't a question of style. Or erudition. Or even truth. It was the way Jane said things. No one could pronounce upon life with the same piercing wit as Jane, the same thrilling precision. She had a way of placing an important word "so personally," said Margaret, that it gave the entire subject a curious significance.

Jane's pithy pronouncements were legendary. She famously called the Paris publisher Robert McAlmon "an epileptic without gumption enough to have fits" and said that Burton Rascoe, literary editor of the *Herald Tribune,* "wouldn't have recognized the Sphinx outside of Egypt." Once, paying tribute to someone who had (briefly) understood her, Jane remarked: "A hand on the exact octave that is me." Another time, responding to Margaret's cry that " life should be ecstasy," Jane laconically replied, "Why limit me to ecstasy?"

But it was impossible to capture the ecstasy of Jane's talk, the odd, biting brilliance, the quirky economy of her words. It was too ephemeral.

In Margaret's view, Jane's arrival was "a new, unexpected extra life that to me was like a second birth." From the moment Jane appeared, there were ruffled feathers, just the kind of drama Margaret thrilled to.

It was February of 1916 and the magazine was now two years old. Margaret had just moved back to downtown Chicago, her lakefront interlude having come to a close. That day an heiress whom Margaret had impishly dubbed Nineteen Millions was visiting the magazine offices. Margaret, of course, was hoping that her wealthy guest might be willing to part with a few pennies in the interest of "Art." The courtship was well under way.

Minutes earlier, Jane Heap had come in. A perfect stranger, she stood quietly to the side, big-boned and imposing, listening as Nineteen Millions spouted opinions. Jane watched with interest. Finally, letting out a tender laugh, she interjected a wry observation.

Nineteen Millions glared at Jane with fury. Then she abruptly stomped out, muttering that, above all things, she "disliked frivolity."

Margaret's reaction was just the opposite. She knew instantly that she wanted to live with this kind of frivolity forever.

FOR THE NEXT six years, Margaret and Jane were inseparable. Once they began talking, said Margaret, they couldn't stop. By June they were lovers.

All that spring Margaret had been casting about for a housing solution to the summer. One day it occurred to her that Nineteen Millions had extended an open invitation to visit her in California. Margaret wrote immediately to say she was coming—she and her "helpmate" Jane

Jane Heap

Heap—choosing to overlook the minor matter of their earlier spat. Nineteen Millions was less forgetful. Margaret was of course welcome, she wrote; Jane Heap was emphatically not.

Undeterred, Margaret insisted they go anyway. Though this time it was Margaret who stomped out in a huff, only moments after Nineteen Millions had pronounced Jane "odious" for a second time. Margaret never doubted their luck would turn. They retreated to Muir Woods, across the bay from San Francisco, and in no time were back on their feet, having secured a dilapidated ranch house with lovely eucalyptus trees leading to the sea. So began the *Little Review*'s second interlude amidst the marvels of nature.

It was a five-month idyll. By day, Margaret and Jane swam and rode horses like seasoned wranglers, standing in their stirrups and emitting whoops and Indian war cries. By night they worked on the *Little Review* by the glow of a kerosene lamp. Jane drew cartoons and Margaret played the piano on a Steinway she'd secured from a shop in San Francisco at no cost. They ate fudge for breakfast and lolled about until noon. They talked endlessly, incessantly. Their talk began at lunch and climaxed at tea. By dinner they were "staggering with it." By five the next morning they were "unconscious but still talking," said Margaret. "This was what I had been waiting for all my life."

IN FACT, THEY were as different as two lovers could be. Opposites in temperament, they were rarely in accord, yet still intensely engaged—especially when they were quarreling, which was always.

"Jane was the earth to Margaret's fire," the cultural historian Steven Watson has written, "the butch to her femme, the depressive to her hysteric."

Margaret was flexible and uncommonly brazen; Jane was brittle and given to brooding. Jane was systematic: tactful and highly composed. Margaret was impetuous: filled with whimsy and mad ideas. She could be charmingly impertinent and often was. When Upton Sinclair wrote, saying, "Please cease sending me the *Little Review*. I no longer understand anything in it, so it no longer interests me," Margaret replied, "Please cease sending me your Socialist paper. I understand everything in it, therefore it no longer interests me."

Margaret was eternally interested in what she called "the created life," all that was artful, even the artful putdown—even when it was aimed at her.

Sometimes Jane resorted to analyzing Margaret's character on paper, enumerating her faults in a gloating letter that would later be slipped under Margaret's door. But it never went as Jane hoped. Instead of reducing Margaret's self-esteem, Jane would see exaltation cross Margaret's face, a flush of excitement.

"Never forget what you wrote in this note," Margaret would exclaim. "It's too good! You must try to put it into the *Little Review*."

So intent was Margaret on bringing Jane's extraordinary verbal prowess to the world that sometimes, in social situations, she purposely antagonized people to draw Jane into a quarrel. Jane complained that Margaret carried her around like a fighting cock to be thrown into the ring. "It's an awkward role for me," she observed. "You're the buzz and I'm the sting."

In truth, both women thrived on the opposition. Jane felt she had never encountered enough resistance before her life with Margaret; Margaret that her argumentative side had never been prized.

IT WAS TIME to bring out a new issue of the *Little Review*. They were living under such a spell, said Margaret, that even breaking up their conversation to undress, or move to the bedroom, seemed an agony. They dragged their beds to the living room, dined in their pajamas, and kept talking. Compared to the brilliance of their talk, observed Margaret, the mediocrity of the manuscripts coming in was maddening. "Why labor to perpetuate the dull?"

In protest, they decided to publish an empty issue, sixty-four blank white pages, accompanied by a statement declaring that "since no art was being produced," they would make no attempt to publish any. "The *Little Review* hopes to become a magazine of Art. The September issue is offered as a Want Ad."

Their idyll in Muir Woods came to an abrupt end as the autumn rains

Jane Heap had a preference for men's suits. Photo by Berenice Abbott.

descended, swamping everything in sight. It was time for a change, said Margaret. New York was where they must go.

THEIR FIRST NIGHT in New York was inauspicious. Margaret had intended to enter the city on a stallion. Traveling with Jane was akin to riding a balky mule. Jane had become hopelessly depressed the minute they boarded the train. As they taxied downtown, she wouldn't even glance out the car window. When they arrived at the Brevoort Hotel, she threw herself facedown on the bed and refused to move.

This was the one part of Jane's character that Margaret couldn't abide: Jane's indulgence of her own gloom. Personal manias were one thing. No relationship, said Margaret, could interest her that hadn't a "thousand dramatized reserves." But Jane went too far. She kept a revolver in a trunk in her studio and was constantly threatening suicide. Sometimes her moods were insupportable.

Margaret sank down into the hotel chair. Eyeing Jane's prostrate body, she tried to muster some fresh unreality to pull things around. What would happen if she allowed Jane to return to Chicago as she seemed to want to do? Jane would squander her priceless talk, that was what would happen. Without a champion, Jane's ephemeral gift would be lost. She, Margaret, was her champion. It was her role to bring Jane's conversational genius to the world. No one else could do it—no one else would. And since Jane had made it clear she would never sit down on her own to write, it was clearly Margaret's job to coax Jane's talk into print.

Her resolve once again rekindled by sheer force of will, Margaret let herself drift off to sleep now. By morning she was astride her steed again.

FROM 1917 TO 1923, there was almost never a week when Margaret and Jane's morning coffee was assured. They rented a small basement office in Greenwich Village for $25 a month and found an equally cheap apartment nearby, four spacious rooms above an undertaker in an otherwise stately old house. After the usual piano arrangements had been made, they concentrated on the furnishings, beginning with the living room, which Margaret insisted should be "a special, haunting" place where all future *Little Review* conversations would commence. They hung a large divan from heavy black chains affixed to the ceiling and covered it with silk cushions they sewed themselves—emerald green, magenta, royal purple, and chartreuse. A large reading table and a single lemon-yellow lamp stood sentry between the windows.

The *Little Review* now entered what Margaret considered its most "creative period." Under her sole stewardship, its contents had been lively but uneven; its editorial voice—part "arty indolence," part anarchy—had been wildly inconsistent. Jane brought focus and organization. Her judgments were astute, her attention unswerving.

To Margaret's mind, editing the magazine with Jane was the ultimate expression of her admiration for Jane's genius. Getting Jane's column onto paper was quite another matter. The ritual was complicated. Margaret would prime Jane with hours of "psychological gossip," then lock the doors, having procured several days' worth of delicatessen food beforehand, and begin transcribing, taking down Jane's pithy, stream-of-consciousness pronouncements in a hurried scrawl throughout the night. Somehow the column came out every month, however, always under the tiny byline "jh." (Jane insisted on signing her name in lowercase letters.)

For all her mercurial enthusiasms, Margaret never doubted her taste and perceptions. She always knew "when writing was beautiful and when it was not," she claimed. Knowing *why* was less important. Asked late in life

Washington Square North, nos. 21–25. Photo by Berenice Abbott.

if she had had standards, Margaret bristled. *"Mon dieu,"* she exclaimed with indignation, "I had nothing *but* standards!" Though she allowed that the magazine had had its weaker moments—"We often printed rot," she once observed—her faith in herself was absolute.

Beyond standards, it took daring to bring out the magazine each month, not only an intrepid will and a brazen theatricality, but a supreme indifference to authority. When bills accumulated, Margaret charmed, coaxed, and cajoled creditors. When this didn't work, she resorted to guile—"tears, prayers, hysterics or rages." Sometimes she simply bent the rules. If a creditor appeared in her office demanding an immediate check for goods sent, Margaret would oblige him with a check. When the fuming creditor returned a few days later waving the same check, returned by the bank, she would coquettishly reply, "But I didn't say it was *good*," and bat her eyelashes.

Once, in response to an infuriated printer who insisted that she send him all the money in the office, she dutifully slipped five cents into an envelope and mailed it. Another time, determined to right their fortunes in a single day, Margaret stormed the wealthiest offices of Wall Street, canvassing tower after tower of CEOs for contributions. Sometimes they ran fewer pages, or did without a cover, or printed on cheap stock. "We may have to come out on tissue paper pretty soon, but we shall *keep on coming out!*" Margaret defiantly vowed.

They found the cheapest printer in New York, a Mr. Popovitch, whose mother had been poet laureate of Serbia. Often they went to his shop and helped set type and fold pages to gain time—the same time Margaret then lost reading aloud Wyndham Lewis to Mr. Popovitch's two daughters.

They were equally resourceful about adjusting the rituals of their private life to their precarious finances. During one especially penniless period, they ate potatoes prepared in every conceivable manner that jh, a "superb" cook, could concoct. During another lean stretch, it was biscuits, made from a single sack of flour, that kept them going. They sewed their own clothes and cut each other's hair, insisting always on a life of beauty.

Indeed, for all their poverty, Margaret never dropped her standards. When the famously overbearing Boston heiress Amy Lowell arrived one morning unannounced and tried to insinuate herself onto the *Little Review* staff, Margaret bravely stood her ground, refusing to be bought. Big-boned and so immense, Margaret remembered, that she could barely squeeze through the door, Amy Lowell was a poet herself.

"I have money," Amy announced. "You haven't."

She was prepared, she said, to offer Margaret $150 a month in return for editorship of the *Little Review* poetry department. "I'll merely direct," she added. "You can count on me never to dictate."

"No clairvoyant was needed to know that Amy Lowell would dictate . . . any adventure in which she had a part," Margaret wryly observed.

She was so sorry, she answered, but she couldn't possibly function "in association."

**Margaret Anderson. Photo by
Berenice Abbott, circa 1925.**

MARGARET'S WILLFUL optimism was paying off, however. Since coming to New York, the *Little Review* had become an important venue for modernist writing, much of it by women. New work by Gertrude Stein, Mina Loy, Djuna Barnes, Mary Butts, H.D. (Hilda Doolittle), Dorothy Richardson, and Marianne Moore now appeared regularly in its pages, adding to the magazine's growing luster. Artists as well as writers courted them now; younger poets dropped by for conversation. Their rooms were becoming an oasis for renegade bohemians.

Margaret expected nothing short of the "exceptional" from her company. "Art," to her mind was "the person." Why entertain if not to be surrounded by exceptional people?

Any guest who displayed too much solemnity was immediately suspect. Once, an aspiring female author, a girl Margaret described as having the kind of "earnestness that would prevent anyone from achieving anything," asked what in fact she should do to become a good writer?

"Use a little lip rouge, to begin with," Margaret suggested. "Beauty may bring you experiences to write about."

Unfortunately, even the presence of exceptional people didn't relieve Margaret's insolvency. Though the magazine steadily gained in stature, it never achieved paying status: "Money absolutely abstained from coming in," said Margaret delicately. "It is much easier to find a public for ideals than for ideas," she observed.

When Gertrude Stein reproached Margaret, telling her that she didn't consider it "a good principle for the artist to remain unpaid," Margaret retorted, "It's a little better than for him to remain unprinted, that's all."

Another time, accused of putting out a magazine that was "a debauch of art for art's sake," Margaret sardonically quipped, "Should it be art for money's sake?"

Compounding their financial miseries, the U.S. Post Office began to interfere with their venture, riffling through each new issue of the *Little Review* in search of "advanced intellectual smut." It was always disheartening, said Margaret, having labored tirelessly for an entire month to put out an issue, to receive an official notification that bluntly stated: BURNED.

SOME OF THE dynamism of the *Little Review* was also attributable to the arrival of Ezra Pound, who became the magazine's foreign editor in 1917, and, like Anderson and Heap, was deeply committed to bringing fresh talent to the eyes of the world. Pound had initially promised to circulate the magazine in Europe in exchange for a place where he and T. S. Eliot were guaranteed publication once a month. In return, he offered to pay contributors out of a fund provided by an anonymous patron, a well-connected lawyer and art collector named John Quinn. At Pound's behest, the *Little Review* now included work by T. S. Eliot, Wyndham Lewis, Yeats, Ford Madox Ford, H.D., and other European modernists, raising its profile even further. Over the next few years, the magazine would not only feature the best modern writers in England, France, and America; it would became the most important outlet for avant-garde literature in America.

It was Pound who first sent Margaret the opening chapter of a "tightly written manuscript," which he highly recommended, though wasn't sure they would care to print, "as it would involve the magazine further with the Post Office censors." The manuscript was James Joyce's *Ulysses*, the still unknown and unsung modernist masterpiece of the century. But Pound had underestimated Margaret, who instantly saw *Ulysses*'s greatness. "This is the most beautiful thing we'll ever have" she told Jane. "We'll print it if it's the last effort of our lives."

For the next three years, the *Little Review* printed monthly installments

Ezra Pound, foreign editor of the
Little Review

of *Ulysses*, despite the fact that four separate issues were burned for alleged obscenity.

When they published the Nausicaa episode, in which Bloom's erotic fantasies about Gerty MacDowell lead to a lyrical moment of autoerotic release—the scene, as Margaret always described it, "where the man went off in his pants"—their luck ran out. Spurred by complaints from the Society for the Suppression of Vice, a pious order headed by a mild-mannered reformer named John Sumner, Margaret and Jane were arrested on charges of obscenity.

By chance, Margaret happened upon her grand inquisitor only a few days after the indictment was served, meeting him at the Washington Square Book Shop, where the two proceeded to engage in a heated exchange. She concluded he wasn't the ogre she had imagined, but a rather courtly fellow, charming and shy. She felt sure, had she been able to entertain him for a month's worth of teas, she could have won him over. "He was the perfect enemy," she remarked. "I won every point and he seemed to like it."

Unfortunately, there wasn't time enough for a month of teas. The next time Margaret saw Sumner was in court. The benches were packed with policemen, pimps, and petty thieves, along with two rows of artsy Greenwich Village women, Mina Loy and the Baroness among them, fashionably dressed for the occasion. Their patron John Quinn insisted on representing them, which they regretted, as Quinn's strategy was at best low-key. Margaret wanted an obstreperous defense worthy of Emma Goldman or the militant Inez Milholland (reputed to be the "most beautiful woman ever to bite a policeman's wrist"), at the very least a fiery speech about freedom and beauty. She felt sure that if Jane had been allowed to speak, she would have cinched the case. Jane felt little but contempt for the proceedings: "Men think thoughts and have emotions about these things everywhere," she noted, but have rarely expressed it "as delicately and imaginatively as [Joyce's] Mr. Bloom."

The trial had more than its share of absurd moments. At one point, the judge wouldn't allow the "libidinous" sections to be read aloud, ruling that the passage would corrupt the innocent ears of the demure-looking Margaret.

"But she is the publisher," Quinn protested.

Two of the three judges slept through most of the proceedings. The third, a young Norwegian, later told Jane that had he known they were country-men (Jane's ancestors were Norwegian), he would have changed his verdict.

Margaret Anderson and Jane Heap, *middle standing;* Ezra Pound, *right standing;*
Man Ray, *with camera;* Mina Loy, *front center;* Tristan Tzara, *to her right;*
and Jean Cocteau, *with cane;* in Paris

To Margaret's disgust, no New York newspapers rose to their defense. They were declared guilty and fined $100, then ushered to the station for fingerprinting.

Margaret, angered by the trial's dearth of drama, decided to stage a little theater of her own at the station. Presented with the inkpad, she bristled with indignation, then announced that before she could possibly submit her fingers to the grubby ordeal of finger-printing, she would require "a cake of very good soap, a bottle of very good eau de cologne and a very clean towel."

Afterward, when a friend expressed disappointment that Anderson and Heap hadn't martyred themselves by going to jail, Margaret nodded in agreement. "It is always a mistake to allow the persuasions of your friends or your lawyer to keep you out of jail," she said.

BY NOW THE *Little Review* editors had moved to a new apartment on West Eighth Street, the top floor of a small brick dwelling that also housed the Washington Square Book Shop, the foremost purveyor of the *Little Review*. It was into this new apartment, in fact, that the eccentric Baroness Elsa von Freytag-Loringhoven strode one morning, having only moments before shaved and lacquered her head vermilion. The Baroness, recalled Margaret, had been despondent for weeks. William Carlos Williams had been treating her deplorably, writing her insulting letters, rebuffing her declarations of love in the most ignoble ways. Unable to bear his rejection any longer, she'd shaved her head in a final, nihilistic act of despair.

Cloaked in a crepe sheet stolen from a funeral home, the Baroness sashayed across the living room and took a few turns, exhibiting her lacquered pate from all angles, the vermilion accentuated by the stygian walls.

"Shaving one's head is like having a new love experience," she purred. Then she abruptly threw off the sheet. "It's better when I'm nude."

IF JAMES JOYCE was the most important male contributor to the *Little Review*, the Baroness, to Margaret's mind, was the most treasured female

Baroness Elsa von Freytag-Loringhoven. Photo by Man Ray.

contributor (after Jane Heap, of course): "The only figure of our generation who deserves the epithet extraordinary," Margaret later wrote.

From the moment the Baroness had waltzed into their office three years earlier, Jane and Margaret recognized her as exceptional. They had already judged her a high talent, having read an astonishing poem she'd sent anonymously with a cryptic dedication to Marcel Duchamp. Now they were able to connect the remarkable poem to the equally remarkable person who stood before them, her black velvet tam-o'-shanter trimmed with dangling spoons, her white spats appliquéd with furniture braid.

"We're taking the poem," said Jane. "It's beautiful."

Pleased, the Baroness nodded, offering the opinion that the *Little Review* was "the only magazine of art that is art." Though she filched five dollars' worth of stamps, as was her wont, before making an exit, from that moment forward she was always welcome.

At about the same time, the *Little Review* editors accepted their first story by Djuna Barnes, beginning an uneasy friendship that, in Margaret's words, "might have been great had it not been that Djuna always felt some fundamental distrust of our life—of our talk."

Margaret had initially been taken by the tall, dashing Djuna, with her mordant wit and elegant voice, her trill of sharp laughter. She was moved by Djuna's maternal side.

"You two poor things," Djuna would say in her warm, laughing voice. "You're both crazy of course, God help you. I suppose I can stand it if you can, but someone ought to look out for you."

Djuna looked out for them by bringing in the first strawberries of spring and the last oysters of winter, said Margaret, "but to the more important luxuries of the soul she turned an unhearing ear. Djuna would never talk. . . . She said it was because she was reserved about herself. She wasn't, in fact, reserved—she was unenlightened."

Right: Djuna Barnes. Photo by Berenice Abbott.

On Djuna's part, she viewed Margaret with wary respect. Though she mocked Margaret's fastidiousness, saying that she even washed her soap before using it, decades later, recalling Margaret in a letter, she wrote: "In her young years I never thought her very good-looking, as many people did, but now she is beautiful—I mean it really. Her serious face is beautifully tragic and her smile has the loveliest, most touching charm."

Later Margaret would accuse Djuna of having an "outside that was often stunning" and an inside that she didn't know anything about. Margaret said it embarrassed her "to attempt a relationship with anyone who was not on speaking terms with her own psyche."

The truth was more complicated. The seed of Margaret's hostility was sown, no doubt, by an affair rumored to have taken place between Djuna and Jane Heap sometime between 1918 and 1919. The only witness to the full fury produced by the incident comes in a short passage from the memoirs of the artist Maurice Sterne, Mabel Dodge's third husband and briefly one of Barnes's lovers. As Sterne remembered:

> I had dinner with Djuna Barnes, the avant-garde writer, occasionally. She ordinarily spoke very little, being more interested in observing the people she was with. One night at Polly's restaurant in Greenwich Village, Djuna suddenly exclaimed that she saw someone she knew. She took me over to a table where a mousy girl was dining with some friends. Djuna began hissing,—*I hate you, I hate you, I hate you* over and over again. The tan mouse smiled sweetly but there was an electric spark in her smile and they had an ominously quiet, violent fight before Djuna stalked out with that long stride of hers.

The "mouse" was Margaret Anderson and the matter in dispute was her lover Jane. Djuna's letters to another friend, written sometime in 1938, refer to Jane Heap as a "shit," perhaps indicating that the affair ended badly. Whatever the depth of the distrust between them, to Margaret's credit, she always published Djuna's work, which she admired despite their personal animosity.

The Baroness, by contrast, had difficulty with Djuna's work. "I cannot

Polly's Restaurant in Greenwich Village. Photo by Jessie Tarbox Beals.

read your stories Djuna Barnes," she said. "I don't know where your characters come from. You make them fly on magic carpets."

Djuna at first didn't appreciate the Baroness either, though later she amended her initial impressions, becoming her most loyal friend. In 1923, sensing that the Baroness's spirits were "withering in the sordid materialism of New York," Djuna, Margaret, Jane, and Berenice Abbott collected money to send her back to Germany. But the Baroness wouldn't stay. She drifted to Paris, and in her last tragic years it was Djuna, when everyone else had grown weary, who supported her by selling portions of Joyce's annotated *Ulysses* to pay the rent on the Baroness's meager flat. It was to Djuna that

Djuna Barnes, Margaret Anderson, and Carl Van Vechten

the Baroness penned her last desolate letters, described as "the saddest and most beautiful letters in English literature."

> I will probably—yes, yes, yes, probably have to die. . . . I cannot any more conceive of the idea of a decent artist existence for me, and another is not possible. . . . My terror is so genuine, so must my end be. Life goes out of life . . . and I marvel that I have been in it. . . . Forgive me my troubled being. . . . I am not truly deranged even, but scattered. . . . Tragedy is written on me. . . . I almost despise myself for the trouble I make and the trouble that troubles me. But what shall I do? I am stunned nearly to exhaustion. Forgive me, but I am mourning destruction of high quality—as I know myself to be. . . . That is the tragedy—I still feel deep in me glittering wealth.

In 1927, the Baroness and her beloved dogs were asphyxiated by gas in her apartment, whether by accident or design it was never known. At her funeral, Berenice Abbott said that she "couldn't believe that anyone as vibrant as Elsa could die."

WHEN THE *LITTLE REVIEW* was approaching its tenth anniversary, Margaret announced to Jane that she felt the time had come to close the magazine. "It had begun logically with the inarticulateness of a divine afflatus," she argued. "It should end logically with the epoch's supreme articulation—*Ulysses.*"

Jane felt nothing so definitive. Now more than ever, she argued, it was important to keep the *Little Review* alive. Closing it would amount to an act of desertion. The issue they had printed on the heels of the trial was an outspoken defense of art. It had featured work, she said, for which there was no other home: a Dadaist novel by Pound, an edgy short story by Djuna, poetry by Mina and the Baroness, along with a riveting portrait of the pair by Man Ray—Mina looking coy under the brim of a mannish hat, the Baroness posing as a bourgeois in dark dress and beads. There were new contributions by Gertrude Stein, Guillaume Apollinaire, Jean Cocteau, and the Baroness waiting in the wings. Besides, Jane added, Margaret couldn't end the magazine—she had founded it.

"I certainly can give it up," Margaret quipped. "I'll give it to you."

They argued for weeks. For the first time in her life, Margaret felt paralysis, an uncertainty of a magnitude she had never before known. Years later, reconstructing her life in writing, Margaret would reflect back only glancingly on this difficult period, recalling somewhat cryptically that she hadn't known what to do next, so instead she "did a nervous breakdown that lasted many months." Whatever the true measure of the crisis, the rift between the two women grew deeper than their clash over the magazine's future, for Margaret would leave Jane for a new lover some months later, a mesmerizing opera singer named Georgette Leblanc.

Georgette Leblanc. Portrait by Djuna Barnes, 1941.

LIKE ALL EVENTS in her life, Margaret's attraction to Georgette was instant and absolute. Less than a year after they met, she and Georgette, who was twenty years her senior, were sailing to France to begin a new life.

From 1924 to 1927, Jane carried on alone, publishing the *Little Review* as a quarterly and, when finances fell short, as an annual. The magazine continued to be a mouthpiece for the latest developments in art nonetheless, running issues on Dada, Constructivism, de Stijl, Surrealism, and the machine aesthetic for the remainder of the decade. In 1926, Jane opened a gallery at 66 Fifth Avenue as an adjunct to the magazine, that year mounting the first show of Russian Constructivist stage sets ever to appear in America. An epoch-making exhibit dedicated to the Machine Age followed the next year, making headlines. Margaret, meanwhile, remained in France.

In 1929, fifteen years after the *Little Review* had begun, Jane finally concluded that the magazine had, in fact, run its course. Meeting her in Paris, Margaret joined in the production of the last and, as it turned out, longest issue, more than one hundred pages. Jane wrote a farewell editorial, saying that the revolution in the arts, begun before the war, "had heralded a renaissance" and that the *Little Review* had been "an organ" of that renaissance, having given space to "23 new systems of art . . . representing 19 countries." The moment had now passed; it was time to move on.

MARGARET ANDERSON never abandoned her lifelong crusade to resist reality. *Dilettante* was a label she always proudly claimed. If ever she was accused of being uneducated, she readily agreed. Learning, she ventured, had always been a dreary activity compared to understanding, which was certainly possible without a lot of study. Though Margaret had once vowed that she would "never, never be a mother," it was a role with which she was not unfamiliar in the end, having not only given birth to the vision of a radical new magazine but served as midwife to the revolutionary visions of countless others, many of them women. For all Margaret's flightiness and inconsistencies, she held to her word. She *did* produce the most daring literary journal America had ever seen, remaining as she promised quite definitely aloof from natural laws, especially the law of probability. Margaret won her perpetual war on reality. She made real her fantasies, willing fancy into fact. Hers was one of the most delectable and original self-inventions ever to flow from a memoirist's pen.

"I shall die as I have lived," she vowed late in life. "I shall just go into a dream."

CHAPTER 3

EDNA ST. VINCENT MILLAY

IMPRISONED IN THE PERSONAL

In the fall of 1918, having just received news of the Armistice, an elfin, red-haired young poet and her two male companions celebrated with an all-night spree. Riding back and forth on the Staten Island ferry, they cavorted until dawn, drinking jug wine and prancing in the moonlight. They clambered up and down the hilly Staten Island shoreline and danced along untamed stretches of beach. They chased each other down the dunes. Striking dramatic poses, they took turns reciting poetry.

When morning arrived, the wild-hearted poet left her two companions and stumbled home to her Greenwich Village garret, a one-room cold-water flat with barely enough space for a table and a typewriter. There she spent the next day and night feverishly composing poetry. She wrote in a hot burn, chain-smoking cigarettes and drinking tea, skipping meals, too excited to sleep. It was a scenario she would repeat countless times.

Neither such ecstatic play nor such driven labors were unusual for Edna St. Vincent Millay. Small-boned and slender, barely five feet in height, with a boyish figure and "wild, gray-green" eyes that squinted when she smiled, she was the woman everyone in the Village was speaking of that year, the precocious young poet from Maine who had already published at the age of twenty-five.

Left: **Edna St. Vincent Millay, 1930. Photo by Herman Mishkin.**

Edna was the model bohemian, a sly-humored pagan who made the rounds of Village parties, a gamine surrounded by a swarm of suitors. Both her name and her bittersweet verse were already synonymous with hedonistic youth. Her sonnets were celebrated for their flippant attitude toward love, their nervy assertion that a woman had the same right to sexual infidelity and amorous adventure as men. "And if I loved you Wednesday, / Well, what is it to you?" Edna archly proclaimed. "I do not love you Thursday— / So much is true."

Legions of men were in love with her. Legions also wrote about her, contemplated her, puzzled over her. None could quite pin her down. In memoirs of the period, she appears as "the fleeing and challenging Daphne," the playful heathen, earthy and flirtatious, yet inaccessible, ultimately elusive.

Edmund Wilson, canny in his reflections of the era, describes her rounding the corner of MacDougal Street, flushed and laughing, "like a nymph," her lover Floyd Dell also laughing, close in pursuit. A Vassar friend, Margaret Lovell, remembers her getting ready for a Village costume ball: Edna kneeling stark naked before a mirror, wrapping scarves borrowed from a friend around her shoulders, breasts, and wild red hair. Another writer recalls her reciting poetry in a smoky Village apartment, a throaty baritone in flowing chiffons, self-consciously dramatic, her voice unearthly, more British than American in cadence.

"She was one of those women whose features are not perfect and who in their moments of dimness may not seem even pretty, but who, excited by the blood or the spirit, become almost supernaturally beautiful," wrote Wilson. She had an intoxicating effect on people. Falling in love with her, he claimed, was an "almost inevitable consequence of knowing her in those days." It "created the atmosphere in which she lived and composed." Even children felt the draw. Whenever Wilson arrived to call for Edna in a cab, the children playing on 19th Street would run and crowd around her, he remembered. "It was partly that she gave them pennies," he said, but it was also her magnetism.

This mesmerizing spell that Wilson and so many others spoke of was

Edna St. Vincent Millay, 1914. Photo by Arnold Genthe.

not, however, without its darker side. There was also "something of awful drama about everything one did with Edna," wrote Wilson. "She was sometimes rather a strain, because nothing could be casual for her; I do not think I ever saw her relaxed, even when she was tired or ill. She did not gossip . . . did not like to talk personalities. It was partly that she was really noble, partly that she was rather neurotic." Though this side of her, he added, was more in evidence later.

She was sometimes "lonely and unreachable," wrote Dell, "at moments a scared little girl from Maine." She seemed "a little aloof from ordinary concerns."

It was this remoteness, this persistent, enigmatic remove that so frustrated and eluded Edna's suitors. She was like an underground stream: impossible to trace or pursue to its depths.

Part of it was the rigor of Edna's mind. She had a searching intelligence, an agility and quickness that startled even her friends. She could think in verse, recalled one, "tossing off a quatrain impromptu."

"Edna had as clear, hard, alert and logical a mind as I have encountered in man or woman," observed the editor Max Eastman. "She surprised me continually too with her large and accurate knowledge about many things —about nature, about language, about everything relating to her art."

Yet part of her inaccessibility also had to do with Edna's commitment to her work, her fierce need to write poetry.

"Her determination to be a poet, and not some man's woman or even some child's mother, was absolute," observed Eastman. Perhaps this is what made people "shy and a trifle constrained in her presence. You felt the strength of character behind that decision, and strength of character is always a trifle alarming."

Edna had learned these things—the high-keyed focus, the tenacity, the conviction—at her mother's knee. She was the product of her mother Cora Millay's making. It was Cora who created her daughter's "will and need" to be a poet, who drove and encouraged her singular gift. Yet it was also Edna's mother who inadvertently set the stage for the poet's tortured emotional life in later years. For, behind the witty seductress of Greenwich Village legend there loomed specters and shadows, a tormented woman quite different from the myth, a poet periodically possessed by demons, driven to alcoholism and psychosomatic illnesses, breakdowns and compulsive love affairs.

Edna St. Vincent Millay would climb as high as any woman poet ever had, publishing more than twenty books of verse in her lifetime, one for which she was awarded the Pulitzer Prize for Poetry, the first woman ever to be so honored. But her stunning ascent was not without its psychic costs.

BORN IN 1892, EDNA was the first of three daughters in an old but impoverished New England family of flinty Irish stock. Her mother, having dreamed of being a writer herself, was determined to give her daughters every possible opportunity to develop their artistic talents. She taught Edna to write verse at four and at seven to play the piano, instilling in her firstborn a stoic New England discipline, as well as a love of play.

The girls lived in a world that was completely female. Cora was a free-thinker who believed in following one's instincts, even if they ran contrary to society's ideas. When Edna was six, her mother politely asked her school-teacher husband to leave, having concluded that life would be no less laborious without him, given his penchant for losing paychecks to poker games. Years later, Edna wrote that she remembered a swamp of cranberries, and her father's walking "down across that swamp . . . when my mother told him to go & not come back," which he never did.

Enduring the small-town censure that inevitably befell any woman with enough mettle to take life into her own hands, Cora filed for a divorce soon after. From that moment forward, she supported the family on her own.

The household had always had a slightly eccentric tenor. Cora had a "freewheeling spirit" and encouraged the same in her daughters. Freedom of expression was affectionately nurtured, inventiveness prized. A sudden flood in the kitchen—the house was unheated and the pipes occasionally burst—was treated as an excuse to don ice skates and glide around the floor. Theirs was a world of earth worship and pagan play. In spring Edna climbed trees in the moonlight; in summer she roamed the nightwoods alone, fueling what she would later call her "Earth-Passion."

Cora was especially adamant on the subject of self-reliance. The family moved from one small coastal town to the next. Beginning when Edna was eleven or twelve, whenever her mother's work as a night nurse took her too far afield to return home by evening, she left Edna in charge, confident that her eldest daughter, whom she called "Vincent" and raised as a son, was utterly capable.

There were times when Cora was away for days—even weeks, which, on the face of it, seemed fine. Answerable to no one, the girls ate what they liked, sometimes sitting down to a pan of fudge for dinner, a pail of blueberries for lunch. They skipped school if they wanted, did their homework at whim. The dishes piled up in the sink, the beds went unmade. Yet they were never idle; there were always activities. They sang and composed songs, took walks and read, played the piano and staged impromptu plays. Edna seemed to thrive. Yet the downside of being given such freedom and responsibilities so early was that it robbed Edna, in particular, of a part of her childhood, for as the nominal head of the household, she had little room for displays of fear, weakness, or need. While Cora, for all her progressiveness, freed her daughters from the constraints of conventional "womanly" behavior, making no distinction between what a boy or girl could do, in her ambitiousness she also perhaps pushed her eldest from the nest too soon, assuming Edna was less needy than she actually was.

Some years later, Edmund Wilson, meeting the poet's mother during a visit to a beach

Cora Millay

house near Provincetown that Edna was given for the summer, recalled how taken he had been by the uncommonness of Cora's spirit: "She was a little old woman who, although she had evidently been through a good deal, had managed to remain very brisk and bright. She sat up straight and smoked cigarettes and quizzically followed the conversation," Wilson recalled. "She looked not un-like a New England schoolteacher, yet there was something almost raffish about her. She had anticipated the bohemianism of her daughters; and she sometimes made remarks that were startling from the lips of an old lady."

Edna *left* with Vassar College friend Corinne Sawyer, circa 1914

If Cora Millay consciously cultivated the poet in her eldest daughter, she could never have anticipated the rapidity with which her ambitions would be realized. In November of 1912, having casually suggested to Edna that she enter a national poetry competition, Edna's poem "Renascence" won fourth prize and was published to enormous acclaim that year. Congratulatory letters poured in from across the country, several of which grew into ongoing correspondences. No one could quite believe that so young a poet—and a poet who was female—had written the astonishing poem. At the age of nineteen, Edna was suddenly a celebrity.

Fate next intervened in the person of a female patron, Caroline Dow, who heard a recitation of the prizewinning poem and volunteered to raise the tuition for Edna to attend college. Plucked almost overnight from the rocky Maine soil of her childhood, Edna left for New York City early in 1913 to study at Barnard. A semester later, she transferred to Vassar College in upstate New York.

At Vassar, the young prodigy quickly made a name for herself, not only as a gifted poet, singer, actress, and playwright, but as an unrepentant hellion who brazenly cut classes, stole out for illicit midnight walks, and openly smoked in the cemetery near campus. Such flagrant displays of insubordination reeked havoc on the equanimity of Vassar's president, who, though besieged with angry complaints, was wary of expelling the rebel poet. "I know all about poets at college," he told Edna one day, "and I don't want a banished Shelley on my doorstep."

Shelley or not, Edna remained unreformable, doing little to change her ways. By autumn of 1917, having almost failed to graduate for disciplinary reasons, Edna was back in Manhattan, this time to put down permanent roots. Now twenty-five, she was for the second time a minor publishing celebrity. In December her first book, *Renascence and Other Poems,* had come out to excellent reviews. Yet, despite her critical success, there was no financial reward, and the means to support herself remained unresolved.

DURING HER LAST months at Vassar, Edna had befriended the eminent British actress Edith Wynne Matthison, whose carriage and celebrated stage voice Edna worshipped. Shortly after graduation, Edith had insisted on taking the young poet under her wing, inviting Edna to come to live with her and her husband in Connecticut for the summer, while she arranged for Edna to give paid poetry readings at the estates of friends.

For Edna, the attraction to Edith had been oddly potent, even at the start. As the summer wore on, her feelings for the older actress grew more complex. She had now been separated from her family for four years. She yearned for the landscape of her native Maine, "the thin sweet sound of leaves in the wind." Most of all, she craved the physical closeness and fraternity of her mother and sisters, to whom she was still deeply bound. She wrote to her mother nearly every day.

Now, in a transfer of her deepest, unrealized longings, she turned to Edith, as if to a lover, seeking the intimacy and emotional shelter she missed.

"You wrote me a beautiful letter,—I wonder if you meant it to be as beautiful as it was.—I think you did," Edna wrote Edith. "For somehow I know your feeling for me, however slight it is, is in the nature of love."

Her letters were tinged with homosexual longings, desires for a level of intimacy the older actress may or may not have shared.

"Love me, please; I love you," Edna pleaded in another. " I can bear to be your friend. So ask of me anything. . . . But never be 'tolerant,' or 'kind.' And never say to me again—don't dare to say to me again—'Anyway, you can make a trial' of being friends with you! Because I can't do things that way. . . . I am conscious only of doing the thing that I love to do—that I *have* to do—and I have to be your friend."

Edna at Vassar, 1917

"When you tell me to come, I will come, by the next train, just as I am," she told Edith. "This is not meekness, be assured; I do not come naturally by meekness, know that it is a proud surrender to you; I don't talk like that to many people. With love, Vincent Millay."

Edith was well past forty, Edna just twenty-five. It was a pattern that would periodically arise throughout the poet's life. Whenever Edna felt the walls of the outside world pressing in on her and the cloistered refuge of her childhood slipping too far away, she sought release through erotic connection, usually with a man, though sometimes with a woman. Wilson had seen as much in Edna's poem "Renascence," which he called "a study of claustrophobia." The voice in the poem is afraid of being "buried alive," forever trapped at home, shut in between the steep Maine hills and the sea, the confining boundaries of her small-town childhood. Yet simultaneously the poet longs for such enclosure too. As with most phobias, a deep undercurrent of desire accompanied Edna's darkest fears: while she lived in terror of being stifled, crushed by the earth of her girlhood landscape, she also craved its all-encompassing cocoon. It was a conflict she was never to resolve completely.

ARMED WITH EDITH'S letters of introduction to big-name theater producers, Edna began auditioning for the New York stage. It was 1917, and America was now at war. Her sister Norma joined her in November, having secured work in an airplane factory. They found a one-and-a-half-room flat on Waverly Place, which, like most Greenwich Village apartments, was unheated. It did, however, have "the luxury of a fireplace," Edna wrote, "for which Joe the Italian brought, every few days . . . a load of firewood at 10 cents a precious stick."

The winter passed in a fever of writing. Huddled beside the fireplace, Edna worked each night until the cold numbed her fingers, at which time, craving heat as much as company, she would repair to one of the neighborhood artist bars, and so begin her legendary night crawl.

Prewar villagers had gathered at Mabel Dodge's, or at the Liberal Club. Later bohemia met in edgier surroundings. As Malcolm Cowley recalled in *Exiles Return*:

> The social centers of the village were two saloons: the Hell Hole, on Sixth Avenue at the corner of West Fourth Street, and the Working Girls' Home, at Greenwich Avenue and Christopher Street. The Hell Hole was tough and dirty; the proprietor kept a pig in the cellar and fed it scraps from the free-lunch counter. The boys in the back room were small-time gamblers and petty thieves, but the saloon was also patronized by actors and writers from the Provincetown Playhouse, which was just around the corner. Sometimes the two groups mingled. . . . The Hell Hole stayed in business during the first two or three years of prohibition, but then it was closed and I don't know where the gangsters met after that. The actors and playwrights moved on to the Working Girls Home, where the front door was locked, but where a side door on Christopher Street still led into a room where Luke O'Connor served . . . the best beer and stout he could buy from the wildcat breweries.

In late winter, after a brief and disheartening experience with the Theatre Guild, Edna auditioned one afternoon for the lead in an upcoming play with the Provincetown Players.

Born on a dilapidated fisherman's wharf in Provincetown, Massachusetts, the Players had begun two seasons earlier as the brainchild of two visionary playwrights, Jig and Susan Cook. Their dream of pioneering a small, experimental theater, free of commercial compromise, had been conceived one drunken evening in a weathered beach shack on the tip of Cape Cod, bohemian Greenwich Village's summer retreat.

The theater was communal on every level. The impromptu troupe, which soon boasted a loyal corps of literary talents—including John Reed, Louise Bryant, Hutchins Hapgood, Max Eastman, and the brilliant young playwright Eugene O'Neill—worked, cooked, ate, and played together, sharing lovers on more than a few occasions as well.

Rehearsals were freewheeling affairs. The thespians swam from the wharf between scenes, sunbathing in the nude as they discussed life and art, gossiped and planned new plays, each of which they wrote, produced, and acted in themselves. On show nights, the audience— usually other artists—brought their own chairs or camp stools, which they planted among the tangle of oars, anchors, and fish nets heaped on the dock.

At the end of the summer, the improvisational theater seemed too vital to cease. Emboldened by their success, the Players decided to reassemble upon returning to the Village that fall. Now in their second New York

Edna St. Vincent Millay

Floyd Dell

season, the Provincetown Players had officially taken up residence in a small converted stable on MacDougal Street, with barely enough room for one hundred seats. Though still unable to pay actors and writers, the troupe had gained a measure of prestige, having caught the eye of uptown critics who regularly taxied downtown to review new productions.

EDNA WAS AUDITIONED by the playwright Floyd Dell, a tall, lanky young writer of thirty, recently divorced and working in the Village for the radical magazine *The Masses*. Like most of his cohorts, he also composed poetry and prose on the side. The lithe young woman with auburn hair who read for the part seemed perfect, he thought. It wasn't until she'd left that he connected the name she had given—Edna Millay—with the beautiful and moving poem "Renascence," which he knew and admired. He gave her the part the next day.

The production went so well that Dell offered Edna the lead in his next drama, even before the first had closed. By now they were close friends. During rehearsal breaks, they often slipped out for coffee, unable to afford much else. Dell was almost always penniless, as his work for *The Masses* paid next to nothing. There were certain perks that came with the job, however, including free tickets to the Greenwich Village artists' balls at Webster Hall, which Dell gladly passed on to his leading actress. Edna shined at these orgies of drink and dance. Dressed in a costume of her own design, she caroused until daybreak, crawling home as the streetlights flickered off. Her circle soon widened. She was now a familiar face at the Provincetown, and through Dell she met many writers and artists who lived in the Village: Theodore Dreiser, Hart Crane, Jane Heap, Djuna Barnes, Sherwood Anderson, Lawrence Langner, Malcolm Cowley, and Susan Glaspell.

It's been surmised that Floyd Dell was Edna's first real lover. Though there had been flirtations at college, Edna's legendary career as a sexual libertine apparently began one night on Waverly Place, in the poet's cold-water flat, after a romantic dinner with Dell at the Brevoort Hotel. Yet if Dell was her first lover, he was hardly her last. As Edna's biographer Joan Dash has written, "It was as if a new form of escape from the bonds of childhood had been made available to her, a new way of battering at the too-close walls of the shelter she both dreaded and required." Having found in Dell's arms "the freedom that was sexual love," Edna now moved through a dizzying succession of lovers, running "from freedom to enclosure to freedom, all the while proclaiming in the poetry of those early years a woman's right to love as willfully and capriciously as a man."

Artist's ball at Webster Hall in Greenwich Village. Photo by Jessie Tarbox Beals.

Whether Edna found satisfaction in these feverish trysts was a matter of much speculation. Dell believed she didn't, though his was the biased perspective of a spurned lover. Edna wanted to be loved, Dell claimed, but was terrified of surrendering herself as a woman fully to a man, afraid she would lose her identity and independence as a poet. He repeatedly accused her of holding back. "Don't you think that our virtues as artists or poets may spring partly from the faults of our nature?" Edna quipped.

Dell was at the time in the midst of psychoanalysis and urged Edna to do the same, to cure her "sapphic tendencies," as he called them. She flatly refused. The prospect of anyone coming too close, she privately admitted, was deeply alarming, and she was vocal about finding Dell's entreaties intrusive. Dell's curiosity, she later told a friend, pried too deeply into that "darkness which was mine alone." Even in the last years of her life, Edna would write that she still dreaded the "fearful thing" she might discover if she should find the "lost and ominous key to the sealed chamber of her mind."

Still, Dell was the lover to whom Edna repeatedly returned. "There began for us a romance that was haunted by her sense of the inevitable impermanence of love," wrote Dell. "She refused to marry me. We parted several times. She fell in love with other men and then came back to me."

Whenever Dell mentioned marriage, Edna bristled. He was trying to shackle her with the old feminine labors of cooking and baby tending, she charged. "I'm not the right girl to cook your meals and wash and iron your shirts." She was "nobody's own," she declared.

This was partly, as Dell claimed, a cry of rebellion against being female. Only alone and with her poetry was Edna safe from the insidious claims of marriage, housekeeping, and babies—womanly roles that would surely subvert the tomboy Vincent, her mother's surrogate son, the brilliant poet and beguiling performer. Certainly the early and abrupt departure of her father must also have contributed to these feelings, as Dash sensitively suggests. For on some level Edna must have felt abandoned. While she knew her mother had sent her father away, she must have wondered why he agreed so readily to go. Surely, if he had loved her more, the child's mind would have reasoned, he would never have allowed the separation. To Edna, for reasons deeply rooted in her past, the act of committing oneself to a man also meant exposing oneself to the pain of his leaving—for there was nothing that guaranteed that a man would not pack up and leave; she had witnessed it herself at the age of seven.

How much safer then, to play the philandering boy-poet, giving one's heart to no one, committed only to poetry and play.

EDNA'S TRYSTS WOULD continue, the list of lovers seemingly endless: among them, Allan Ross Macdougall (future editor of Edna's collected letters); the writer Scudder Middleton; the musician Harrison Dowd; and Rollo Peters, an artist connected with the Theatre Guild. Each fling followed much the same pattern. After a fiery onset, there would be passionate vows, followed by a period of sweet companionship. Then Edna's old fears of being trapped would begin to creep in, making her restless and increasingly remote. Suddenly she would break things off, only to begin the feverish cycle again, just days later, her rogue heart alighting on some new and tantalizingly prospect.

There was, however, one exception, one man whom Edna wanted to possess and who always remained unattainable. In the spring of 1918, an old friend of Floyd Dell's from Davenport, Iowa, a poet by the name of Arthur Ficke, came through town on his way to military service in France. Broad-browed, with chiseled features and thick, wavy hair, Ficke cut a handsome figure. Dell insisted on taking his friend to Waverly Place to meet the woman he was smitten with, the actress he'd mentioned from the Provincetown Players. By some uncanny coincidence, she turned out to be the same woman, Ficke quickly realized, he had been corresponding with for years.

Half a decade earlier, having read the astonishing "Renascence," Ficke and his colleague Witter Bynner, both established poets, had written admiringly to its creator. They were convinced that the author's identity was a hoax, that whoever the poet was, she couldn't truly be a twenty-year-old woman. The trail of letters that followed had grown increasingly flirtatious, as Edna, writing back to Ficke and Bynner, had archly insisted she was indeed a "full blooded female" and could prove it. Later that year, while at Barnard, Edna had met Bynner and was soon on such familiar terms that she was calling him Hal in her letters, as he was fondly known by friends. But she'd never met Ficke, though they had continued to correspond.

They were five in number that first afternoon when Dell and Ficke came by Waverly Place. Norma, Edna's sister, was also there, along with her lover, the painter Charles Smith. They sat cross-legged on the apartment floor, talking as they ate a delicatessen dinner. A giant pickle was passed "hand to hand" and Norma suggested it was "like a loving cup," at which point Ficke began to compose a sonnet on the idea, scrawling it on the top of a pastry box. Edna felt herself falling irretrievably in love with Ficke, which, clearly, he could see, for the sonnet alluded to "a promise in your eyes," though also to something else: a coyness and a certain staginess he thought he saw. The poem spoke of her hair as "a little challenge of lies." Edna was challenging him to fall in love with her. This was the implicit message he got, though he was unsure.

They spent the next two nights and a day together, unable—or unwilling—to name the feverish thing that flew between them. The war was on, and the situation was impossible anyway: Ficke wasn't free; he was married.

After Ficke left, Edna threw herself into a frenzy of writing, trying through her poetry to come to grips with her feelings. The sonnets she produced sounded an ongoing theme: that love was too powerful, impermanent, and painful to sustain; that love would always die; it was a false promise, fool's gold. It would be better to be free and in control again: "that I would be / From your too poignant lovelinesses free!"

Yet there were also strains of a second theme—Edna's shadow self: the voice of the reckless pagan, the prodigal lover keenly aware of fugitive time, certain that, given the choice, it was better to love freely and wildly and deplete oneself, than not to love at all.

It was the old debate that raged within her: the clash between the austere

Edna with Arthur Ficke and Inez Millholland

Arthur Ficke

New England puritan self, committed only to her poetry, and the Celtic pagan, pleasure-loving and devoted to play.

Edna sent Ficke the sonnets along with a storm of letters. He was "the first man [she] ever kissed without feeling [she] would be sorry for it afterward," she told Ficke. The tone of her letters was alternately reckless and thoughtful, at moments philosophical about the impossibility of their love, at others sharply despairing, lonely, and filled with frustrated longing. She was trying desperately to write her way out of the emotional maelstrom, to escape into poetry, as she always had before; trying to use her work to order her feelings. "My time, in those awful days after you went away to France, was a mist of thinking about you & writing sonnets to you," she wrote. "You were spending your time in the same way, I believe."

But Ficke wasn't exactly. Despite the charge that had passed between them, the sonnets he wrote were more circumspect. There were intimations that he was wary of "the pure white heat" of Edna's passions, that perhaps he saw in her something unslakable, an emotional intensity that was impossible to meet. Whatever it was, it appears that Ficke felt something cooler, though Edna didn't see this.

SOMETIME THAT SAME year, Edna began writing satirical sketches and clever, fast-paced potboilers under the pen name Nancy Boyd for the commercial magazine *Ainslee's*. She earned enough now to spend the better part of each day on the more serious business of her poetry. Often, in the afternoons, she sat in the basement of the Grand Ticino, a small Italian restaurant on Thompson Street, drinking tea at a back corner table, her chin resting on the heel of her hand, her red hair falling over one eye as she scrawled.

Increasingly assured as a writer, Edna was feeling the first satisfactions of success, with three books of verse ready for publication. Yet in the two years since she had come to the Village, she had continued to live dangerously, subsisting on little sleep and erratic meals, too much alcohol, pushing each day to meet deadlines, feverishly socializing each night.

Her friends could see the strain. Elizabeth Haight, dropping by one afternoon, voiced concern that Edna might be squandering her poetic gift, spending herself on lovers and not her work. Edna assured her friend she was fine. "I always know exactly what I am doing, Elizabeth; I take no risks. Don't worry about me," she insisted.

Yet her poetry belied a different truth: "My candle burns at both ends; / It will not last the night; / But ah, my foes, and oh, my friends— / It gives a lovely light!" These famous words became emblematic of a generation.

Jessie Rittenhouse, seeing Edna again after some years, was dismayed by the fragility in her eyes. "One could see upon her face the marks of New York and its struggle. . . . Rarely does one see a face more mobile and expressive. Even when she was gayest there seemed to be a certain element of tragedy looking out of her eyes."

BY THE SUMMER of 1918, Edna's income from *Ainslee's* was so steady that she was able to send for the rest of her family. Her mother arrived from Maine, her sister Kathleen from Vassar, and they settled into a flat on Charlton Street with room enough for four. Within months, the place had become a Village institution. Every evening, as one habitué recalled, "swarms of young painters, writers and poets made pilgrimages" to their apartment. "Those evenings at 25 Charlton Street were a perpetual soiree with Edna holding court in one room . . . while Mother Millay fluttered on guard over her fledglings, hopping from one room to another."

To Edna's great disappointment, Ficke didn't stop in New York after the Armistice, as he had promised, or if he did, he didn't call. Yet the poems he sent her for critique continued to arrive at regular intervals, as did his letters, allowing her to falsely hope. She tried to suppress the feeling that she was still waiting expectantly. Then Ficke wrote that he and Witter Bynner would soon be leaving for an extended junket to Asia. It was a wrenching blow, though, writing to Bynner, she made light of it: "Hal, dear,—My heart is breaking with envy of you. The day you sail I'm going down to Chinatown . . . and if Arthur goes with you there is only one thing left: I shall asphyxiate myself in Pell Street punk-smoke. Good friend, write me sometimes."

For the first time, Edna admitted to herself that something about Ficke's sonnets oppressed her; perhaps it was their "harsh and somber restraint."

With the war over, a wave of cynicism had swept the country, further complicating Edna's mood. The noble fight that was to have made the world safe for democracy hadn't changed anything. As Malcolm Cowley reflected in *Exiles Return*: "We had lost our ideals. If any of them survived the war, they had disappeared in the midst of the bickerings at Versailles. . . . But they did not leave us bitter. We believed . . . that the Germans were no worse than the allies, no better, that the world consisted of fools and scoundrels . . . that everybody could be bought for a price."

Echoing these views, Edna had been working on an acerbic little anti-war drama, a one-act called *Aria da Capo* that captured something of the disaffection in the air, the sense that the old platitudes were dead, that life was incongruous, even cruel.

When the Provincetown Playhouse produced *Aria* in December of 1919, with Edna directing and Norma as the lead, even Edna was startled by the critic's unanimous raves.

"I find myself suddenly famous," Edna wrote to a friend, ". . . and in this unlooked-for excitement I find a stimulant that almost takes the place of booze! . . . There is scarcely a little theater or literary club in the country . . . that isn't going to produce it."

It was soon after the opening of *Aria,* at a late-night party in Greenwich Village, that Edna met Edmund Wilson, then a young and ambitious editor

Right: **Edna St. Vincent Millay**

at the fashionable magazine *Vanity Fair*. Edna had arrived that evening after eleven, having come directly from the theater. Though she complained of exhaustion, she was persuaded to recite several of her poems.

"She was dressed in some bright batik, and her face lit up with a flush," Wilson remembered. "She had a lovely and very long throat that gave her the look of a muse, and her reading of her poetry was thrilling."

Wilson had been interested in meeting Edna for some time. He had been struck by one of her early sonnets and then saw *Aria da Capo.* "I was thrilled and troubled by this little play," he recalled. "It was the first time I had felt Edna's peculiar power."

Determined that it shouldn't be the last, Wilson began to court Edna's attentions by way of *Vanity Fair*. At the time she still had no real market for her poetry. Though Edna occasionally sold verse to the highbrow *Dial*, she mostly published in the more trashy *Ainslee's*, which paid writers well but carried little critical weight. Wilson was in an excellent position to advance her career, which he now consciously set out to do, bringing Edna to the attention of his editor Frank Crowninshield, who soon began to publish her regularly. It was the beginning of Edna's far-reaching fame and would change her life.

Wilson was but one suitor among Edna's many, however, as he was all too aware. Even John Bishop, his fellow editor, was actively pursuing the fiery young poetess, causing a strain in office relations. It was difficult, complained Crowninshield, to have both his assistants in love with one of his most brilliant contributors.

According to Wilson, Edna was a part of at least two ménages à trois during this period. One, it seems, involved Bishop and himself. As the story goes, one evening, having renewed their good relations, both men made love to Edna at the same time.

Edna liked to flaunt her lack of inhibitions, making sport of prudishness whenever she could. Max Eastman, in his memoir *Great Companions*, recalls a round of charades that was typical of Edna's style. A group of friends had gathered at a house party in the country and on impulse had decided to play charades. At the last moment, a bashful young man from Yale had decided to join the game. The word to be enacted was *Bathsheba,* and in the final scene Edna was to play the part of Bathsheba bathing on a rooftop, with the young man from Yale playing the part of David passing by.

"This high table will be the rooftop," he said excitedly. "I'll enter from the side door, and you'll be up there in a bathing suit—"

"Bathing suit!" Edna said. "You don't take baths in a bathing suit!"

The Yale man played his part with "heroic fortitude," Eastman remembered, though he was blushing.

Edna's disdain for bourgeois proprieties was legendary. It was people's prudishly conventional ideas about sex, she told Eastman, that kept psychoanalysts—who were all "pathologically inhibited"—in business. At a party one evening, Edna was sitting alone nursing a bad headache when a young psychiatrist approached. He'd been watching her, he said, and believed he might be able to help. He suggested they repair to the library to talk privately.

When they were well isolated, he closed the door and then requested her permission to ask a few questions. After an awkward start and several bizarre digressions, he finally blurted out what he wanted to ask: "I wonder if it has ever occurred to you that you might perhaps, although you are hardly conscious of it, have an occasional erotic impulse toward a person of your own sex?"

"Oh, you mean I'm homosexual!" she exclaimed. "Of course I am, and heterosexual too, but what's that got to do with my headache?"

Though Edna gently mocked the psychiatrist, in truth her homosexuality was something she chose to keep concealed. While a persistent thread of homosexuality runs through many of her letters to

Edmund Wilson

111

women friends, she was always extremely discreet about the precise nature of her lesbian leanings, choosing not to leave much of a paper trail. Veiled references to an affair she had with Thelma Wood, the love of Djunas Barnes' life, appear in certain memoirs from the period, though only selectively and not in Edna's own journals. (Apparently the affair occurred sometimes in 1922 during Edna's difficult year in Paris.) Why she chose to remain silent on the subject remains a question of some speculation. Certainly, her complicated relations with men left her with more than enough to sort out. And her shifting sexual identity was further complicated by the ambiguous role her mother played in the family drama. Once Edna's father had left, her mother had filled in as both lover and protector, father figure and alter ego, pushing Edna to independence and worldly accomplishment, at the same time fostering a visceral attachment so powerful it was at times incapacitating. Later, writing to her mother from Europe, Edna would remark, "If I didn't keep calling you mother, anybody reading this would think I was writing to my sweetheart. . . . Do you suppose, when you & I are dead, they will publish the *Love Letters of Edna St. Vincent Millay & her Mother?*"

EDNA ADORED THE theater and often went to plays with Wilson. One evening, as they sat together in the audience, she became visibly tense. She was apparently upset by the heroine, Wilson remembered, who was playing cat and mouse with one of her suitors.

When the curtain fell, she turned to him. "I hate women who do that," she said.

She was expressing the truth, Wilson felt. Though Edna was capable of being "sternly sharp with an admirer who proved a nuisance, she did not like to torture people or to play them off against one another," he observed. With the "dignity of her genius" came a lack of malice.

"Those who fell in love with the woman did not, I think, seriously quarrel with her . . . and they were not, except in very small ways, demoralized or led to commit excesses, because the other thing was always there, and her genius, for those who could value it, was not something that one could be jealous of. Her poetry, you soon found out, was her real overmastering passion."

Withdrawal, Wilson felt, was her natural condition. When Edna left for Europe, neither he nor Bishop dared to see her off at the dock, fearful they would be faced with too many other suitors. "Her relations with us and her other admirers had . . . a disarming impartiality," he ruefully observed. She didn't give the impression that, "aside from her mother and sisters, her personal relations were important except as subjects for her poems." What interested her was "seldom the people themselves, but her own emotions about them."

This was not, he felt, because Edna was coldhearted or touchy but rather because this was where the deepest drama took place—among the cabal of four in her family, or else within herself, hammered into art.

She had grown up in isolated rural towns, her intellect and character formed in solitude, under "hard conditions," he felt. Her "cramped" emotional life had found its sole outlet and satisfaction in the poems she wrote. For this reason, he added, "this life of art, by which she had triumphed in a little Maine town that offered few other triumphs, was to remain for her the great reality that made everything else unimportant."

Edna's elusiveness only heightened Wilson's interest. He felt the city had begun to frighten her. The old claustrophobic feeling she had described so powerfully in her poem "Renascence" had returned, pressing in on her even more menacingly. And though she was surrounded by lovers, they seemed to be the wrong lovers. Arthur Ficke had failed to keep his promise of returning after the war. "It is a pity you are so far away," Edna wrote him. "There are so few people in the world to whom one has a word to say, Arthur!"

That April Edna sent a letter to a friend saying: "I'm having a sort of nervous breakdown."

She'd become preoccupied with death, yet Wilson believed "it was not the deaths of the body that she suffered: it was the deaths of all those human relations—it was her rejection, day after day . . . of all the natural bonds and understandings which make up the greater part of human life—comfort, security, children, the protection and devotion of a husband . . . so that she was still . . . an outlaw living from hand to mouth . . . bedeviled day and night by all the persons she no longer had the energy to excite to her own pitch of incandescence."

IN THE SUMMER of 1920, Wilson visited Edna in Truro on Cape Cod, where she was sharing a beach house with her mother and sisters. He'd never seen a bohemian household like it and was fascinated. They had almost no furniture, he remembered, and were "rather vague about meals, only really concentrating on dinner," which was casually served on a plain board table by the light of an oil lamp. "But they never apologized for anything." The house was also without plumbing. On their first night there, Norma told him, it had started raining. The girls and their mother had immediately stripped and run outdoors to take a shower under the rain spout from the roof.

That night, he remembered, they entertained him with humorous songs, then played Beethoven's Fifth on an ancient phonograph. Finally, stepping outside alone with Edna to sit on the porch swing, Wilson summoned the courage to formally propose marriage. Edna paused, then told him she would think about it, though Wilson also thought he heard her mumble under her breath, "That might be the solution," though he wasn't sure.

But Wilson was not the solution, it seems, nor were any of the others who proffered their proposals. Edna had come to a crisis in her life. "I'll be thirty in a minute!" she cried one day to Wilson. All that summer she'd hoped for a letter from China, but when a letter finally arrived, it turned out to be from Bynner, not Ficke, making her wonder if Hal might not actually be a better choice. Reading the letter, she casually remarked to Norma that she "might marry this man some day." But it was clear her heart wasn't in it.

AT WILSON'S URGING, Edna decided to go Europe. She had never been, and she desperately needed a change of scene. Wilson devised an arrangement by which she could continue to write the Nancy Boyd stories for *Vanity Fair* from abroad, ensuring her a regular salary, even offering to pay her more money if she would sign her own name to the pieces. But on this last point she wouldn't agree. She was adamant that her real work should never be mixed with the lighter, loosely written Nancy Boyd pieces. Her serious writing had a tough intellectual side, an unmistakable rigor and form, which she wouldn't compromise. "No matter how confused her life became," he observed, "she was always clear about this."

That fall, a few months before leaving, Edna sent letters to both Bynner and Ficke. "When are you two boys coming back here?" she wrote Bynner. "Where you used to be, there is a hole in the world. . . . I miss you like hell." Her letter to Arthur was sadder, more wistful:

> It doesn't matter at all that we never see each other, & that we write so seldom. We shall never escape from each other. . . . It is very dear to me to know that you love me, Arthur,—just as I love you, quietly. . . . It is a thing that exists simply . . . there is nothing to be done about it. . . . There are moments, of course . . . that it is different. One's body, too, is so lonely. And then, too, it is as if I knew of a swamp of violets, & wanted to take you there . . . you must never think that I don't understand.— You will never grow old to me, or die, or be lost in any way.

She waited eagerly for a response. When none appeared by December, Edna's anxiety increased. Yet she revealed none of this in the letter she dashed off to her mother that same month: She was going to Europe, she said, "as a free woman, a business woman, & because I want to travel." Her going had "nothing to do with any love affair, past or present."

She had been sick, Edna explained, and had had "another small nervous breakdown." My poetry, she added, "needs fresh grass to feed on. . . . New York is getting too congested for me." She left for France that January. It was 1921.

Wilson visited Edna in Paris later that year and got the impression she was having a good time. But her letters home betrayed something else: loneliness, homesickness, and a mounting fixation with her own health. It had now been a year since her first open declaration to Ficke, and Edna wrote him again, this time more pleadingly. "Arthur, it is wicked & useless,—all these months apart from you, all these years with only a glimpse of you in the face of everybody.—I tell you I must see you again, " she said. Without reconsidering, Edna posted it.

BY SUMMER EDNA'S third book of poems, *Second April,* had come out in America to wildly enthusiastic reviews, deepening Edna's renown. The critics now habitually referred to her as one of America's finest lyric poets. The youthful defiance of the early verse had been tempered by a darker, more contemplative side, they said. The promising young prodigy had ripened into a mature poet, whose artistry had only grown more refined.

There was other news from America as well: both Edna's sisters had married. Though Edna wrote back enthusiastically, telling them that "Now I have two bruvvers! And two such nice bruvvers," her effusiveness seemed forced, barely masking the note of desperation in her voice.

Lately she'd been feeling painfully alone and was suffering from a stomach affliction she couldn't shake. Ficke and Bynner were back in the States; it was she who was on the move now. From Albania she wrote to Ficke that: "when I start to write you all I can think of to say to you is—Why aren't you here? . . . When I come back to the States, won't you come east to see me? . . . That is what I want of you—out of sight & sound of other people, to lie close to you & let the world rush by. . . . Oh, my dearest, dearest, would it not be wonderful, just once to be together again for a little while?"

From Vienna Edna confided to him that she was broke, but he wasn't to tell a soul. "It seems a long time since I have seen anybody I cared anything about," she added.

Now a bizarre three-way correspondence between Edna, Bynner, and Ficke developed, confusing Edna further. Evidently Bynner had written to her proposing marriage, but she had missed the letter. Instead she had received a note from Arthur saying that he thought she and Hal should wait before making such a serious decision. Yet Arthur had said nothing about his own feelings toward her, which was deeply unsettling. She knew he had recently been in New York and that his marriage was failing. She wondered why he hadn't written her from there.

Lonely and confused, Edna sent a halting and uncertain letter back to Bynner: "Do you really want me to marry you?" she probed. "Because if you really want me to, I will." She had thought for a long time that some-day she should marry him, she confessed. "You have known me since I was a little girl," she added. The reference to her childhood was an indication of the emotional dislocation she felt, the reeling displacement. She wished he could be there, she said, so they could speak. "You will let me hear from you at once, Hal, won't you? Oh, if you knew the comical state my mind is in!" A few days later she wrote a second letter. If he had since changed his mind, she would understand and they would be friends once more. Otherwise, she was thrilled that he was coming to Europe so they could talk things over. And yes, she admitted, he was right about her loving Arthur. She had never hidden it, but wasn't it true that one could love sev-eral people, she reasoned. It was nothing to feel troubled about. "For surely, one must be either undiscerning, or frightened, to love only one person, when the world is so full of gracious and noble spirits. Besides, I should not wish to marry Arthur, even if it were possible," she added. It was not "be-cause you are free and he is not, Hal."

But Edna was dissembling. She had just learned that Arthur had fallen in love with a young artist by the name of Gladys Brown. Privately, she was grap-pling with the news, struggling to main-tain a stiff upper lip. To Arthur, she dashed off a breezy and brave letter. She had known "all about the girl in

Witter (Hal) Bynner

New York, long before you told me," she said. She'd sensed it in his letters. It didn't matter "with whom [he] fell in love, nor how often, nor how sweetly," she added gamely. "All that has nothing to do with what we are to each other."

For some months Edna had been planning to bring her mother to Europe, though when marriage to Bynner had suddenly seemed imminent, she'd hastily postponed the trip. Then she changed her mind, imploring her mother to come.

Meanwhile, the circular exchange of letters between Bynner, Edna, and Ficke continued. Both Ficke and Bynner had decided the marriage was a bad idea. Bynner believed Edna still loved Arthur and Arthur, who no doubt agreed, thought that they were too confused to make any decision for a while. Edna now began a sequence of sonnets that would be her saddest and most melodic work. "Pity me that the heart is slow to learn / What the swift mind beholds at every turn," she wrote. "I only know that summer sang in me / A little while, that in me sings no more."

The marriage to Hal was definitely off, though by the time Cora Millay arrived in Paris, Edna's spirits had lightened. Together, mother and daughter walked the city arm in arm, drinking in the sights. Even when Edna learned in a letter that Arthur and Gladys had slipped away and were now together in Paris, she seemed to take the news in stride. Then at the close of 1922, she got a second, more jarring, bit of news: Arthur and Gladys were to be married.

Edna's intestinal complaints abruptly worsened. She was in such pain she had to put aside the novel she was writing. Once again, she summoned her courage and bravely sent Arthur her congratulations: "Isn't it funny about you & Gladys?—My God—it's marvelous," she wrote. She closed by repeating her vow that she would love him always, until the day she died.

Right: **Edna St. Vincent Millay**

IN EARLY 1923—months sooner than she had planned—Edna and her mother returned to America. Edna found a tiny apartment on Waverly Place; Cora went on to Maine.

The months slid by now, Edna hardly conscious of time. She felt so tired, so sick and dispirited, she could barely lift her pen. If ever a visitor appeared, she feigned a certain "high, bright gaiety," a friend remembered, masking her despair with a rush of feverish talk. Yet, as soon as the visitor left, Edna collapsed again. Even the news that she'd won the Pulitzer Prize for Poetry for her long poem "The Ballad of the Harp-Weaver" barely lifted her spirits. Though in the eyes of the world, she was a romantic figure—fabulously popular, the most adored, copied, quoted and envied poet in America—Edna felt broken.

EDNA RARELY LEFT the apartment that long winter. Finally in April, friends persuaded her to join them for a house party in the country. Some years earlier, Max Eastman had introduced Edna to a Dutch businessman friend named Eugen Boissevain, who at the time hadn't made much of an impression. Now she encountered the genial Dutchman again. Tall and handsome, with a rugged build and a quick, contagious laugh, he was charming and "lighthearted as a troubadour." This time Edna found him deeply attractive.

Within hours a parlor game had evolved into an impromptu play. Edna and Arthur Ficke, also among the guests that afternoon with his wife Gladys, hastily blocked out several amusing scenes. Then the drama commenced. Edna and Eugen, cast as a guileless married couple, acted their parts wonderfully—so much so, Floyd Dell later wrote, that it became apparent that it wasn't just acting. "We were having the unusual privilege of seeing a man and a girl fall in love with each other violently and in public . . . and doing it very beautifully."

When the party finally dispersed the following afternoon, Eugen insisted on taking Edna to his country home, apparently recognizing that she was dangerously sick and needed medical attention. Over the next several weeks he nursed her back to health "like a mother," Dell wrote, calling in a fleet of doctors. By the end the month, they'd decided to marry.

Eugen was unlike Edna's former lovers, who had always been artists and writers, actors and intellectuals. A maverick and a businessman; daring, yet deeply stable, he was a gentleman. Bold-spirited and boisterous in conversation, he had "a Gallic" appetite for the pleasures "both of the mind and of the flesh," yet was free of the extrovert's need to be the focus of attention. He was most comfortable, in fact, as an appreciator and promoter of other people's gifts. What he had about him,

Edna St. Vincent Millay

said Max Eastman, was "a strain of something feminine that most men except the creative geniuses lack."

Eugen's former wife had been the notorious feminist lawyer Inez Milholland, to whom he had been slavishly devoted. Content to take a backseat to his wife's high-profile career, he'd served as her manager, secretary, chauffeur, and political strategist, until the day she had collapsed onstage without warning while delivering a speech. She had died a few hours later of pernicious anemia at the age of twenty-eight.

Seven years had passed since then, yet in Edna, for the first time, he must have recognized a role for himself requiring the same qualities of character. Edna's fierce independence and her insistence on the primacy of her own artistic ambitions must have seemed the perfect counterpoint to the feminine traits he so comfortably claimed within himself, for he took up the roles of nursemaid, business manager, and doting husband with unabashed energy and commitment. Not only was Edna's worldly stature unthreatening to his masculine identity; in many ways it seemed to serve it.

The wedding was a rushed affair, celebrated in Eugen's Croton house just hours before Edna entered the hospital for an intestinal operation. For the remainder of the summer she convalesced, while Eugen hovered over her sickbed like an indulgent parent, standing in as secretary and editor whenever needed. Often he took dictation while Edna recited new poems she composed in her head. And he and Ficke spent days helping her prepare her new collection, *The Harp Weaver and Other Poems*, which came out in November.

Earlier in the fall, Eugen had found them a charming brick house on Bedford Street in Greenwich Village. Three stories high and known, famously, as the narrowest house in the Village, they were just moving in when Edna was asked to give a reading tour through the midwest. *The Harp Weaver* had received glowing reviews and Edna was not only collecting sizable royalties but commanding huge lecture fees, with more speaking offers than she could accept. Her poems, by contrast, were filled with dejection, withdrawal, and abject defeat.

And there was yet another disjunction. Despite Edna's enormous popular appeal, the mainstream poetry world was changing. Experimental magazines like the *Little Review* and *The Dial*, which would soon become the most important cultural journal of the 1920s, were interested in modernist work that broke the forms upon which Edna's work was built. That same year, 1922, *The Dial* had published the *The Waste Land* by T. S. Eliot, a long and magnificent poem written in a radical new idiom. Contemporaries like Mina Loy and Djuna Barnes, whom Edna knew through the Provincetown Playhouse, were writing in forms that were frankly experimental. Their terse poetic satires mirrored the dislocation of modern life, a densely ironic and fragmented vision no longer in consonance with Edna's romantic pathos, nor with her chosen form, the traditional sonnet. The world of American poetry in which Edna had occupied such a prominent place was slowly heading off in a different direction, one which she would not follow.

There was one female poet, however, with whom Edna *did* feel a personal and poetic kinship: the glamorous Elinor Wylie, who at the time was poetry editor of *Vanity Fair*. Tall and aloof, with bronze, swept-back hair and an aristocratic face, Elinor looked, said the critic Louis Untermeyer, like Nefertiti: "the same imperious brows; the high cheekbones . . . the long smooth column of the throat."

Elinor had long been a creature of scandal. Born into a socially prominent Philadelphia family, she had married a well-born schizophrenic and borne him a son. Four years later, abandoning her child, she ran off with a lover, Horace Wylie, and lived for a while incognito in Europe. Then in 1922, leaving Wylie (whom she had subsequently married), she moved to New York, where she rented a large, high-ceilinged room on the parlor floor of One University Place, still one of the great old houses overlooking Washington Square.

Her poems, which she read with "a shy fire," said the critic Carl Van Doren, began to be noticed, as did her style. She both wrote and spoke, he added, with "a lovely, amused formality." She was a woman who was endowed with both beauty and genius. "Doubly driven, she was doubly sensitive," he said, which made her both capricious and steadfast, desperate and hilarious, "profound" and also "exquisitely superficial." Like Djuna Barnes, she somehow always managed to convey high style with scant funds. Dressed in glittering silver sheaths from Paris, her hair sleekly marcelled, she had a way of transforming her modest parlor into a place of glamour by the time her guests arrived; among them Edmund Wilson and the poet Bill Benet, whom she married in 1924.

Edna's first contact with Elinor was in the form of a congratulatory letter she sent Elinor from England in 1921:

> Dear Elinor Wylie:
>
> I have just read with keen delight your beautiful *Nets to Catch the Wind*, of which I am writing a review for the *New York Evening*

Post. Not since I discovered Ralph Hodgson have I had such happiness in a new volume of poems. . . .

A thousand people will be waiting, as I shall be waiting, with assurance, for your next book. . . . Wishing you all good things and the success which you so unquestionably merit.

Most heartily yours, Edna St. Vincent Millay

A year later, after Edmund Wilson introduced the two poets, a rare and remarkable friendship began. Often the two would talk for hours, comparing notes on technique, discussing preferences in poets, arguing endlessly about the emotional travails of Shelley, whom Elinor loved. When Elinor married Benet, she and Edna drew closer still, amused to find they made an equally spirited foursome when they went out on the town together.

Edna was beginning to tire of the city, however. She felt increasingly unnerved by the noise, hemmed in by the tall buildings. As a spoof, she had laid out a burlesque miniature garden when their landlord didn't make good on his promise of planting the yard. But what she really wanted was the country, the isolation and remove she associated with her childhood. It was an old and insidious longing, one that promised refuge and creative release yet also carried with it the darker penumbra of entrapment.

Eugen felt no such ambivalences. That spring he bought them a farm in the foothills of the Berkshire Mountains, seven hundred acres of land three miles from the village of Austerlitz, New York, with meadows and woods and a stream. Edna gave it the name of Steepletop. It was "one of loveliest places in the world," she wrote.

To an outside observer it must have seemed idyllic. Edna was able to write in solitude. Eugen, sufficiently wealthy at this point to give up his import business, farmed. There was foreign travel: trips to Europe, India, and the Far East; forays into New York to see old friends and attend the theater; weekend house parties with literary cohorts; elegant meals and home-brewed wine. There were parlor games and tennis matches, nude swimming parties and nocturnal escapades, and always hours of disciplined

Edna's farm, "Steepletop"

writing. Best of all, Eugen took care of all domestic and business matters: he managed the farm, planned poetry readings, and booked hotels.

He'd observed that his wife didn't keep regular working hours. "If I let her struggle with problems of order . . . she doesn't write. . . . So I solve it quite simply: I look after everything," he told a reporter some years later. Eugen even did all the housework.

"She must not . . . have too many of those other mundane moments in a woman's life. . . . She must not be dulled by routine acts; she must ever remain open to fresh contact with life's intensities."

In the early 1930s, interviewed on the subject of their unorthodox household, Edna claimed she thrived on their unconventional domestic arrangements. It was her freedom from quotidian matters, she said, that released her from the things that dissipate a woman's energies. "But I haven't made the decision to ignore my household as easily as it sounds," she added. "I care an awful lot that things be done right. . . . But if I had to live in a mess, or live in a neat room and give up my writing, I prefer the mess."

BY THE WINTER OF 1926, Edna was hard at work on an opera collaboration with a composer friend; she was responsible for the libretto. That summer she had begun complaining of a headache that wouldn't lift and of dark spots that jiggled before her eyes. While the doctors assured her there was nothing wrong, the symptoms persisted.

Aside from the headaches, though, she had few complaints. Life with Eugen was filled with gaiety. On weekends there were always houseguests: Elinor and Bill Benet, Eliena and Max Eastman, Arthur and Gladys Ficke, and occasionally the poet Louise Bogan and her husband, who owned a house in nearby Hillsdale.

In February of 1927, the opera finally opened in New York to enthusiastic reviews. After a handful of performances, it was taken on the road, where it met with equal success. Yet the year, which had begun so auspiciously, was the beginning of a new and troubling phase in Edna's life. In December of 1928, Elinor Wylie died quite suddenly of a stroke. She was just forty-two. It was a devastating blow. Edna wrote Elinor's son: "There was only one of her. I was in New York at the time it happened. I was just at the end of a long and tiring reading-tour. . . . I said to myself, As soon as this darned chore is over, I'll rush to see her. And just as I was dressing to give my last reading . . . somebody who didn't know that I even knew her, casually mentioned that she had died. How do we bear these things?"

Writing to Bill Benet, she urged him not to torture himself with thoughts about how he might have loved Elinor better. "It was you just as you were that she loved, & loved so truly," Edna assured him:

> Yesterday we were in the cellar, sampling the new wine which Pierre our cook has made, and there on a shelf we saw the tiny keg labeled *Seven Shires* which we had been keeping for Elinor. It was that wine we had that she liked so much, you remember. We were keeping it for

her; Nobody was allowed to touch it. . . . She is not out of our minds or off our tongues for very long. We talk of her for hours at a time. . . . She was so wise. . . . I remember the happy times we had together, & how delightful she was, & how funny, so gay & splendid about tragic things, so comically serious about silly ones. . . . There was nobody like her at all.

Meanwhile, Edna's headaches were getting worse. It was increasingly hard for her to write, so she often didn't. Her new poetry collection, *The Buck in the Snow and Other Poems,* had come out in September to negative notices, adding to her fragility. Meeting Edna in New York one afternoon, Wilson was vaguely troubled by Eugen's "protective attitude," which he sensed was adding to Edna's burdens. On a weekend visit to Steepletop soon after, he could see that Edna was trying to recover her old fire. "She had now, she told me, taken up music again and was trying to work regularly at it. She was studying a sonata of Beethoven and played parts of it with her bright alive touch, dropping them, however, with impatience at the rag-gedness of her own performance." Then she got out a lot of new poems, over which they had a long session. "It brought her back to her old intensity. She was desperately, feverishly anxious not to let her standard down."

But there was a strain in the air, Wilson felt, as if Edna was grasping at something she feared was slipping. To distract her, he changed the subject, entertaining her with an amusing story. She laughed, he remembered, though at one point he thought he heard her blurt, "But I'm *not* a pathetic character!"

Visiting a year later, Wilson found Edna much subdued. She seemed qui-eter, more remote. "While we were talking, it began to grow dark, and the living room was half in shadow. . . . I had a curious and touching impres-sion, as Edna sat quiet in a big chair, that—torn and distracted by winds that had swept her through many seas—she had been towed into harbor and moored, that she was floating at anchor there."

Edna had been led back to something like the rural isolation of her girlhood, Wilson felt, and in her retreat, with no children to tend or compel her to outgrow her own childhood, she'd lost something of her adult self. This was the darker side to Eugen's patience and devotion. The more he took charge of Edna's life and health, the more childlike and dependent she seemed to become. "Though I did not see much of her through all those years, I got the impression," Wilson later wrote, "that she was alternating between vigorously creative periods . . . and dreadful lapses into depression and helplessness." He thought he recalled her telling him once, not long after her marriage, that she had spent weeks in bed weeping.

As the years passed, Edna's health continued to deteriorate, the headaches giving way to more mysterious afflictions, and her habit of convalescence grew.

"She seemed to be mysteriously sick a great deal of the time," her friend Max Eastman wrote. "She cultivated for all it was worth the privilege of being sick. She lived largely upstairs in her bedroom, and would fly up there from the slightest annoyance. . . . One felt on entering Steepletop that some very fragile piece of china, inestimable in value, was in unstable equilibrium upstairs, and that even the airwaves, if too much agitated, might unbalance it."

Eastman felt she "babied herself" and "Eugen babied her" and that there was too much alcohol; it was getting in the way of her work. There was no doubt, he later reflected, that "chemical stimulation blunted the edge of Edna's otherwise so carefully cherished genius. It also caused our four-sided close friendship to dwindle away, for the old gay conversations came to depend upon a preludial pepping-up, which required more alcohol than Eliena and I could . . . take." Sometime in the 1940s, Eastman recalled sending Edna and Eugen a letter, gently warning them that there was too much drink. They wrote back immediately, thanking him, promising to correct it. But they never did.

AS TIME PASSED, Edna's drinking grew more acute, dulling her capacity to retreat into writing, the one realm where she'd always found release. But what few besides Eugen knew was that Edna's substance abuse had now gone beyond alcohol.

After an automobile accident in late 1938, Edna had begun to complain of back pain. Eugen had taken her to a local doctor, who prescribed morphine, which Eugen was taught to inject. By late 1939, at Edna's insistence, a highly respected New York doctor had not only increased her morphine dosage but augmented it with a cocktail of other drugs, including barbiturates to help Edna sleep (this on top of the hard liquor Edna still drank). For the next four years, Edna was in and out of hospitals, putatively for "recurrent depression." The real reason, though unacknowledged even in her medical records, was Edna's drug addiction, which her doctors finally succeeded in breaking in the spring of 1946.

That summer, Edna began to correspond with Edmund Wilson again after a lapse of fifteen years. She told him that she had recently been in the hospital, where she'd had "a very handsome—and, as I afterwards was told, an all but life-size—nervous breakdown." She added that she'd been unable to write during her illness, and instead had been memorizing vast amounts of poetry. "Anyway, I have them [the poems] all now. And what evil thing can ever again brush me with its wings?"

What she didn't say was that she'd been addicted to morphine.

Wilson had not seen Edna since his call of 1929, nineteen years earlier. Though they'd exchanged letters since Edna had reopened communications, it was not until the summer of 1948 that Wilson and his wife finally stopped in at Steepletop. "As we drove through the tunnel of greenery that led to the house," he recalled, "I felt, as I had not done before, that Edna had been buried out there."

When Eugen came out, he was gray and stooped, dramatically aged. "I'll go and get my child," he said. At first Wilson didn't realize he was referring to Edna. They made their way into the living room, which seemed to contain most of the things that had been there on his last visit, but the couches looked badly worn. "The whole place seemed shabby and dim," he wrote.

Edna with her husband Eugen Boissevain

When Edna finally appeared, it took a moment before Wilson recognized her. "She had so changed in the nineteen years that, if I had met her unexpectedly somewhere, I am sure I should not have known her. She had become somewhat heavy and dumpy, and her cheeks were a little florid. . . . Her hands shook; there was a look of fright in her bright green eyes."

Eugen brought them martinis and then sat down. "Very quietly he watched her and managed her. At moments he would baby her in a way that I had not seen him use before but that had evidently become habitual. . . . My wife said afterwards that Gene gave the impression of shaking me at her as if I had been a new toy with which he hoped to divert her."

Edna told Wilson she'd been writing and was very much excited, because for two years she had been unable to work. She then pulled out some of her poetry, which was, he said, "of an almost unrelieved blackness." He could see she was "just emerging from some terrible eclipse of the spirit."

The shock of seeing Edna and Eugen like "deteriorating ghosts" in their own home was more than Wilson could bear. He soon insisted on leaving, though he asked if Edna and Eugen might like to join them later that evening for a musical concert, which they declined.

Dorothy Thompson, a journalist friend, reported an equally disturbing visit to Steepletop soon after. Eugen, she remembered, had led Edna into the living room by the hand, "as if she were a recently invalided small child." Edna was wearing a Chinese mandarin coat and Eugen "fussed over her, speaking in language just short of baby talk; and she answered him like a little girl getting over a mild case of measles and wanting to be babied." When Eugen saw she was settled, he went out and closed the door. "As soon as he was gone, Edna's whole manner changed; she began talking in the customary hearty way" her old friend remembered, and the two women "gossiped like a pair of old cronies."

Dorothy was thinking of leaving when the door suddenly opened again. "Eugen entered carrying a table tray . . . announcing that his child must have her supper now. Edna instantly reverted to her earlier role, allowing herself to be docilely led over to the low table."

Infantalized for years, Edna's fiery creative self had somehow been stifled. Her safe "harbor" had become an entombment she couldn't escape. Something vital inside Edna had gone silent and she was trapped now somewhere in her past.

There remains, however, a curious sequel to Edna's story, as Wilson would later write. Eugen died of lung cancer in 1949. Edna followed a year later, in October of 1950, dying of a fatal fall. She was just fifty-eight.

After Eugen's death, no one had thought Edna would be able to take care of herself at Steepletop alone. Her friends had urged her to come to New York, where there would be company and diversions. But Edna had insisted on returning to the country. She wanted to be home, she said, where she could be writing. She liked to work late at night, often padding off to bed at daybreak.

When Edna's sister Norma arrived at Steepletop after her death, she was surprised to find the house "in perfect and beautiful order: the floors were waxed; furniture polished; couches and chairs newly and brightly recovered."

Edna, on her own again, had apparently recovered her old fire. On her last evening, she had stayed up all night reading proofs of a new translation of the *Aeneid* by a friend, having promised Scribners she would give them a jacket quote. The table beside the chair where she'd worked that night was covered with pages of small, careful notes she'd made. Nearby lay an open notebook with the penciled draft of a new poem.

CHAPTER 4

ENTERTAINING BOHEMIA

THE HOSTESSES AND
THEIR SALONS

Late in 1912, Mabel Dodge, a restless millionaire with a nose for intellectual fashion, entered the cramped top-floor gallery of Alfred Stieglitz at 291 Fifth Avenue. There, in the last of three skylit rooms hung with paintings, she found the prophet of modern art standing amidst a clutch of friends— artists and backroom regulars drawn, like herself, to the gospel of the avant-garde. Though she knew very little about modern art, with the exception of what she'd gleaned from Leo and Gertrude Stein during a brief visit to their fabled apartment in Paris, Dodge had come prepared to play the role of patroness. What she saw in Stieglitz was entrée to a world she wanted to possess, a brave new bohemian life that would relieve the boredom of her wealth and free her, she hoped, from the curse of her class: the habit, as she wrote, "of never experiencing anything . . . first hand." She knew that Stieglitz, like the Steins, was someone to cultivate, someone who had vision into a radical new consciousness still in its infancy.

"It was always stimulating to go and listen to [Stieglitz] analyzing life and pictures and people," Dodge recalled. "There were always attractive people at [his] place. And strange, alluring paintings on the walls that one gazed into while he talked. . . . In those early years he launched nearly all those painters who count."

Left: **Mabel Dodge in Florentine costume**

It was not within Dodge's powers to come to such judgments on her own. Though armed with a keen sense of what she sought, she depended on others to discern who the important figures in this new world would be. Once identified, however, she pursued them with the avidity of a true collector, driven to possess all those whom she drew into her orbit.

"I became a Species of Headhunter," she wrote, with no apparent irony. "I wanted to know everybody. . . . It was not dogs or glass I collected now; it was people." This ravenous urge to acquire, if not dominate, all in her world, was not a trait Dodge seemed inclined to disavow. Rather, it appeared that she took a certain perverse pleasure in flaunting this part of her nature.

Mabel Dodge

"I have always known how to make rooms that had power in them," she famously pronounced in a not-altogether-flattering four-volume memoir published in the mid-1930s. Dodge, never shy about estimating her own endowments, was exulting over her social eminence as the Gertrude Stein of prewar Greenwich Village. The comparison, however, was not unjustified. Just as Stein played host to avant-garde Paris as modern art was being born, Dodge gathered together at her legendary New York salon the preeminent artists, writers, and radicals of her day. The difference was that Stein entered bohemia on the wings of literature, while Dodge slid in on a mix of hubris and money.

Mina Loy, a close friend, called Dodge the "most ample woman personality alive." Others were less charitable. Her enigmatic air reminded the painter Jacques-Emile Blanche of "a fleshy odalisque, worn out by the heavy perfumes of the harem." "While many salons have been established by women of wit and beauty," wrote Max Eastman, editor of the radical

Postcard from Gertrude Stein to Mabel Dodge

magazine *The Masses*, "Mabel Dodge's was the only one established by pure will-power."

Dodge's style was unabashedly self-indulgent. No stranger to dramatics, she draped herself in flowing silk robes and gauzy chiffon turbans, officiating her Evenings from a divan near the hearth with a sphinxlike remove that even friends found perplexing.

It was done, according to memoirists of the period, with the briefest of gestures—a nod of the head, a furrowed brow, a rapt gaze that somehow conveyed attentiveness.

She was "a dynamo with a face that could express anything and nothing more easily than any I have ever seen before," observed Carl Van Vechten. It was "a perfect mask."

Dodge's inscrutability carried with it a peculiar and compelling power, however. There was something in her manner that encouraged people to feel, in the journalist Lincoln Steffens's words, as if they could "think more fluently." Max Eastman likened the spell Dodge cast to "a magnetic field in

Mabel's villa in Florence

which people become polarized and pulled in and made to behave very queerly." "Like yourself," the artist Marsden Hartley wrote to Alfred Stieglitz, "Mabel Dodge is a real creator of creators."

In truth, Dodge's most sustained creative project was ultimately herself, yet her commitment to the modernist credo was nonetheless real, as was her generous financial support of other artists and causes. Her life story piqued the imaginations of everyone from Gertrude Stein to D. H. Lawrence, both of whom used aspects of her character in their writing. Her fame, though it edged into hucksterism, was not unjustified.

NORMALLY, A WOMAN of Dodge's gilded class would have settled on Manhattan's upper East Side. Born into the commercial aristocracy of Buffalo, New York, in 1879 and educated in exclusive boarding schools, she was well versed in the ways of the rich and privileged. But at thirty-three, Dodge had just returned to America after a decade of willful indulgence in fin de siècle Florence, where she had played host to some of the century's most brilliant provocateurs—among them Bernard Berenson, Gertrude Stein, and Mina Loy. In her ten years abroad, she had acquired a taste for the eccentric and unusual, especially when they served her own affectations.

In Florence, Dodge had tried her hand at the role of femme fatale, making something of a cult of the orgasm. No matter that she was married to a mild-mannered architect from Boston. "He was a wet blanket," she reported, too dull to use the rope ladder she had devised for him to descend into her bedroom from the story above. "I so deep, so fatal, so glamorous—he so ordinary and matter-of-fact!" she wrote, in a rare moment of self-parody. She tried, she said, "to wish him away." After filling her magnificent Tuscan

Mabel Dodge in New Mexico, circa 1918

villa with exquisite objects, then with a steady stream of amusing guests, Dodge threw herself into a series of steamy affairs, always with inappropriate men. But the pattern was discouragingly the same. When the heat of conquest cooled, and after she had broadcast her latest escapade in a flurry of torrid confidences, the mood precipitously darkened.

It was her friendship with Gertrude Stein, who was living in nearby Fiesole, that ultimately refocused Dodge's sights, making her reconsider her life of suffocating excess. Gertrude was "prodigious," Dodge wrote, "her body seemed to be the large machine that her large nature required." She had "a laugh like a beefsteak" and would wear "a sort of kimono made of brown corduroy in the hot Tuscan summertime, and arrive just sweating, her face parboiled." Yet with all this, "she was not at all repulsive," Dodge said, "she was positively, richly attractive in her grand *ampleur*."

"*Why* are there not more real people like you in the world?" she scrawled to Gertrude, after one of Stein's visits.

Gertrude's eccentric antiformalism was the perfect antidote to Dodge's ennui, which is what, finally, the extreme aestheticism of her life in Florence had produced. Gertrude convinced Dodge that modernity was the path forward, and for Dodge, New York was her New Jerusalem.

THE APARTMENT DODGE chose—four high-ceilinged rooms in the heart of Greenwich Village—sat not at the fashionable top but at the foot of Fifth Avenue, just off the tree-lined green of Washington Square. While the houses overlooking the north side of the square were mostly Georgian, having about them the dignified air of old London, those on the south side had a more tatty feel. Here stood an assortment of artists' rooming houses. For $30 a month the more prosperous could rent an entire floor; for as little as eight, a single bedroom. But it was the maze of crooked streets beyond the square, which had the "slightly raffish look of the Left Bank in Paris," that was most typical of the Village. It was here, where rents were cheap and the ragtag streets were lined with tearooms and bohemian restaurants, storefront theaters, and fledgling magazine offices, that Mabel Dodge insinuated herself in late 1912. Her salon-to-be was two doors north of the famous Brevoort Hotel bar, the nightly haunt of the neighborhood's artists, writers, and eccentrics.

Dodge's new world called for a new image. She bobbed her hair, began wearing simple sack dresses, and, in contrast to the indulgent decor of her Florentine villa, decorated her airy rooms all in white. Here, finally, was an elegantly empty stage on which she would conjure her newfound sense of the modern. The actors, she was confident, would arrive.

Fate soon intervened in the person of a dandy and "flaneur-at-large" whom Dodge met one night at a dinner party: Carl Van Vechten. Her first impression of the foppish, pudgy-faced man seated across from her was that he was distinctly "funny-looking," with "large teeth with slits showing

Mabel's apartment in the heart of Greenwich Village

between them that jutted out and made him look like a wild boar," though the rest of him, she conceded, "looked quite domesticated."

Van Vechten was an influential music and theater critic for *The New York Times,* and as such had access to the most voguish inner circles of the dance, theater, and music worlds. He seemed to know everyone and to be everywhere. His special passion, however, was Harlem. Van Vechten adored the blues and often prowled Harlem's hot spots, searching out music and seductive stories, which he churned out for several tony white newspapers. He was fast becoming black Manhattan's most ardent champion, not to mention Harlem's most ubiquitous white guide.

Though married, Van Vechten made no secret of his affairs with men. There were rumors that he kept a flat in Harlem, black with silver stars on the ceiling, for nocturnal trysts. Officially he lived with his wife, the actress

Carl Van Vechten. Photo by Nicholas Muray.

Fania Marinoff, in an elegant apartment on West 55th Street, later the scene of his famous integrated parties of the 1920s, where a daringly mixed crowd of black and white notables—everyone from Bessie Smith and Paul Robeson to George Gershwin, Edna St. Vincent Millay, and Tallulah Bankhead—would drink their way through the decade. Gossip thrilled him, as did all manner of salon exotica. An accomplished photographer, Van Vechten specialized in black portraiture and prided himself on his growing collection of black male nudes.

In no time, he had installed himself as a regular guest in Dodge's rooms, bringing with him a dazzling entourage of writers, Harlem dancers, poets, actresses, playwrights, Broadway soubrettes, and musicians.

"You have a certain faculty," Lincoln Steffens said to Dodge one evening. "You attract, stimulate, and soothe people," he observed, "men like to sit with you and talk to themselves!"

Why not put this gift of hers to use? "Organize all this accidental, un-planned activity," he told her; hold official "Evenings."

And so Mabel Dodge's famous Evenings were formally born, and with them Greenwich Village's reputation as a place of art, intellectual foment, freedom, and controversy that quickly spread beyond its borders.

By 1913, Dodge was writing gleefully to Gertrude in Paris, urging her back to America. "Life in New York is one long-protracted thrill," she told Stein. By now, New York's gathering avant-garde had become a fixture of Dodge's salon. Here, collected in the same room, was an improbable mix of characters—not only poets and painters but people of all professions and political views, all classes: "Socialists, Trade Unionists, Anarchists, Suffragists, Poets, Relations, Lawyers, Murderers, "Old Friends," Psycho-analysts, IWW's, Single Taxers, Birth Controlists, Newspapermen, Artists, Modern Artists, Clubwomen, Women's place-is-in-the-home women," is how she described it. Dodge's salon was where black Harlem first met Greenwich Village bohemia and, conversely, where white bohemia got its first taste of a parallel black culture that it would soon not only glorify but actively try to emulate.

Margaret Sanger

Sometimes as many as a hundred guests assembled. Every Wednesday evening, a throng ascended two broad flights of red-carpeted stairs and entered Dodge's rooms. Guests included Djuna Barnes, John Reed (briefly Dodge's lover), Emma Goldman, Alfred Stieglitz, and the French painter Francis Picabia. Some arrived in jewels and formal evening clothes, others in handmade batiks and sandals. Weaving discreetly through the hordes was Vittorio, Dodge's Florentine butler, who poured Pinch Scotch and passed trays of Gorgonzola sandwiches and ham, artfully arranged on Catagalli plates. (Djuna Barnes, at the time a struggling journalist, wryly allowed that she would be forever grateful to Dodge for letting her "eat as many sandwiches as my suburban stomach could hold.") Later, amidst the din of tinkling glasses and late-night talk, gold-tipped cigarettes, proffered in large white bowls, circulated the room, and women—to the scandal of the press—openly smoked.

On most evenings, there was a set subject and designated speakers, followed by general discussion, which, because of the crowd's eclecticism, was often fiercely partisan. Notorious anarchists sparred loudly and aggressively with well-fed capitalists. Poets and Modernist painters—John Marin, Marsden Hartley, Andrew Dasburg—debated effete critics and the editors of glossy magazines. Birth control advocates like Margaret Sanger, espousing Havelock Ellis's theories on sex—"a sacred, all-pervasive and spiritualizing urge," as he defined it—tangled with prudish society matrons.

Sanger was among the circle of feminists whom Dodge had met at the Heterodoxy, a club, Dodge wrote, "for unorthodox women . . . women who

An evening at Mabel Dodge's salon

did things and did them openly. Women who worked." Poised, alluring, deeply articulate, Sanger was to Dodge a mesmerizing figure:

> It was [Sanger] who introduced to us all the idea of birth control, and it, along with other related ideas about sex, became her passion. . . . She was the first person I ever knew who was openly an ardent propagandist for the joys of the flesh. This, in those days, was radical indeed when the sense of sin was still so indubitably mixed with the sense of pleasure. . . . She made love into a serious undertaking.

For the communards who gathered at the Heterodoxy—Sanger, Dodge, Emma Goldman, Mary Heaton Vorse, Charlotte Perkins Gilman, and Marie Jenny Howe, among others—the writings of Freud, Havelock Ellis, and the Swedish feminist Ellen Kay had become requisite reading, giving rise to the growing sense among them that the psychological revolution that would

145

ultimately liberate the human female would only be won *after* all constraints on sexuality had been removed.

On this point Emma Goldman was famously outspoken. On Goldman's first official Evening, guests crowded into every corner of Dodge's rooms, expecting to see before them a wild-eyed, bomb-lobbing extremist. Instead they encountered a remarkably level-headed and charismatic lecturer, who looked more like a "hausfrau," Dodge said, than a dangerous subversive. (Far more terrifying, Dodge later confessed, was the kiss Goldman's lover Sasha tried to steal from Dodge one night in a taxi.) The high point of Goldman's lecture always came at the end, when, having just delivered an impassioned argument for equal sex rights for women, she dared any man in the room who had never experienced premarital sex to come forward and be counted. When no one did, titters rippled through the crowd, only proving her point.

Red Emma knew firsthand what she preached. Both she and Isadora Duncan, the barefooted high pagan of modern dance, openly took lovers —this at a time when attempts to advocate birth control, even for married women, were brutally prosecuted and wife beating was an accepted part of domestic life. Goldman's most notorious affair was with the anarchist Alexander Berkman, who, after shooting the millionaire tycoon Henry Clay Frick, was jailed for fourteen years. In 1912, Berkman, just released from prison, had rejoined Goldman in Greenwich Village, where she was now living with a younger male lover. As for Isadora Duncan, she liked to say that she took lovers because her body "had endured so much pain from assorted headaches, backaches and battered toes that she felt it owed her all payment possible in sexual rapture."

THE INTEMPERATE AND frankly titillating talk about subjects still deemed dangerous, if not taboo, by the rest of the country—sex, psychoanalysis, homosexuality—assured the success of Dodge's Evenings as pure entertainment. Yet it was also what made them so radical. There were those, certainly, who were privately scornful of Dodge. Stieglitz, Picabia, and Hartley attended Dodge's evenings, wrote Agnes Ernst Meyer, but "they also resented her; she played with life as if it were a game in which the stakes were not very high." But there were many who genuinely admired her too, and few who didn't come to her soirees. As Max Eastman wrote, "Everybody in the ferment of ideas could be found there."

Mabel Dodge

Dodge, for all her airs and misplaced ambition, gave the avant-garde its first meeting place and forum for conversation. It was she who served as the social glue connecting people who would never otherwise have met or had occasion to publicly air their ideas. Her Greenwich Village salon was where bohemia's revolutionary ethos—a conflation of art and political activism, visceral experiment and utopian ideals—first coalesced.

IF MABEL DODGE was the social doyenne of early Greenwich Village, Harlem had its counterpart in the person of wealthy A'Lelia Walker, who also held sway as one of the era's most audacious and unforgettable hostesses. What Dodge's evenings were to downtown bohemia before the war, A'Lelia's lavish parties were to Jazz Age Harlem. "You should have known A'Lelia," Van Vechten once remarked to a friend. "Nothing in this age is quite as good as *that*."

A'Lelia, an extravagant figure who liked to wear bejeweled turbans and often carried a riding crop, was the richest black woman in America. Her mother, Madam C. J. Walker, a former washerwoman, had built a mighty beauty empire from a secret patented hair straightener that "dekinked" Negro hair, turning her almost overnight into a multimillionaire. A pillar of

Harlem society, Madam Walker was already known as a tireless philanthropist when she died suddenly in 1919, leaving her fortune, her beauty empire, an Italianate villa overlooking the Hudson River, and several elegant Harlem townhouses to her only child, A'Lelia.

A'Lelia's political convictions, by contrast, were decidedly vague. Six feet tall and voluptuous, "a gorgeous dark Amazon" surrounded by her "light-skinned ladies in waiting," according to Langston Hughes, A'Lelia preferred spending money to giving it to charity, as her mother had so regularly done. She spent freely at Manhattan's most exclusive jewelers, couturiers, and car dealerships. And, like Mabel Dodge, she entertained often and always in high style.

A'Lelia's glittering interracial parties of the 1920s, like those of her friend and cohort Van Vechten, were the stuff of legend. On any given evening, besides the usual throng of artists, dancers, jazz musicians, poets, journalists, critics, and novelists, one might see English Rothschilds, French princesses, Russian grand dukes, mobsters, prizefighters, men of the stock exchange and Manhattan's social elite, elegant homosexuals, Village bohemians, white movie celebrities, and smartly dressed employees of the U.S. Post Office.

On most occasions, A'Lelia entertained at her palatial double brownstone on 136th Street, though for more intimate gatherings she used her pied-à-terre at 80 Edgecombe Avenue. Here guests might be treated to a poetry reading by Langston Hughes, a sultry blues performance by Alberta Hunter or Nora Holt, or a few song-and-dance numbers by Harlem's latest rising star.

On weekends, A'Lelia moved her grand entertainments to her thirty-four-room mansion on the Hudson, a place so spectacular it was sometimes called the "Xanadu of Harlem's artistic and intellectual elite." Built in the Renaissance style by her mother in 1917, its luxuries included marble staircases, a wood-encased library filled with rare books, a frescoed dining

Right: A'Lelia Walker

Products sold at the Walker beauty emporium

room ceiling, Aubusson carpets, a gold grand piano, a basement gymnasium, and a large garden pool surrounded by statuary. Black male servants dressed in doublets and hose and white wigs attended to the guests. "One couldn't help being impressed with the brilliance of the evenings," one visitor recalled. "Literature, politics, painting and music were always discussed. Something interesting was constantly happening."

Not everyone in Harlem concurred. A'Lelia's parties were also the subject of some controversy. She was "no judge of character and easily won by flattery," recalled Carl Van Vechten. Wherever she went, she was surrounded by "parasites, jesters and well-meaning courtiers." Among Harlem's upper crust, the commercial origins of A'Lelia's wealth—hairdressing—and the fact that she wasn't college educated, made her "a parvenu." Certain upstanding Harlemites wouldn't deign to attend her galas. Others enjoyed her champagne, smiling scornfully, however, if ever her name was mentioned in conjunction with social leadership. After seven minutes, it was said, conversation with A'Lelia "went precipitously downhill." Friends, however, defended the lively and sociable hostess. "She made no pretense of being intellectual or exclusive," said Langston Hughes, but she was undeniably gracious, and gave you the impression that she could engage you in conversation on most any topic. Asked once how she stayed so well informed, she breezily told a reporter that she had learned "the art of reading headlines and the trick had served her well."

But A'Lelia was no fool. Like Mabel Dodge, she never said more than was required, careful always not to interject her views into the brilliant conversations that swirled about her rooms. She usually made a brief, dazzling appearance early in the evening, after which she retreated to her private quarters to play bridge with her circle of women friends. If she was snubbed by Harlem's class-conscious elite, A'Lelia was remarkably non-judgmental herself (except, that is, if someone got in her way). According to David Levering Lewis, "she was especially fond of homosexuals"; those Harlemites who might otherwise have been openly critical of such lifestyles learned to hold their tongues. "She made no effort to limit society in any strict sense," Van Vechten remembered. "She invited whom she pleased to her own apartment when she entertained, and frequently they invited whom they pleased." Yet the guest lists were always impressive. And A'Lelia's imperial self-possession and captivating style were not themselves without significance.

Being wealthy and extremely dark-skinned was a combination that both intrigued and repulsed black and white Manhattan in the 1920s. Even in African American circles, there existed a deep-seated prejudice against dark-skinned blacks. Lighter skin conferred superiority and, by extension, privilege. Skin hue determined who was hired for the chorus lines at the most desirable clubs, who landed menial work; even who gained admission to Negro schools and colleges, regardless of academic qualifications. "There are near-white cliques, mulatto groups, dark-skinned sets. . . . The snobbery around skin color is terrifying," observed the white English heiress Nancy Cunard, who shocked her contemporaries by living openly with a black musician in the 1930s. So entrenched was the stigma against darkness that Harlem newspapers were crowded with ads for skin-bleaching creams.

A'Lelia's statuesque blackness stood as a bold challenge to these biases. Rather than try to diminish her racial identity, A'Lelia seemed to thrill at displaying it. Wherever she went, she comported herself with a queenly splendor and a theatricality calculated to turn heads. In Paris, during a solo five-month trip to Europe, Africa, and the Middle East, she made headlines

in her plumed hats and spellbinding jewels as she strolled the Champs–
Elysées. In Cairo she was pictured riding among the pyramids on camel-
back. In London, a friend reported, her appearance one evening at an opera
box in Covent Garden "was so spectacular that the singers were put completely out of countenance."

"She looked like a queen and frequently acted like a tyrant," wrote Van
Vechten. "She was tall and black and extremely handsome in her African
manner." She often dressed in red or in rich brocades of gold and silver with
her trademark turbans. As Carole Marks suggests, A'Lelia was the ultimate
racial modern, a self-invented woman who delighted in creating a stage
on which to parade her blackness before whites. So brazen was her self-
confidence (or her sense of entitlement) that even in the face of the usual
hierarchies of class and race, she was seemingly blasé. When informed one
night that a Scandinavian prince had not been able to negotiate the
crowded hallway leading to her apartment, she "sent word back that she
saw no way of getting His Highness in . . . nor could she herself get out
through the crowd to greet him. But she offered to send refreshments down-
stairs to the Prince's car," Hughes recalled. On another notorious occasion,
legend has it, whites were served chitterlings and "bathtub" gin, while black
guests gorged on caviar, pheasant, and champagne. Such was her racial
pride that A'Lelia could make sport of the color bar, even amidst mixed
company. In this, at least, she had absorbed her mother's message.

MADAM WALKER, A'Lelia's mother, had displayed a passion for racial up-
lift coupled with a flair for commerce few could match. She had started her
sprawling beauty empire with $1.50 in savings and a wonder formula that
came to her, according to company literature, one night in a dream. "A big
black man appeared to me and told me what to mix up for my hair," she recalled. "Some of the remedy was grown in Africa, but I sent for it, mixed
it, put it on my scalp, and in a few weeks my hair was coming in faster than
it had ever fallen out."

Madam Walker initially sold her product door-to-door. But within a year, she had added a mail-order operation, which she farmed out to A'Lelia, who, however reticently, took on the job in deference to her mother's wishes. By 1908, aware that the success of her product was dependent on proper application, Madam Walker had opened a beauty salon and training school as well, choosing Pittsburgh as her base of operations.

Lelia College for "Walker hair culturists" was unique among beauty schools, for the essence of what Madam Walker taught was racial pride. The idea was to cultivate inner and outer beauty in customers, to instill a sense of confidence and self-worth by helping each woman find her own personal style, not a derivative one. Madam Walker stressed the importance of feeling good about being black and being female. Salon agents were instructed never to use the word *straightener* when referring to their product. What they were selling was a grooming tool to heal and condition the scalp. But Madam Walker's message went beyond beauty techniques. She also preached financial independence, insisting that women were too reliant on men for their physical survival. Crisscrossing the country with A'Lelia at her side, she urged women to strive collectively to create business opportunities and economic self-sufficiency. "I want to say to every Negro woman present, don't sit down and wait for the opportunities to come," she told an audience in 1913. "Get up and make them."

A'Lelia felt no such compulsion. It had never been easy to meet her mother's expectations, as A'Lelia was the first to admit. Though while alive Madam Walker had indulged her daughter's every whim, A'Lelia could never escape the sense of obligation that came with her mother's largess. After Madam Walker's death, A'Lelia stepped back from the business, no longer impelled to please her mother, and delegated most of her responsibilities to F. B. Ransom, her chief manager. For the next several years, the Walker Company continued to prosper. But by 1923, competitors had begun to sprout up on every Harlem corner. When Ransom petitioned A'Lelia for suggestions about boosting sales, she had little to offer. "I feel we have exploited this field thoroughly and are getting as much right now out of this business as any concern is getting or can get," she wrote. Whereas Madam

A'Lelia Walker

Walker would have leapt to the challenge, A'Lelia's attentions had by now turned elsewhere. Lacking her mother's business zeal and only mildly interested in the betterment of her race, A'Lelia dedicated herself instead to making a place for herself amid Harlem's social whirl. "She wanted to miss nothing," recalled a friend. As hostess and impresario to Harlem's artistic elite, A'Lelia had found a role well suited to her indulgent nature.

Early in 1927, after several well-liquored brainstorming sessions, A'Lelia decided to convert a ground-floor section of her 136th Street town house into a private club for artists and writers. What she had in mind, she said, was something "completely informal . . . homey [and] comfortable," a place like the Century Association downtown, where artists could meet and bring their friends, and "eat for prices within their very limited reach." At the suggestion of a writer friend, Bruce Nugent, whom she hired as her decorator, she called it the Dark Tower, in homage to Countee Cullen's "Opportunity" column of the same name.

A'Lelia assembled a group of fifty artists—a "breed of chiselers," Nugent later called them—to help her flesh out the concept. But after meeting several times without producing anything she liked, A'Lelia became annoyed and hired a new decorator. The walls were soon covered with costly gold and buff French wallpaper and framed texts of a several prize-winning poems by Hughes and Cullen. What had originally been envisioned as a casual setting was now decidedly upscale.

In the engraved invitations sent out late that October, A'Lelia wrote: "We

A'Lelia Walker's salon, the Dark Tower. Photo by James VanDerZee, 1928.

dedicate this tower to the cultured group of young Negro writers, sculptors, painters, music artists, composers and their friends. A rendezvous where they may feel at home."

But by then, A'Lelia had all but abandoned her original idea. The multitudes who appeared at the reception opening night were anything but the struggling artists she allegedly wanted to support. Like all of A'Lelia's galas, the party seemed a paean to the rich and influential. The hall "was a seething picture of well-dressed people," wrote one friend. "One of the artists was nearly refused admission because he had come with open collar and wore no cravat, but someone already inside fortunately recognized him and he was rescued." Colored faces "were at a premium," Nugent recalled. "The place filled to overflowing with whites from downtown who had come up expecting that this was a new and hot night club." Instead of affordable food, the prices on the menu were scandalously high. Beyond the means of most artists, few patronized the place. Within a year, the Dark Tower was officially closed.

In a moment of petulance, A'Lelia sent out a curt notice blaming not herself but the "members" for its failure:

Dear Members and Friends:

Having no talent or gift but a love and keen admiration for art, The Dark Tower was my contribution. But due to the slothfulness on the part of the members to make use of The Dark Tower, it will be closed November 1 as a private institution.

In a brief coda, she added that the Dark Tower *would,* however, be available henceforth to rent for private parties.

A'Lelia's inflexibility and lack of diplomacy interfered with more than the success of the Dark Tower. Her obstinance also made it difficult to maintain any long-term relationship. Although she was married twice, both unions were bitterly contentious and ended in divorce. As Van Vechten wrote years later, "In love and in marriage she was unsuccessful as was but natural. She was too spoiled, too selfish, too used to having her own way to make any kind of compromise."

EXTRAVAGANCE ON THE scale to which A'Lelia was accustomed could not be sustained forever. Walker Company coffers had been steadily declining for years. But when the stock market crashed in the autumn of 1929, the beauty industry was especially hard hit. Though A'Lelia's lawyers repeatedly warned that post-crash revenues had plunged to devastating levels, A'Lelia turned a deaf ear, either unwilling or unable to curb her spending. Finally in 1931, keen to stem the tide of losses, and under mounting pressure from the trustees of her mother's estate, A'Lelia tried to find a buyer for Villa Lewaro, her Hudson River mansion. Her first thought was Van Vechten, to whom she wrote, "I have been holding on to this place through sentiment (my mother), but I've arrived at the conclusion it is foolish of me to maintain such a large and expensive home with no family ties and I spend all my time in New York City. It is assessed at $190,000. I'll let it go for $150,000. . . . There isn't a person I'd rather have Villa Lewaro than you."

But Van Vechten had neither the interest nor the means to come to her aid. "But, dear A'Lelia, what would I do with a house? I am always away all summer. And where do you think I'd get all that money? A'Lelia, behave!"

By this time A'Lelia had auctioned off the villa's contents. On Thanksgiving weekend of 1930, bargain hunters had swarmed the house and grounds, snapping up art and antiques for prices well below what they'd cost. "White Buyers Strip Villa of Treasures," one headline read. "Sale of Villa Lewaro Nets $58,000 in 3 Days as Millionaires Bid," reported another. Bessie Bearden, mother of the artist Romare Bearden, was quoted as saying, "A few of us who had once enjoyed the hospitalities of the mansion stood with wet eyes and looked on."

The villa remained on the market and most of A'Lelia's jewelry was pawned. But she managed to hold on to her silver, her baby grand piano, and her beloved Lincoln. That August, determined to make the best of things, A'Lelia drove to Long Branch, New Jersey, for a weekend party to celebrate a friend's birthday. On Sunday, after a day at the ocean, disregarding her doctor's warnings about high blood pressure and overeating, A'Lelia consumed a whole lobster, a chocolate cake, and champagne. At 4 A.M. that morning, she awoke complaining of a headache that was interfering with her vision. A few hours later, she died of a cerebral hemorrhage. She was forty-six.

WHEN HE LEARNED of her death, Langston Hughes, whom A'Lelia had counted as one of her closest friends, wrote a poem, "To A'Lelia," which was read at the funeral a week later.

> So all who love laughter,
> And joy and light,
> Let your prayers be as roses
> For this queen of the night.

A'Lelia had given Harlem a hostess as wildly extravagant and grandly subversive as any the age boasted. In her role as "queen of the night," she had played her part to the hilt, bringing gaiety, glamour, and intoxicating style to the Renaissance. If New York in the 1920s was, as F. Scott Fitzgerald famously described it, the greatest, "gaudiest spree in history," then A'Lelia's opulent galas were no small part of the binge. If hers was only a supporting role in the fiercely inventive, barrier-breaking performance that was Jazz Age Harlem, the mark she made was no less significant. A'Lelia passed through the Renaissance like a bright comet, drinking and dining and entertaining on an imperial scale. If she didn't devote her fortune to black charities, as her mother might have wished, she did open her houses to the cultural elite of the moment—white as well as black—in this way giving some of her fortune back. Though A'Lelia wasn't an artist herself, she had genuinely appreciated their company, and acted in her capacity as a hostess as a vital social bridge.

When she died in 1931, the writers and artists of the Renaissance lost one of their most faithful admirers. A'Lelia's death, Langston Hughes later recalled, "was really the end of the gay times of the New Negro era in Harlem. . . . That spring [1931] for me (and, I guess, all of us) was the end of the Harlem Renaissance."

CHAPTER 5

BESSIE SMITH

'TAIN'T NOBODY'S BUSINESS IF I DO!

In February of 1925, Bessie Smith, queen mother of the blues, pulled into the southern town of Chattanooga, Tennessee. She was filled with anticipation. It was the first time Bessie had returned to perform in her hometown since her ascent to stardom in New York. After the performance that evening, she and her niece Ruby, along with three girls from the show, were planning to go to a pigs'-feet party at the home of an old family friend.

The house was in a dark, isolated section of town. It was a moonless night, but the noise and the lights of the house drew them forward. Bessie and Ruby hiked up their slinky skirts as they crossed the muddy yard and stepped onto the sagging front porch.

The festivities were well under way. Inside, the smell of food, sweat, smoke, and liquor filled the air. The bright, fast-paced hammerings of a blues pianist mixed with the boisterous din of the guests. Bessie nodded approvingly.

"The funk is flyin'," she said. Bessie moved through the crowd to the kitchen, Ruby and the girls just behind. Grabbing a plate, she ladled out collard greens, black-eyed peas, and scallions from the pots on the stove, then dug into the steaming vat of pigs' feet. Six feet tall and over 200 pounds, she was a big woman. Looking contented, she sat at the kitchen table to eat, washing down her food with homemade liquor.

A man entered the kitchen. He wore a shiny dark blue suit and had gold caps on several of his teeth. He stank of liquor and perspiration.

Left: **Bessie Smith performing**

"C'mon, baby, let's dance," he said, grabbing for Bessie's girls as they backed into the corner.

Bessie looked up, then slowly rose. Hands planted on her hips, she spat a small bone belligerently in his direction.

"We don't want to be bothered," she said, "so you just get back in there and let them alone."

"Who in the hell are *you*?" he smirked.

Bessie paused. "Did that fucker say something to me?" she asked. All at once she jumped the man, punching him in the head. Stunned, he stumbled to the floor.

Calmly, Bessie sat back down and resumed eating. "This here sure is some delicious food, uhm, uhm, uhm," she said, nodding her head. The man staggered to his feet and slipped out of the kitchen.

When Bessie and the girls finally left the party around four o'clock in the morning, the incident had long since left their minds. Laughing and trading stories, they were halfway down the block when the kitchen aggressor edged soundlessly from the shadows and plunged a carving knife into Bessie's ribs.

With a moan, Bessie held her bleeding side. The man took off running. Bessie, the knife still lodged in her side, started after him, chasing him for three full blocks before sinking to her knees in pain. When the girls caught up with her, Bessie turned to Ruby, groaning: "Baby, take this thing out of me."

Ruby tried, but she was too squeamish, she remembered. One of the other girls had to do it. The police and an ambulance arrived soon after, and Bessie was rushed to the hospital. The doctor who stitched up the wound recommended that she stay for a few days. Bessie, however, wouldn't hear of it. She had performances all that week. At two o'clock the following afternoon, Bessie Smith stood onstage, belting out the blues, just as scheduled.

THE STORY, ONE of many Ruby would later tell Bessie's biographer Chris Albertson, was pure Bessie. Earthy and famously hot-tempered, Bessie was a wild, violent, hard-drinking woman who loved raucous parties, cheap corn liquor, and home-cooked southern food. As Albertson writes, "Bessie cared remarkably little for the good opinion of others." She was rarely intimidated and indulged her appetite for alcohol and sex to extremes. Black and proud long before it was fashionable, Bessie wore her color—and her hardscrabble origins—as a badge, refusing to treat them as handicaps. She was a hardworking performer, not only fiercely determined but immensely talented. Though her stardom eventually crossed racial boundaries, Bessie always remained defiantly herself, seeing no reason to alter her behavior or temper her ways.

If many pronounced her foul-mouthed, ill-mannered, and vulgar, few were immune to her powerful singing. "That wasn't a voice [Bessie] had," wrote one enthusiast, "it was a flamethrower licking out across the room." Langston Hughes said Bessie's blues were the essence of "sadness . . . not softened with tears but hardened with laughter; the absurd, incongruous laughter of a sadness without even a god to appeal to." While Bessie Smith might have been a "blues Queen" to the society at large, wrote the black novelist Ralph Ellison, "within the tighter Negro community where the blues were a total way of life . . . she was a priestess." Alberta Hunter said simply: "Bessie Smith was the greatest of them all."

SHE WAS BORN in 1894 in Chattanooga, Tennessee, one of seven children. Her father, a Baptist preacher, died soon after Bessie's birth. By the time she was eight her mother was dead as well. The child-rearing fell to Bessie's older sister Viola, though soon Viola was pregnant herself, leaving her little time to look after her siblings. They were desperately poor. At age nine, to earn pocket money, Bessie began singing for nickels on street corners. At eighteen, she got a job with a vaudeville troupe touring the South. "She was a natural singer, even then," recalled the producer. Nevertheless, he soon dropped her, claiming Bessie wasn't beautiful enough to be in the chorus line. What he really meant was that she was too black.

Bessie had little trouble finding another job. Film actor Leigh Whipper remembers seeing her perform in Atlanta in 1913: "She was just a teenager, and she obviously didn't know she was the artist she was. . . . She just sang in her street clothes—but she was such a natural that she could wreck anybody's show."

By 1922, when Bessie moved to Philadelphia, she was already well known in the South, and was considered a blues singer with astonishing draw. Two years earlier, Mamie Smith had become the first solo black singer in history to record, alerting the New York record companies to the untapped potential of black talent. Mamie's hit single "Crazy Blues" sold over 100,000 copies in the first month of its release, giving rise to a new phenomenon called "race records."

Bessie, however, didn't make her own recording debut until three years later. It was 1923 and she had just fallen in love with Jack Gee, a handsome but illiterate night watchman whom many have described as an opportunist. But Bessie didn't see it that way. Jack pawned his watchman's uniform to buy her the dress she wore for her first New York recording session, something she never forgot. And that spring, after Bessie cut four more discs, Jack discovered she was being cheated by her pianist-manager Clarence Williams, who was pocketing half of her pay. Jack and Bessie stormed Williams's office, punching him to the floor and beating him until he released Bessie from all contractual obligations. Then they marched into the Columbia recording offices and secured Bessie a new one-year contract.

Bessie Smith, Empress of the Blues, 1920

Bessie was having the time of her life. By night she and Jack prowled the hot spots of Harlem. By day she rehearsed in the foyer of Jack's mother's home on 132nd Street, amid potted palms and Victorian settees, while Jack's teenage niece Ruby looked on, transfixed by her uncle's new girlfriend. "I just stood there and watched her, and my whole life changed," Ruby recalled years later, unaware at the time how true her words would prove.

"Down Hearted Blues," Bessie's first single, hit the market just days after Bessie and Jack were married. There wasn't even time for a honeymoon. An instant hit, the record sold more than 2 million copies in six months. Bessie rushed back to New York to record seven more songs. Immediately after, she began packing for her southern tour, the first of many she would do over the next eight years while under contract with Columbia records.

She was an electrifying performer. Though her show in those early years was unassuming, consisting of a few simple dance steps, her hips swaying wantonly to the music, her powerful voice possessed a red-hot pathos all her own. Bessie belted out songs of love, grief, yearning, and neglect with a lusty, soulful realism. She sang of low-down, philandering lovers and no-good husbands, of poverty, loneliness, and physical abuse, making it clear that she knew of hard times firsthand. Yet even beyond the bitter truth of her lyrics, it was Bessie's extraordinary ability to connect with her audiences, not only to feel their woes but to make them feel her own, that made her the envy of other performers. Bessie captured the hard realities of being a black woman in a white man's world with tragicomic flair, exploding timeworn taboos with a proud, shouting defiance. "If I should get the feelin', To dance upon the ceiling, / Taint nobody's business if I do," she sang with sassy self-assurance.

If Bessie was famously generous onstage, sharing herself openly with audiences and those she loved, offstage she was equally extravagant. Bessie gave away money as fast as she made it. She bailed friends out of jail, bought luxury gifts for Jack, and supported her extended family. Once, hearing that a fellow performer was in the hospital and unable to pay his bill, she grabbed a cab during a break in her show, taxied to the hospital, and settled the debt. Another time, on the way to a concert in Detroit,

Bessie Smith and her husband, Jack Gee in 1923

she got off the train on impulse and bought Jack a car—a 1924 Nash, which she paid for in cash. Bessie liked to throw her money around, her niece Ruby remembered: "We'd walk into a joint and Bessie would say, 'Here's a hundred dollars. Set the house up and don't let nobody out and nobody in,' and she enjoyed getting everybody drunk with her."

What Bessie didn't like sharing, however, was the same venue with another blues singer, especially if it was a woman. Ethel Waters, one of the few performers who might have posed a threat, recalled an incident with Bessie in Atlanta sometime before 1920: "Bessie was in a pretty good position to dictate to the managers," Ethel remembered. "She had me put on my act for her and said I was 'a long goody.' But she also told the [manager] that she didn't want anyone else on the bill to sing the blues."

Ethel deferred. "I could depend a lot on my shaking, though I never shimmied vulgarly," she said.

Later, however, when Ethel stood onstage, before she could even finish her first number, the audience started howling, "Blues! Blues! Come on, Stringbean, we want your blues!"

After the show, the manager paid Bessie a visit. He was revoking the order forbidding Ethel from singing the blues, he announced. He couldn't have "another such rumpus." The next Ethel heard was an irate Bessie "yelling things about 'these Northern Bitches.'"

"Now nobody could have taken the place of Bessie Smith," Ethel allowed. "People everywhere loved her shouting with all their hearts. . . . But they wanted me too."

At the close of the engagement, to Ethel's surprise, Bessie summoned her. "Come here, long goody," she said. "You ain't so bad. It's only that I never dreamed that anyone would be able to do this to me in my own territory and with my own people. And you damn well know you can't sing worth a . . ."

Another time, Bessie and a rival blues singer, Clara Smith, were scheduled to perform together for a "blues night." But Bessie never sang that evening. "I don't know *what* happened," an observer recalled. "All of a sudden . . . I saw Bessie throw a chair at somebody who was mashing his way through the crowd. . . . Then I saw them drag her out of there. It took three strong men—she was a powerful woman and she could cuss worse than a sailor."

The story surprised no one. Few in the music world hadn't heard of Bessie's violent temper or her lacerating tongue. She was known to be a barroom brawler who raised her fists with little reservation, taking on men or women with equal ferocity. People also knew that Bessie was a binge drinker; that the cheap corn liquor she carried in her purse fired her temper like gasoline to a flame.

None of this, however, diminished the power of Bessie's work. Her first year of recording had been wildly successful, earning her more cash and acclaim than she ever thought possible. Fans fought outside theaters, jostling for seats to her shows. In little more than twelve months, she had become the hottest of Columbia's recording artists, with more offers for big ticket engagements than she could accept.

Bessie, to her credit, took it all in stride. The only noticeable change in her bearing was her wardrobe. "Bessie liked to dress well," remembered Ruby, twenty years younger than her famous aunt. "And she liked for her men to dress well, so she'd buy expensive suits for Jack and she got herself some fur coats and jewelry—real diamonds." At home, however, "she was still the same old Bessie, slopping around in her slippers . . . cooking up a lot of greasy food."

That December, four months before Bessie's old contract had expired,

Columbia signed her to a new one. Though she was tired and overworked, her spirits were high. She felt lucky to have a husband she loved and with whom she could share her good fortune. Jack, for his part, was too busy enjoying Bessie's newfound riches to notice Bessie's fatigue.

More money meant more elaborate shows. Bessie could now afford a traveling cast of sixty, as well as props and opulent costumes. She was partial to outlandish headgear: huge ostrich-plume headdresses; hats that looked like tasseled lampshades. The gowns she donned were regal as a queen's, shimmering satins beaded with gems or trimmed in fur.

Bessie's fee for a week's performance, which had started at $350, escalated to $1,500 a week. In Memphis, a reporter praised Bessie for "a voice that will never be mistaken for another's. She is in a class by herself in the field of 'blues.'" An article in the *Pittsburgh Courier* reported record-breaking crowds awaiting her show. "Bessie Smith is 'Queen of the Blues' . . . positively the biggest attraction," wrote the correspondent for the *Cincinnati Defender*.

As Bessie's bookings increased, so did the pressure she was under. On tour for months now, she had less and less time to spend with Jack, and it was starting to take a toll on their relationship. Bessie was hitting the bottle more and more, and she'd begun to cancel dates for trumped-up reasons to cover up drinking bouts.

In April, Bessie was called back to New York to record. Jack's niece Ruby, more awed than ever by her famous aunt, begged Bessie to let her accompany her on her next tour. Secretly pleased, perhaps, at the prospect of having company on the road, Bessie agreed. She taught Ruby to dance, so she could perform during set changes.

Their first stop was Chicago, a city that already had its own local blues divas, including Ida Cox, Alberta Hunter, and the incomparable Ma Rainey. Heavy-set, with gold caps on her teeth and "straightened hair sticking out all directions," Ma Rainey, as Albertson writes, "was no beauty." Some said she had the "ugliest face in show business." But Ma was the Mother of the Blues, "the earliest link between the male country blues artists who roamed the back roads of the South and their female counterparts." As such, she was a legendary figure.

Chicago was a sizzling music city with a nightlife equal to Harlem's. However, for Bessie it was untried turf, so she was pleased to learn that an old friend, Richard Morgan, whom she had known in Alabama, had recently moved to the South Side, becoming the neighborhood's most celebrated bootlegger and party host.

As Morgan's teenage nephew, jazz great Lionel Hampton, recalled: "My uncle was a real cool dude. . . . He furnished whisky and bathtub gin for almost all the

Bessie Smith dancing the Charleston, 1924

dives on the South Side. . . . The musicians used to love to come to his place because they could meet all the chicks there, and my uncle would give them all the whisky they could drink. . . . I used to dream of joining Ma Rainey's band because she treated her musicians so wonderfully . . . but my uncle always said that Bessie was the greatest singer—he was always very fond of her."

AFTER A SUCCESSFUL run in Chicago, Bessie went on to play Indianapolis. From there, her next scheduled stop was New Orleans. But Bessie didn't make it. Though the newspaper claimed she had been "called back to New York," the truth was more complicated. In the year since Bessie had cut her first record, she hadn't had a break in her work schedule. To relieve the pressure, she had begun to party whenever Jack stepped out of sight. Only Jack, it seemed, could keep Bessie straight, though his reasons weren't altogether altruistic. The truth was, the more Bessie worked, the more money there was for Jack to spend—it paid to insist that Bessie hold to her exhausting schedule. Jack's way of ensuring this was to beat her up every time he found her drinking. A musician friend described Jack as a "mean man, a really mean man who she had a hard time with."

Bessie sometimes went for weeks without drinking, Ruby remembered, "but when she went on one of those benders, she would stay on for weeks." When she and Jack were on good terms, "you couldn't pay her to touch a drop, but when they had their fights she . . . would drink like mad. . . . You see, Jack . . . was all right for her when she felt like being quiet. . . . But when it came to a good time and she wanted to go off, Jack wasn't the one for her. . . . Jack couldn't see it that way, that's why every time you looked he was knocking her down."

Though Bessie was the highest-paid black performer in the country, regularly referred to now as the Empress of the Blues, she was beginning to feel lonely more often than not.

Back in New York again for a recording session, Bessie learned that Columbia had just added Ethel Waters to its list of black singers. Though Ethel hadn't cut as many records as Bessie, she was gaining popularity with white Northerners. Her songs were "more literate" and less ribald than Bessie's; her humor never too "ethnic" for whites to understand.

SUMMER WAS FAST approaching and it was time for Bessie's traveling tent tour. In a rented rehearsal room in Harlem, Bessie began assembling her new show *Harlem Frolics,* an extravaganza featuring seven chorus girls, a song and dance trio, a tap dancer who doubled as a juggler, three comedians, a seven-piece band, and Bessie herself. The cast was jubilant to learn that this year, for the first time, they would be heading south in Bessie's private railroad car.

Living conditions for touring black entertainers were historically abysmal. Barred from even third-rate white hotels, blacks had to stay in rooming houses for "coloreds" or with black families, if they would take them in.

Showgirls sometimes found beds in local whorehouses, though it was necessary to register with the police so they wouldn't be mistaken for "house girls." When nothing better turned up, performers were forced to sleep in abandoned buildings, empty warehouses, or the train station—all dangerous choices, since harassment by the Ku Klux Klan was common, as were lynchings. Now the entire troupe could live on the train.

Canary yellow with lush green lettering, Bessie's seventy-eight-foot-long custom-made car boasted seven staterooms, each of which slept four; a kitchen; a bathroom with hot and cold running water; and a lower level that could accommodate thirty-five people. A room in the rear held the canvas, as well as cases of soft drinks, peanuts, and souvenirs. It also doubled as sleeping quarters for the "prop boys" picked up en route to do manual labor.

Bessie saved on overhead by feeding everyone on the train. Often she cooked herself, conscripting her musicians to chop vegetables. When the weather was good, the troupe ate picnic-style near the tracks, adding to the familial spirit. Only the prop boys were excluded. Ostensibly this was to discourage them from fraternizing with the chorus girls, though Bessie's emotions toward the girls were complex. Young and seductive, usually in their teens, the girls aroused maternal feelings in Bessie as well as a degree of jealousy. The situation was further complicated by the fact that Bessie sometimes had affairs with women.

After supper, the band members trooped through the town streets, announcing the upcoming show with hand-painted signs and a medley of tunes. Vendors were strategically placed by the tent doors to greet eager customers with hot dogs and cheap novelty items. The tent, huge and circular, was divided into two segregated sections, one for whites, the other for blacks.

Tent seasons usually went smoothly. Bessie's fans weren't limited to blacks; rural southern whites were equally devoted. Though there were always racist incidents, Bessie was rarely surprised or bothered when they occurred, having grown up in the Deep South, home to the most virulent factions of the Ku Klux Klan. It was hardly farfetched, in fact, to assume that

**Cathedral Parkway, no. 542. Photo by
Berenice Abbott.**

some members of her tent audiences, the same white faces who enthusiastically applauded her every evening, were Klansmen enjoying a night on the town without their ghostly sheets.

Occasionally the mood was more ominous, however. One hot July night, Bessie was performing in a small rural town in North Carolina. Inside the oversold tent, the press of bodies made the heat unbearable. Midway through the show, one of the musicians, afraid he was about to faint, stepped outside for a breath of air. As he strolled around the tent, he heard dim voices and a grunting sound somewhere just ahead. Nearing the voices, he glimpsed six hooded figures, the moonlight catching the folds of their sheets. They were pulling up stakes, trying to collapse the tent on the unassuming audience inside.

The musician rushed back around the tent to alert Bessie. She was just coming offstage when he got there, blurting out the news. The frenzied audience was shouting for an encore.

"*Some* shit!" Bessie spat, commanding the prop boys to follow. She hurried around the tent to the clutch of hooded Klansmen. Raising a clenched fist, she shook her knuckles angrily in the air. "What the fuck you think you're doin?" she roared. "I'll get the whole damn tent out here if I have to. You just pick up them sheets and run!"

Stunned, the Klansmen stared at her, backing awkwardly away as she unleashed a barrage of obscenities into the night air. Then she strolled back to the tent, seemingly unruffled.

ATLANTA WAS ALWAYS the last stop on Bessie's tent tour. The railway car was parked for the winter, while the troupe slowly worked its way back to New York, playing short gigs at various TOBA houses. TOBA—short for the Theater Owners Booking Association—ran a chain of vaudeville theaters along the Eastern Seaboard and throughout the South. As the only major venue for black talent in the early years of the twentieth century, the circuit was a mixed blessing. Working conditions in most TOBA theaters were substandard. Stages were cramped, lighting hazardous, dressing rooms often nonexistent. Most managers were white and openly exploitative. Salaries were shockingly low. Performers quipped that the TOBA initials stood for "Tough On Black Asses."

Bessie, of course, had her own ways of dealing with callous TOBA officials. Before leaving Atlanta, Bessie had promised TOBA theater owner Charles Bailey that she'd do a few special shows for whites. It was Bailey's policy that performers were never to enter the theater from the front. Instead, to get to the stage entrance, they were told to walk through the garbage-strewn, rat-infested lot abutting the theater. One glance at that lot and Bessie bristled. Grabbing Ruby's arm, she marched to the front door, stepped defiantly into the theater, and was halfway down the aisle when a flustered-looking Bailey caught up.

"It's me, goddammit," hissed Bessie, "and I ain't goin' no other way."

"Take it easy, Bessie," gasped Bailey under his breath. "If they see you before the show, they won't find you as interesting."

"I don't give a fuck," said Bessie "and if you don't like it, kiss my black ass."

Bessie was equally brazen on behalf of her chorus girls. One night, while playing at the Apollo in Harlem, the manager suddenly appeared. He wanted to replace Bessie's dark-skinned girls with lighter-skinned dancers.

Bessie, striking her characteristic hands-on-hips pose, looked him straight in the eye.

"If you don't want my girls, you don't want me," she announced. "I'm tried of wearin' myself out. I can go home, get drunk, and be a lady—it's up to you." The matter was quickly dropped.

Bessie's sense of justice also applied to her own. One night, a jealous showgirl cut up a pair of new silk dancing shoes Bessie had just given Ruby as a present.

You're fired, Bessie told the girl.

"You ain't so much," the girl retorted, hurling a Coke bottle at Bessie's head. In seconds the two women were brawling.

Bessie's behavior toward her own sex was complicated and often inconsistent. Though many felt Bessie was competitive with other women, Ruby claimed it wasn't always the case. She recalled a visit she and Bessie paid Ma Rainey one evening in Birmingham, Alabama. Ruby had always heard the two blues divas were bitter rivals. But that night, as soon as Bessie heard Ma was in town, she had insisted on seeing her. The moment their eyes met, Ma and Bessie flew into each other's arms, filling the next twenty minutes with excited talk punctuated with squeals of raucous laughter as they regaled Ruby with details of an incident that had occurred in Chicago earlier that year. Apparently Ma, who was openly homosexual, had been jailed one night for partying with naked girls. Bessie, by chance in town that evening, had bailed her out the next morning.

Seeing them joking that night, said Ruby, she "never believed stories about bad feelings between Ma and Bessie."

BESSIE'S MARRIAGE continued to deteriorate. In the beginning Jack had been supportive, joining her on tent tours, sitting in the audience, watching as she sang. Now he seemed to put in an appearance only when he needed money. As Albertson writes, Bessie wondered if perhaps she wasn't the only promiscuous member of the couple.

She had been having sexual relationships outside the marriage for some time. It was one of her ways, she said, nothing serious. With Jack away, she was also drinking more, carousing every chance she could. If Jack suddenly showed up, they would fight. Reconciliation would follow and for a brief time Bessie would be on her best behavior. But then Jack would leave, and the cycle would begin again.

Soon the whole troupe was afraid of Jack. "Jack was the fightingest man you've ever seen," said Ruby. "He'd walk into a room hittin'. Every time they had their fights he'd hit her so hard I'd think he was going to kill her, and I'd butt in and he'd slap me down like I wasn't even there—and I got tired of getting beat up on account of Bessie."

Perhaps to save the marriage, in the spring of 1926, Bessie decided to adopt Snooks, a friend's six-year-old son, whom she and Jack renamed Jack Jr. The boy accompanied an ecstatic Bessie on tour that summer. When they returned to Philadelphia, Bessie began making plans to bring her family up from Chattanooga.

Around this time, a brief item appeared in Harlem's gossip paper, the *Interstate Tattler*, alluding to certain intimate goings-on between Bessie and the singing piano player Gladys Bentley, who was known for her wide-ranging sexual tastes. Some said Gladys was a male transvestite, others a lesbian.

As for Bessie's own tastes, no one is certain when her erotic liaisons with women began. What *is* known is that by late 1926, Lillian Simpson had come into Bessie's life.

Bessie was back in New York for a recording session the day she met Lillian, a schoolmate of Ruby's. Lillian had convinced Ruby to arrange a dance audition for her with her famous aunt. Bessie didn't need another chorine, but she was always a soft touch. Though reluctant, she agreed to take both Lillian and Ruby back with her to Alabama, where she was rejoining her show.

Jack had been traveling with the company while Bessie was away. The day Bessie returned, a chorus girl pulled her aside, divulging that Jack, in her absence, had "messed around" with another girl. Furious, Bessie immediately found the girl, beat her up, and threw her off the railroad car, along with all her clothes. Then she stomped to her stateroom to get Jack's gun. When she reemerged, Jack was standing over the weeping girl, trying to piece together what had happened. Bessie shot into the air.

"You no good two-timing bastard," she shouted, waving her gun. "I couldn't even go to New York to record without you fuckin' around with these damn chorus bitches. Well, I'm gonna make you remember me today."

As Jack tried to approach, Bessie shot again, sending him running down the tracks, with Bessie close behind, shooting as she ran. A few hours later, Bessie and her railway car pulled out of Ozark, without Jack on board.

As Albertson writes, Jack's absence after his "alleged indiscretion" became both an opportunity and a justification for Bessie. Shortly after the incident, Bessie first took Lillian to her bed. Soon the two women were sleeping together regularly. The troupe was sworn to secrecy, but they assumed the worst—that Jack would undoubtedly appear unannounced and discover the truth. They braced for his inevitable return.

With each passing day, Lillian grew more afraid of Jack's wrath should he learn of her relations with Bessie. In Chicago, Lillian tried to leave the show. By the time they got to Detroit, Bessie couldn't convince her to stay any longer; she let her go. Bessie hadn't been drinking throughout the affair. But the night Lillian left, an inconsolable Bessie went on a bender.

By now Bessie knew Detroit pretty well. On an earlier trip, she'd befriended the proprietress of one of the town's most notorious "buffet flats." Buffet flats, writes Albertson: "were small, privately owned establishments featuring all sort of illegal activities: gambling, erotic shows and sex acts of every conceivable kind. These buffet flats were usually owned by women, who ran them with admirable efficiently, catering to the occasional thrill-seeker as well as to regular clients whose personal tastes they knew intimately."

Reputed to be safe, buffet flats were always in private homes or apartments. Bootleg liquor was abundant, and there was usually a different show in each room, which patrons could participate in for an additional fee.

Whenever Bessie came to town, her proprietress friend sent several cars to the stage door to ferry the Empress and a few cohorts to her establishment after the show. That particular evening, the place was packed by the time they got there, Ruby recalled. People wandered up and down the linoleum-clad staircase, drinks in hand, pausing in the various rooms to take in the shows. "It was nothing but faggots and bulldykers, a real open house. Everything went on in that house—tongue baths, you name it . . . Bessie was well known in that place," she added.

After several hours, Bessie and her gang went back to their rooms at Kate's, the boardinghouse where they always stayed. Kate's was a run-down joint, not the sort of place that a star of Bessie's stature would be expected to stay—at least, if she was white. In truth, Bessie liked the informality of Kate's, where she could cook her own meals, and where there wasn't even a lobby, just long, narrow halls lined with rooms.

The next evening was the troupe's last performance in Detroit; as was Bessie's habit, she planned to throw a closing-night party. After the show, it was customary for the cast to change into nightgowns and pajamas and wander from room to room, drinking and carousing. On this particular night, however, everyone congregated in Bessie's room. Spirits were high. Marie, one of the younger showgirls, stood up and did a few comic dance steps.

"C'mon, Marie, show your stuff," howled Bessie, letting out a raucous laugh.

Ruby passed out early that night and was carried to her room. Several hours later, she awoke to shouts and a stampede of footsteps. Leaping from her bed, she rushed to the door and peeked out. Marie was flying down the corridor, coming toward her, with Bessie right behind. The next thing she knew, Bessie came hurling in, bolting the door closed behind her. Jack, it seems, had made a surprise visit and caught Marie and Bessie in delicate circumstances.

"If Jack knocks, you don't know where I'm at," Bessie hissed under her breath.

"Come out here," Jack thundered. "I'm going to kill you tonight, you bitch."

There was silence; everyone waited; then more shouts and threats from

Jack. Finally, Kate came out into the hall and called for calm. All went quiet again. They heard Jack mutter something about coming back, then the sound of his footfalls fading down the hall.

Bessie waited a few moments; then, when the coast seemed clear, she poked her head out into the corridor and told the troupe to collect all they could carry and hurry to the train depot. No one even took the time to change. Clutching armloads of clothes, they rushed through the chilly night toward the unlit railroad car. All lights remained off, at Bessie's orders, as they filed in. Within moments, the dark car was hitched to the next outbound train. An hour later, the Empress and her troupe slid quietly out of Detroit.

As the summer wore on, Bessie and Jack's cat-and-mouse game intensified. "Oh, the blues has got me on the go," she sang. Bessie and Jack would clash, split up, and then reconcile their differences, only to repeat the painful cycle once again. The songs Bessie recorded that season reflected her growing despair: "I cried and worried, all night I laid and groaned," she sang. "It's all about a man, who always kicks and dogs me aroun' / That man put somethin' on me; oh, take it off of me please."

"I think [Bessie] wanted to break away from [Jack]," recalled a friend, "but it seemed like every time they had a fight he'd find some way to sweet her up again. He knew she couldn't leave him . . . but Gertie changed all that."

"Gertie" was Gertrude Saunders, a far less talented performer than Bessie, who had starred in several short-lived shows. Precisely when Jack's relationship with Gertrude Saunders began is unknown. Bessie first got wind of it in March of 1929, in Cincinnati, less than an hour before going onstage. A friend had shown Bessie an article in the *Amsterdam News* featuring Jack as the successful producer of the "Gertrude Saunder's show," showcasing in nearby Columbus, Ohio. Bessie was visibly stunned. But it

Left: **Harlem Street, Eighth Avenue and West 140th Street. Photo by Berenice Abbott.**

Bessie Smith.
Photo by Carl Van Vechten, 1936.

didn't take her long to put two and two together: Jack had used *her* hard-earned money to finance another woman's show: a young, slim, light-skinned woman—a woman in every way her opposite.

Bessie didn't break down until after she got to her dressing room. But she cried, Ruby said, as she had never seen Bessie cry before. "Ruby, I'm hurtin'," she said. "I'm *hurtin'* and I'm not ashamed to show it." Later that night, after Bessie's performance, she and Ruby rode all the way from Cincinnati to Columbus in a cab, arriving at Jack's hotel at 2 A.M.

Bessie and Jack fought hard that night, tearing the room apart. Afterward, the floor was strewn with shattered furniture. Bessie was bleeding. Jack later claimed that he abandoned Gertrude after the fight, that he and Bessie made up. But Bessie and Jack's marriage never recovered after that violent night in Ohio.

BY 1926, HARLEM, according to *Variety*, had "attained preeminence." It was now the nightclub capital of the world. Nowhere was the entertainment more titillating, the after-hours scene more glamorous or seductive. There were amusements to suit every taste and mood: hotspots like the Lenox, where the late-night crowd often stayed for breakfast; Small's Paradise, famous for its big-band jam sessions and its waiters, who "danced the Charleston while balancing full trays on their fingertips;" and the rowdier Pod's and Jerry's, home to Harlem's best stride piano (a mix of ragtime and jazz). In Harlem, one saw "as many limousines from Park and upper

Fifth Avenue parked outside its sizzling cafés, 'speaks', [and] night clubs" as in any high-toned white locale in America.

None of this, however, meant much to Bessie. Though she was now a superstar who dressed in ermine coats and diamonds, she had no more desire to mix with white millionaires from Sutton Place who came to the neighborhood to sin, slum, and shed their inhibitions, than she did with uppity black socialites who lived on Strivers Row. Mistrustful of haughty people of either color, she was more comfortable in a lowlife bar, keeping company with the street folk. There was one exception, however: the wealthy, white music critic and arts patron Carl Van Vechten, whom Bessie grew to know and trust.

On the face of it, Van Vechten's reputation as an upper-class dandy and shameless voyeur made him an unlikely ally for someone as wary of pretension as Bessie. Alfred Kazin, describing Van Vechten years later, called him a man who "thrived on his own affectations." Yet to Harlem's poets, writers, and musicians, Van Vechten was anything but a figure to dismiss. James Weldon Johnson, one of Harlem's most celebrated authors, claimed that no one in the country "did more to forward the Harlem literary movement." Van Vechten arranged for countless poems and stories by black writers to be published in the pages of *Vanity Fair,* work that would never otherwise have been read or seen by the white literary mainstream; he also set up book contracts with Alfred A. Knopf. He wrote dozens of magazine articles and reviews promoting the Harlem arts, including two trailblazing pieces on the blues for *Vanity Fair,* which definitively introduced Bessie to white readers.

By 1925, the year Van Vechten first saw Bessie live in concert, he'd already amassed a sizable collection of her recordings. Decades later, reflecting on the Empress's performance that night, he remembered "a voice full of shouting and moaning and praying and suffering, a wild, rough, Ethiopian voice, harsh and volcanic, but seductive and sensuous too, released between rouged lips and the whitest of teeth." The crowd that evening had burst into "hysterical, semi-religious shrieks of sorrow," he went on. "When Bessie proclaimed, 'It's true I loves you, but I won't take mistreatment any mo', a girl sitting beneath our box called 'Dat's right! Say it, sister!'"

If the language Van Vechten chose carried an unfortunate, if unintentional, edge of condescension, the sentiments behind his words were above reproach. Van Vechten's support and friendship with black artists like Bessie Smith, Langston Hughes, and Ethel Waters was never theoretical. His appreciation for the power and uniqueness of black culture was passionately felt, his advocacy years ahead of his time.

BESSIE'S FIRST APPEARANCE at one of Van Vechten's famous integrated parties on West Fifty-fifth Street came in 1928. She arrived wrapped in a white ermine coat and was met by a sea of white faces at the apartment door. As always, the elegant drawing room was filled with celebrities. That night they included George Gershwin, the opera singer Marguerite D'Alzarez, and Adele Astaire. Bessie, however, was the honored guest. She insisted on a stiff drink.

"How about a lovely dry martini?" Van Vechten purred.

"Whaaat—a *dry martini*?" Bessie roared. "Ain't you got some whiskey, man? . . . I don't know about no dry martinis, nor wet ones either."

Soon Bessie, whiskey in hand, and her pianist Porter Grainger were heading for the piano, Grainger looking painfully embarrassed. Bessie drained her drink, then handed her glass to Van Vechten and began to sing. The guests listened in rapt silence. At the close of each song, amidst clamorous applause, Van Vechten passed Bessie another whiskey. "I am quite certain that anybody who was present that night will never forget it," Van Vechten recalled. "This was no actress; no imitator of woman's woes; there was no pretense. It was the real thing: a woman cutting her heart open with a knife until it was exposed for us all to see, . . . exposed with a rhythmic ferocity, indeed which could hardly be borne."

After six or seven songs, Bessie had slugged down six or seven whiskeys; Grainger and Ruby were getting worried. Both knew it wouldn't take much to set her off. Bessie sang one more number, at which point Grainger gave

Ruby the signal that it was time to go. Sliding into place, Ruby and Grainger moved Bessie toward the door. They were three steps away when Van Vechten's wife, Fania Marinoff, suddenly stepped forward, throwing her arms around Bessie's neck.

"Miss Smith," she cried. "You're *not* leaving without kissing me goodbye." This was all it took.

"Get the fuck away from me," Bessie thundered, knocking Fania to the rug. "I ain't never heard of such shit!"

A moment of silence ensued. The guests looked horrified, speechless. Grainger and Ruby grabbed Bessie's arms and hustled her out the door and down the long carpeted hall.

"It's all right, Miss Smith," Van Vechten cried out solicitously, trailing behind. "You were magnificent tonight."

Once in the elevator, Bessie sank to the floor. "I don't care if she dies," Grainger muttered to Ruby under his breath.

"TROUBLE, TROUBLE, I'VE had it all my days," Bessie sang. By 1929, though Harlem still sparkled, the blues craze had peaked. "Talkies" were beginning to replace vaudeville, Bessie's main source of income. Her Broadway debut that summer, a part in a show called *Pansy,* received scathing reviews. Though she was still able to sell records and continued to perform and draw crowds, her career had hit a lull. Those close to Bessie said she was taking the breakup with Jack hard.

1929 would not be a good year for anyone. That September, as Columbia was releasing Bessie's single "Nobody Knows You When You're Down and Out," few could have guessed how

Van Vechten's wife, the actress Fania Marinoff, 1922

prophetic it would be, not only of Bessie's future but of the entire country's. A month later the stock market crashed. Like a stage curtain dropping to the floor, the giddy 1920s came crashing to a close.

Bessie soldiered on nonetheless. Though her fees had dropped dramatically, she continued to live as she always had: performing in two-bit Southern towns, living in shabby boardinghouses. Other black performers were beginning to move in more worldly circles, however. Ethel Waters was headlining at the London Palladium; Alberta Hunter was starring in the London hit *Show Boat.* Though she didn't know it, Bessie was quietly being left behind. Still, people who knew Bessie insisted she had no interest in European high society. She remained optimistic about her singing career, they said.

Bessie was less sanguine about her private life. Everything she loved seemed to be turning to dust. Her sisters Viola, Tinnie, and Lulu were drinking too much, bitter over the cut Bessie had made in their allowances. Ruby had left, bribed away by Jack's promise of a choice part in Gertrude Saunders's show. The railroad car was gone too, sold when Bessie realized she could no longer afford it. But most devastating was the loss of little Jack. In an act of vengeance, Jack Sr. had gone to the authorities, charging Bessie with being an unfit mother. Soon after, Jack Jr. was taken away.

Bessie was lonely and despondent. "She wouldn't cry, she'd just sit there, staring," remembered a dancer in *Moanin' Low.* "It was strange, Bessie used to carry on so when her and Jack were together, but—I don't know, sometimes I just couldn't believe this was the same woman. That man really broke her down, strong as she was."

Bessie buried herself in work. Columbia Records, on the verge of bankruptcy, slashed the fees on her new contract. To economize, Bessie abandoned the elaborate costumes she loved, the wigs and ornate headgear. She decided to tour the Deep South on her own, a daring plan . . . given the deepening grip of the Depression. It was 1930.

Passing through Chicago, Bessie, as always, looked up her old friend Richard Morgan. But this visit had a different mood from those of earlier times. Richard had heard of her split with Jack; he and his wife had recently separated too. Sometime that week, the perameters of Bessie and Richard's relationship changed. When the Empress left Chicago a few days later, she was accompanied by a new lover, and her show had a new manager.

"She was like a new person," Bessie's sister-in-law, Maud, remembered. "Richard was everything that Jack should have been. . . . They both loved a good time, and they respected each other. Richard was very jovial when he'd had a few drinks, but he never got nasty. . . . He was perfect for Bessie, he understood her."

THE DEPRESSION ENTERED its third year and bread lines grew. It was becoming a way of life. By the spring of 1932, when Bessie and Richard returned to Harlem, rumors were circulating that Connie's Inn, the Cotton Club, and the Lafayette Theater, three of the most glamorous Harlem hot spots, were about to go under. Bessie was hardly surprised when Columbia announced it was dropping her. For nine years, Bessie had been one of the label's mainstays. Now she was on the street. For the first time, she felt pessimistic about her career.

The music world, meanwhile, was shifting gears, moving to a new, stepped-up beat, a beat more in sync with the speed of modernity and moving pictures. The jazz riffs of Louis Armstrong were turning people's heads in New York and Paris. Harlem insiders were talking about a singer named Ella Fitzgerald and a young newcomer, Billie Holiday, whom Duke Ellington called "the essence of cool." The rise of swing was just around the corner. Many saw Bessie now as a has-been, a salty blues mama whose day had passed.

In February of 1936, Billie Holiday's star was rising as fast as Bessie's was falling. Then fickle Lady Luck turned Bessie's way. Billie was singing in a new show at Connie's Inn, which had recently moved downtown to 48th Street and Broadway, when she came down with ptomaine poisoning and had to quit the show. Bessie was asked to replace her. It was Bessie's first break in years.

Herald Square, West 34th Street and Broadway. Photo by Berenice Abbott.

The Broadway audience was new to Bessie, and what she gave them at Connie's was hot new material. For the first time in memory, she was free to reinvent herself. Abandoning the blues, Bessie belted out the latest songs to the stepped-up rhythms of an accompanying swing band; this audience, too, gave her their hearts.

With news of the new, updated Bessie, old friends suddenly reappeared, including Van Vechten, who asked Bessie if he might photograph her. That February day, Van Vechten remembered, Bessie came to his apartment between shows, "cold sober and in a quiet reflective mood. . . . She could scarcely have been more amiable or co-operative. . . . I got nearer to her real personality than I ever had before and the photographs, perhaps, are the only adequate record of her true appearance and manner that exist."

Word traveled fast. Audiences were so enthusiastic, reported one music columnist, that Bessie was being held over at Connie's for the sixth week. "Still Tops" read the headline over her picture in the May 1936 issue of the *Chicago Defender.*

Bessie was on a roll. A week after Billie returned, Bessie opened at the Apollo Theater in Harlem, where she played to a packed house. Her next engagement was in Philadelphia. Bessie was feeling like her old self. For the first time in years, she had her own show; she had bought a car, a used Packard; she was getting good press, drawing large and enthusiastic crowds; she was even, on occasion, philandering a bit.

"I never saw so much life left in someone who had lived so much," said one gospel singer who saw her that spring in Philadelphia. "I don't think anybody or anything could break that woman's spirit."

Even Bessie's moribund recording career showed signs of life: "We were going to make records," said Lionel Hampton. "I told everybody in the Goodman band about Bessie being tight with my uncle, and Benny said, 'Oh, man, we *gotta* make some records with her.' And I had just signed a contract with Victor Records to do a lot of small-band dates with people like Nat King Cole, and all those guys . . . [and they] told me, 'Be sure to get Bessie,' because she was just coming back into prominence then. . . . You know the stories she sang became so true—this was reality."

In September of 1937, Bessie accepted a part in a show that was touring the South. Richard Morgan, who had remained steadfast throughout, went with her. They traveled in Bessie's old Packard, with Richard driving. The Empress had never taken the time to learn to drive herself.

The show was in Memphis. It was Saturday night and Bessie had just finished her last performance. They weren't expected in Darling, Mississippi, until the next afternoon. Feeling restless, Bessie suggested that she and Richard get a jump on the troupe by leaving that night. They could drive as far as Clarksville, she said, and sleep there.

Richard tried hard to dissuade her. That night there was a card game in Memphis he wanted to get into. They argued, but Bessie was adamant, threatening to get someone else to drive if Richard wouldn't. Finally, Richard gave in.

They left Memphis at one in the morning, heading south on Route 61. It was a long, straight stretch of road, dark and silent. They'd driven about seventy-five miles and Richard was tired. A huge truck loomed in the darkness ahead. Richard misjudged the distance of the taillights. He braked hard, but it was already too late. They were skidding as the car hit the truck; the Packard flipped from the force of the impact.

WHEN THE OBITUARY appeared in *The New York Times* the next day, September 27, 1937, it was barely a paragraph long: "Show folk on Beale Street mourned today the death of Bessie Smith, 50, 'queen' of blues singers, who was killed in an automobile accident."

A week later the funeral took place. As news of Bessie's death spread through the black community, her body had been moved from the small Philadelphia funeral home where she lay in state to a larger building that could accommodate the estimated ten thousand mourners who filed past her coffin to pay their respects.

It was a farewell that befitted the Empress she had become. Bessie lay in splendor in a long silk gown and slippers, which, according to the black press, went well with the "pink two-tone velvet" that lined her silver casket. Her expression was serene, belying nothing of the wild, tempestuous life she had lived or the fierce pride that had fired her spirit.

On October 4, at dusk, after a day of record crowds, Bessie's body was at last buried. But her story was not so easily laid to rest. A month after her death, an article by John Hammond appeared in *Down Beat* magazine, alleging that Bessie's death had been the result of southern racism. The piece, based on hearsay, claimed that Bessie had died unattended after the white hospital where she was taken refused to treat her because she was black. The controversy burned, growing with the years and becoming part of music legend. When Edward Albee's play *The Death of Bessie Smith* opened in West Berlin in 1960, based on John Hammond's piece, the stories flamed again.

It wasn't until the early 1970s, after Bessie's biographer Chris Albertson tracked down the one remaining witness to events that sad Mississippi night, that a more complete picture of what probably occurred was finally pieced together.

It seems that a Memphis doctor and a friend, out early for a fishing trip, had come upon the wreck of Bessie's car, lying on its side across the dark highway, just moments after it overturned. As they slowed, their headlights revealed the large figure of Bessie, motionless on the road, and a man, Richard Morgan, signaling frantically for them to stop. In the far distance, two red taillights were receding into the blackness. The lights, the doctor later theorized, were from the truck Bessie's car had struck, which had been pulling slowly away, having stopped briefly for a tire check—perhaps just a moment before the Packard hit.

The doctor hurried over to see how badly Bessie was hurt. She had sustained severe injuries on her right side, he said. Her arm was nearly severed and her ribs were crushed; she was having difficulty breathing. They moved her to a grassy spot near the road while the doctor's friend ran to a nearby house to call an ambulance. About fifteen minutes had elapsed when they heard a car approaching. The doctor's car was in the middle of the road, making it impossible for the oncoming vehicle to pass—but the car didn't seem to be slowing. Seconds later, it tore into the doctor's car, driving it straight into Bessie's wrecked Packard before skidding into the ditch. Inside sat a stunned young white couple who had been drinking. They were injured, but not badly.

When the ambulance at last arrived, Bessie was lifted in. It drove to Clarksville, to the black hospital. The ambulance driver said Bessie was never taken to a white hospital.

But many people, including Bessie's family, believe there was more to the story. Jack Jr. said he was told by Richard Morgan that when the ambulance arrived, the white woman was taken away and not Bessie. When a second ambulance at last appeared, Bessie was driven to a white hospital first, where she was refused treatment. Only after that was she taken to the black hospital, where she died.

BESSIE'S GRAVE REMAINED unmarked for thirty-three years. While Jack Gee and Bessie's family fought over her estate, no one purchased Bessie a headstone. Benefits were held to raise the funds, the proceeds of which went to Jack, say relatives. Asked why he never bought Bessie a stone, Jack commented, "I never saw three cents of all that money."

In 1970, Janis Joplin and the wife of the local NAACP chapter at last bought Bessie a headstone. Jack was invited to the unveiling but, predictably, he never made it. Joplin's involvement, which she stressed was an expression of her admiration and indebtedness to Bessie, spoke volumes about the deep and enduring impression that Bessie's raw and powerful blues had made on generations of women singers.

Bessie had risen higher in her profession than any black woman of her time had climbed. And she'd done so without ever hiding the truth of who she was. "I've got the world in a jug; The stopper's in my hand," she'd sung in 1923. Bessie had never stopped believing the world was hers to live, capture, and express. As the inscription on her gravestone reads: "The Greatest Blues Singer in the World Will Never Stop Singing—Bessie Smith—1895–1937."

CHAPTER 6

ETHEL WATERS

AM I BLUE?

"I never was a child.
 I never was coddled, or liked, or understood by my family.
 I never felt I belonged.
 I was always an outsider."

Such were the words Ethel Waters wrote in the opening of her brave and startling autobiography, *His Eye Is on the Sparrow*. They were no exaggeration. Born out of wedlock, Waters began life unwanted, untended, and for the most part unloved. Her mother Louise was twelve years old when she was raped by John Waters, a teenager from the neighborhood who was "dark brown in color though he had white blood." John was the son of Lydia Waters, a wealthy white woman of Dutch descent who lived—after her marriage to a black man—"as a Negro and among Negro people," according to Ethel.

When Louise's mother, Sally Anderson, learned of the rape, she went immediately to Lydia Waters, who coolly denied her son's crime. By the time John Waters confessed, Sally Anderson's heart was so set against the Waters family, she not only refused to ask for financial support, she wouldn't allow the Waters name to be uttered in her home. Her granddaughter Ethel, as a consequence, never knew her father, a playboy and a pianist. Nor did she ever use her last name while growing up, though she did see her white grandmother again, briefly, fourteen years later.

Left: **Ethel Waters**

Lydia Waters, perhaps conscience-stricken, sent word one day asking Ethel to visit. She'd heard that her light-skinned granddaughter bore a striking resemblance to her family.

"I'm Lydia Waters, your grandmother," Lydia said when Ethel arrived, taking her into her arms. But it was too late, Ethel recalled. "I couldn't think of her as anything but a stranger whom Mom had regarded as our enemy."

Lydia Waters reached out to her granddaughter several times again. But Ethel, who would struggle all her life to reconcile these two visions of self—one black, one white—chose not to answer her summons. It was a division that would ultimately be expressed in her art.

ETHEL WATERS WAS fraught with contradictions: she was tough, but she was also genteel; she was sexy, but she was also deeply spiritual. She wasn't a jazz singer, but she would influence countless jazz singers and musicians. She wasn't a blues diva per se, yet she would play a pivotal role in popularizing the blues among white audiences. Though disdainful of genuine blues singers, whom she called crude "shouters" who gave out "with unladylike growls," she also boasted of her own rough, unmannerly side. "By the time I was seven, I knew all about . . . life in the raw," she wrote. "I could outcurse any stevedore and took sadistic pleasure in shocking people."

Waters was a performer of unusual versatility, and her image changed with every decade. She was a sultry sex symbol and recording star in the 1920s, a Broadway actress in the 1930s, and in the 1940s a Hollywood film star—the heavy-set, white-haired persona of her later years.

Music historian Gary Giddins called her "the mother of modern popular singing, the transitional figure who combined elements of white stars like Nora Bayes and Sophie Tucker . . . with black rhythms, repertoire, and instrumentation." Lena Horne said she "was the mother of us all." Waters adapted white diction and performing styles to a black image, opening up the world of white entertainment to blacks. She also inspired white singers to venture into jazz and blues. Envious of her style and dramatic phrasing,

Sophie Tucker, the white sensation of vaudeville, paid Ethel for singing lessons in the 1920s, although Ethel was her junior by twelve years.

Black music, wrote Giddins, "captured the sensuous stance of rebellious youth; traditionalists found it a heart of darkness, and accused it of undermining the nation's morals. Without meaning to—the divisions in [Ethel's] temperament mirrored the divisions in the nation—Waters played both sides against the middle. She was irrepressibly erotic at one moment, and abundantly high toned the next."

Perhaps, as Ethel liked to say, "her mixed blood" explained it.

"I've always thought that I inherited the better qualities of both my grandmothers," she wrote. "From little Sally Anderson, who died in defeat and the grimmest of poverty, I got my fighting heart. From Lydia Waters, who died rich but heartbroken and quite possibly tortured by a bad conscience, I think I inherited poise, dignity, and whatever intelligence I have."

ETHEL ARRIVED ON the morning of October 31, 1896. Her grandmother Sally Anderson took over as soon as she was born. Still a child herself, Louise, Ethel's actual mother, could barely look at the baby. "She never wanted me," Ethel wrote. "So it was natural for her to resent me, the child she had conceived against her will."

Sally worked long hours as a live-in domestic for a white family and was rarely home, and her mother, Louise, had moved away, so Ethel's upbringing fell to her two alcoholic aunts, Vi and Ching. They lived in a series of run-down shanties in the red-light district

Ethel Waters (with inscription to Carl Van Vechten)

south of Philadelphia, "a plague spot of vice and crime," in Ethel's words. Vi and Ching rarely noticed Ethel. They didn't cook, though it hardly mattered; what little money they had went to liquor, not food. Ethel lived as a wild child, stealing to eat, the leader of a gang of neighborhood toughs. She slept where she could—on the floor, the broken-down couch; sometimes even on the street, on the warm iron grates by the bakery. "I came to know well the street whores . . . their pimps, the pickpockets, shoplifters and other thieves," she later wrote.

For pocket change, she worked as a "lookout" girl for the prostitutes. Whenever a cop ventured into the alley, she and the other slum kids would sing out the words to their street game in high, lilting voices. Within moments, the streetwalkers would vanish and the doors of the whorehouses would be locked.

Sally had one night off a week. Usually she arrived to find the trash-strewn house full of men, with Vi and Ching drunk or out cold. Fiercely proud and hungering for respectability, Sally would try to make order. Ethel always looked forward to her grandmother's night off because Sally brought food, stashed in the pockets of an apron hidden under her petticoat. As soon as Ethel spotted Sally, she would dive under her grandmother's dress, squealing, "What did you bring me? What did you bring me this time?" Never mind that it was food retrieved from the trash, leftovers that Sally's white employers chose to toss rather than share with the servants.

Starved for affection as much as for food, she befriended a beautiful young prostitute named Blanche, who sang songs and read her stories. In return, Ethel picked up narcotics for Blanche at the pharmacy. Blanche had syphilis and was dying. "Prostitutes and dope never could afterward tempt me," Ethel later wrote. "Blanche, poor soul, did more to keep me straight in the tough years to come than any person I ever knew."

A quick-witted girl with a ferocious imagination, Ethel amazed her teachers with her gift for mimicry, though they were shocked by her toughness and her vulgar tongue. When Sally enrolled her in a new Catholic school, she thrived under the gentle encouragement of the nuns, impressed that she could call them "sister," a familiar term Negroes used among themselves.

She was eight when she saw her first stage show. Thereafter, whenever Ethel could, she sat in the back rows of the ten-cent storefront theaters on South Street, transfixed by the vaudeville performers; or she slipped into the Standard Theater, where the black stock companies appeared. As soon as she got home, she imitated every song.

One day, to everyone's surprise, Louise reappeared. Ethel had never known her mother, whom she dubbed "Momweeze," but she decided she liked her. Louise barely tolerated Ethel.

Not that it really mattered; what little childhood Ethel had had was about to end. Sally got sick and could no longer work, after which the family moved from one squalid hovel to the next. As Sally lay dying, Ethel took her failing grandmother into her arms and sang a favorite hymn, "His Eyes Is on the Sparrow."

"I held Mom tight," she wrote. "Mom who had been all heart and fighting fury. I thought of how hard she'd worked for the little she'd wanted from life and how she never got that. . . . But she'd kept her head up, never quitting or whimpering." When Sally Anderson died, Ethel lost the one person who had possibly loved her. She had just turned thirteen.

At thirteen Ethel was also married, betrayed by Louise, who promised her to Buddy Purnsley, a local man twice her age. "I thought . . . she'd agreed only because marrying me off . . . was an easy way of eliminating me as a problem." Buddy turned out to be an angry, paranoid man who unjustly accused Ethel of infidelity and beat her. Ethel left him within a year.

With the aid of a glowing recommendation from a now-penitent Louise, Ethel landed her first hotel job. An enthusiastic worker, Ethel scrubbed, mopped, waitressed, and washed dishes with equal fervor, though what she liked best was working as a chambermaid: "I had about a half hour to clean up each room, but I'd hurry and get them done in ten minutes. That left me twenty minutes to act. I'd get in front of the mirror and the show would begin. There I'd be, mugging and acting for all I was worth."

Harlem Street, 422–424 Lenox Avenue. Photo by Berenice Abbott.

Still, Ethel's big ambition was not show business: "What I dreamed of," she wrote, "was becoming the ladies maid and companion of some wealthy woman who was traveling around the world and would take me with her."

On Ethel's seventeenth birthday, her life took a sudden and precipitous turn. Prodded by friends, she was coaxed into performing at a Halloween party in a local saloon. Though a decent singer, "I seldom depended on my voice," she wrote. "I had developed into a really agile shimmy shaker." That evening, in addition to her agile shimmy, Ethel sang a blues ballad, which the crowd loved. In the audience that night was a black vaudeville team, Braxton and Nugent, who approached her after the show with an offer of $10 a week to join their troupe. It was three times what she was making as a chambermaid. Yet Ethel was still uneasy about giving up the security of her scullion's job. Before she let Louise sign the contract (falsely claiming she was twenty-one), Ethel made her promise to hold her cleaning job until she got back.

Ethel's first performance was in Baltimore in 1917, at the Lincoln Theater, a run-down vaudeville house with no wings or dressing rooms. Many nights, Ethel remembered, the audience was more boisterous than the entertainers: "Rugged individualists all, they did whatever they pleased while you were killing yourself on the stage. They ran up and down the aisles, yelling greetings to friends and sometimes having fights. And they brought everything to eat from bananas to yesterday's pork chops.

"But they also were the most appreciative audiences in the world if they liked you. They'd scream, stomp, and applaud until the whole building shook."

Ethel wanted to add a new song, "St. Louis Blues," to the show, and to take it in a new direction, to sing it more slowly, with more pathos. It was the first time a black audience had let "my kind of low singing get by," she remembered of her first night. "You could have heard a pin drop in that rough, rowdy audience." Afterward, "the money fell like rain on the stage," she wrote. Ethel sent most of it home to Louise, Vi, and Ching, as she would all her life.

Though teamed up with two other singers, as an act called the Hill Sisters, Ethel was soon singled out by audiences. Tall and lean, with a fetching coyness, she quickly earned the nickname Sweet Mama Stringbean, as well as the distinction of being the show's biggest draw. One night she overheard Braxton and Nugent discussing the money they were pocketing from her act: almost triple her pay. Enraged, she marched in and quit, followed the next day by her two partners. The three women decided to go out on their own.

They traveled through the South, playing in ramshackle theaters and dingy saloons, working like coolies. Every time Ethel stepped onstage, she was showered with coins, while no one, she said, was tossing even "an old doughnut" at the Hill Sisters, which was souring relations. Though Ethel was getting top billing, she wasn't sure the bitterness and backstage rivalries were worth it. "I still had no feeling of having roots," she wrote. "I was still alone and an outcast." What she wanted more than anything was what she'd still never had—a family, "clean surroundings, a decent, quiet place to sleep, some sense of order."

In 1918, on a highway near Birmingham, Alabama, Ethel was gravely injured in a car accident. At the hospital, a victim of racism and gross neglect, she almost lost her leg. By the time she made it home to Philadelphia three months later, she was weary of the road, disillusioned with show business. Broke and still partially crippled, she moved in with Louise and Vi and took a job washing dishes at a Horn & Hardart automat.

By her own account, Ethel never made a career move without being pushed. This time it was Joe Bright, a black actor-producer from New York, who coaxed her back to the stage. Bright was producing stock shows at the Lincoln Theater in Harlem when he wired Ethel offering work. As always she was ambivalent—at once insecure about her chances in New York and driven to defy her fears. This was the smart, unwanted slum child locked inside the woman; the tough street urchin who swung between extremes of neediness and aggression, one moment longing desperately for a show of affection from the mother who all but abhorred her, the next terrorizing the other ghetto kids with savage threats. Ethel accepted the New York offer, albeit warily. The year was 1919 and Ethel had just turned twenty-three.

New York was the big time, Harlem the pinnacle for black entertainers. Though only ninety-seven miles north of Philadelphia, it was a different world. In those days, Ethel recalled, "Harlem was anything but an exclusively Negro section." Blacks were unwelcome on 125th Street, and they were barred from all but the balcony of the Alhambra Theater, a major showcase for black entertainers. Many white showhouses didn't allow colored audiences at all.

Ethel's performance at the Lincoln Theater went so well that she was asked to stay a second week. One evening, an acquaintance, Alice Ramsey, stopped by and invited her to Edmond's Cellar, the Harlem dive where Alice was employed as a dancer. For singers, "the last stop on the way down in show business was Edmond's Cellar," recalled Ethel. "After you had worked there, there was no place to go except into domestic service. Edmond's drew the sporting men, the hookers, and other assorted underworld characters." Ethel's visit to Edmond's would inadvertently land her a job, two roommates, and an apartment in Harlem. It wasn't the Lincoln, but at least it was full-time work.

Edmond's was a crowded, low-ceilinged joint with cramped tables and "a handkerchief-size" dance floor. The pay was a stingy $2 a night. The real money came from customers' tips, which were thrown into a kitty and divided at the close of what was always an endless evening. "There was no set closing time. . . . I used to work from nine until unconscious," Ethel recalled.

A new pianist, Lou Henley, challenged Ethel to expand her repertoire, urging her to tackle more complex "cultural" numbers. At first she resisted. "It's the story told in the songs that I like," she said. "If I don't like the stories in these songs . . . I won't sing them." But, to Ethel's surprise, she found that she could characterize and act out the songs just as she did with her blues. And audiences were enthusiastic.

Word began to spread. Soon Ethel was such a draw that people had to wait upstairs because there wasn't enough room on the main floor. "White society folks began to come in to hear me," Ethel wrote. The tips were so good that singers from all over Harlem were suddenly vying for work at Edmond's.

Ethel's versatility and inventiveness were beginning to serve her well. She had the sexual swagger of singers like Bessie Smith and Ma Rainey, yet her voice was softer. While Ma and Bessie were "Deep South talents," whose blues were steeped in black rural life, Ethel's style was crisp and urbane, more northern. At once flirtatious and commanding; softly insinuating and tough; proud of her blackness yet enamored of the worldly poise of the white vaudeville women, Ethel was somehow incorporating these contradictions in her work. She was soaking up everything around her, combining the subtle humor and enunciated clarity of white singers like Sophie Tucker with the sexy intonations of the black blues, complete with growls, riffs, and down-and-dirty moans. Intuitively she seemed to know what to absorb and what to discard as she shaped her own definitive art. As Ethel herself said, she tried to be "refined" even when she was being her most outrageous.

Ethel would later look back on this period as the happiest in her life. She was rooming in Harlem with two other women performers; taking her meals at Eva Branche's boardinghouse, where the theatrical people talked shop; and performing nightly at Edmond's. Afterward she would hit the Harlem dance halls, unwinding at the Renaissance Ballroom or the Rockland Palace. Music was undergoing a revolution and everyone seemed to know it. Black blues, so long relegated to the margins of the culture, had come of age.

In 1921, "the clarity of Ethel's diction" and the "relative whiteness of her style" attracted the eye of Black Swan Records, who paid her a lump sum of $100 to record two sides. The record, which featured "Down Home Blues" on one side and "Oh, Daddy" on the other, sold 500,000 copies in six months, pulling the company out of the red. Fletcher Henderson, a pianist with classical training, was Ethel's accompanist. Embarrassed, apparently, at the idea of working with a girl who sang the blues, Henderson wasn't sure it would be dignified enough for him. But the success of their record changed his mind. At Black Swan's urging, Henderson organized a band to tour with Ethel through the South, where they became the first black musicians to broadcast on the radio.

Ethel returned to Harlem after six months on the road and once again went to work at Edmond's. But the continuing success of her recordings soon forced her back out onto the vaudeville circuit. Teamed up with a female pianist now, Pearl Wright, and the dancer Ethel Williams, whom many suspect was Waters's lover, they played up and down the Eastern Seaboard.

Ethel's salary and expenses climbed with each engagement. Ethel loved fine clothes and wasn't shy about buying them. The cabaret artist Bobby Short, at the time a child performer in Chicago, remembers seeing Ethel for the first time. She was dressed in "black velvet and pearls," he recalled. "I saw her from a distance, and I was awestruck. She was every bit the star in her demeanor, carriage, and performance. You really knew you had met somebody. And God knows where it all came from."

The three women played the South next, starting in New Orleans. When they arrived in Macon, Georgia, however, they sensed something "grim and forbidding about the place." It wasn't long before they learned the truth: a colored boy had been ac-

Ethel Waters (with inscription to Carl Van Vechten), 1920s

cused of talking back to a white man, and for this he'd been lynched. There had been no trial, no possibility to mount a defense. That night, Ethel also learned that their boardinghouse was next door to the home of the boy's grief-stricken family. She went over and sat with them until daybreak.

In truth, it was never easy playing in the South. Black performers were applauded by whites in the theaters, only to be spurned and insulted by them on the streets. In some towns, they were spat at; backstage, the theater hands taunted them with racist slurs. But the worst was the theater in Atlanta, Georgia, which was managed by Charles Bailey, one of the meanest, most abusive bigots in the business.

Ethel didn't like working with men like Bailey, but there was no avoiding his theater; it was part of the TOBA circuit. On arriving in Atlanta, she and Pearl dropped by the theater to check the piano, as they always did before

Ma Rainey and her band at the beginning of the 1920s

a performance, and found it badly out of tune. Ethel went to speak with Bailey immediately, assuming he would send for a tuner. When he refused, she braced for a standoff. If the piano wasn't tuned, she explained, it would be impossible to go on and do the act.

Bailey narrowed his eyes. "Did I hear you say you can't go on? You WILL go on," he thundered.

Ethel now volunteered to pay for the piano tuning herself.

"Who do you think you're talking to?" he spat. "No Yankee nigger bitch is telling me how to run my theater."

This was too much for Ethel, who had contained herself until now.

"And no Georgia cracker is telling me how to run my act," she retorted.

At this Ethel calmly sat down and waited. Bailey didn't say anything more. But several hours later, just before Ethel's show, Bailey had a second piano wheeled into the theater.

The week seemed to be passing quietly. Then one of the black stage-hands warned that Bailey was planning an awful revenge. Ethel knew she and her girls had to leave Atlanta fast. But when they got to the train station, she found Bailey had put out an order not to sell them tickets. Even worse, when they returned to the hotel, there were three white cops standing sentry across the street. The hotel owner, who also detested Bailey, felt that their only hope was to get to a small train station outside of town, where Bailey wouldn't have thought to go.

The three frightened women sat up all night, taking turns by the window, waiting for the cops to go off duty. The clock ticked, but the cops didn't move. Three o'clock passed, then four, then five. Ethel's group was beginning to despair when suddenly, at 5:30 A.M. the police sauntered off—no doubt to grab a quick cup of coffee before returning for the morning watch. Ethel and her girls hurried down the hall, then silently out the side door, praying for a car with a driver who would ferry them out of town. It wasn't a car they saw; it was an old colored man driving a horse and buggy, but he agreed to take them. An hour later, settled in their train seats, the three women watched with relief as the Atlanta skyline dissolved into a distant blur.

ETHEL'S SEX EDUCATION, she always said, began early: "By the time I was seven, I was repelled by every aspect of sex." As a child, sharing the same bed with her aunts and their transient lovers, Ethel witnessed the sex act with horror. By age eleven, she was going around with girls who were fourteen or fifteen, accompanying them on after-school visits to neighborhood stores owned by middle-aged men who had a yen for nubile young bodies. Ethel would watch as the men fondled the other girls' breasts, slapped them on the behind. But the men never touched her, she claimed. Her icy stare was sufficient armor. Later, when the same girls slipped into the alleys at night for more potent sex experiments, Ethel made no such assays.

Unlike her blues rival Bessie Smith, whose wild and bottomless appetite for sex was the stuff of legend, Ethel, to judge from the tenor of her auto-

Ethel Waters in duet with Eubie Blake in
Blackbirds, 1930

biography, was indifferent to men. On the road with the Hill Sisters and later, performing solo in Philadelphia and Harlem clubs, Ethel was often romanced by admirers from the audience. Her "girlish reticence" always seemed to attract the "wolves," she said. Usually she was unresponsive, though now and again there were exceptions.

One night a man named Rocky sent word asking her to join him for a drink. "Tell him I don't drink nothing but milk," Ethel told the waiter, assuming her suitor would be dissuaded. (Unlike most of her peers, Ethel didn't touch liquor.) But night after night, Rocky invited her again. Finally, Ethel's curiosity got the better of her: she began sitting with him between sets. Rocky was charming and courtly and he spoke with a silver tongue. "I'd never heard anyone talk like that," she wrote, "in language that rippled and sang and danced."

By the time Ethel learned that her paramour was a junkie and a thief, a smooth-talking Jekyll-and-Hyde character who was in and out of jail, she was too involved to walk away. Like so many of Ethel's short-lived love affairs, this one would end on a rancorous note. She and Rocky fought incessantly—and often physically—over Rocky's drug habit, until whatever passion Ethel once felt was obliterated. There would be other similar relationships, including two more bad marriages, about which she would say little.

Given Ethel's early awareness of her mother's rape, followed by her own traumatic teenage marriage to Buddy Purnsley, there were reasons, certainly, for her sexual ambivilence. Until Buddy, staying a virgin had been Ethel's most fiercely held goal. Buddy had wanted to marry her only because he couldn't get her into bed any other way, she said. Their wedding night couldn't have been "nastier or more unpleasant."

Unfortunately, the men with whom Ethel was later involved never seemed to disprove her initial instincts, which were that a woman was better off without a man than with one. Yet there were also other, more veiled, impulses behind Ethel's coolness toward men, among them her homoerotic leanings, a side of her sexuality that goes unmentioned in her autobiography.

Alberta Hunter, a rival singer with impeccable manners, makes several disparaging allusions to Ethel's bisexuality in interviews, the implication being that in certain quarters, Ethel's lesbian relations were well known, if not "notorious," in her day. Yet Ethel always remained silent on the subject, both in print and in her songs. According to Alberta, who kept her own lesbian lovers discretely out of view, Ethel physically fought with her girlfriends in public, a sight that always made Alberta recoil.

LIKE THE STOCK compositions of the great blues "shouters" Ma Rainey and Bessie Smith, Ethel's repertoire included plenty of "grief-and-rage-struck" songs about two-timing husbands and murderous wives. Yet Ethel's style differed from theirs: besides the sweeter quality of her voice, she was just as likely to take a more droll, comedic view of male-female relations, making mischievous sport of both sexes. Ethel had a certain coquettish charm, an insouiance and sparkle that set her apart. She could deliver a slyly suggestive song with fetching innocence or cleverly milk an off-color pun, then slide into a devilish imitation of a musical instrument with equal appeal. As much a comedienne as a singer, Ethel was the queen of double entendre, as Giddins writes. Her humor was quick and cosmopolitan, wickedly sure. Though she could stir the heart, she also knew how to entertain; and when it came to her views about love, more often than not, Ethel chose to entertain.

EARL DANCER, A Harlem showman with shrewd instincts, had been urging Ethel to try "the white time" for years. Although her high-toned blues
were well suited to white audiences, Ethel always resisted. Whites are "off
the beat most of the time," she said. "They wouldn't understand my blues."

Ethel felt that most of the blacks "getting by on white time" were cari-
catures still performing in the old minstrelsy tradition, gagmen perpetuating
the debasing stereotypes of "darky" routines. She refused to exaggerate her
characterizations to please a white audience. "I ain't changing my style for
nobody," she said.

But Earl continued to press; and finally in 1924 Ethel gave in, agreeing
to play to a white audience in Chicago. The night she debuted, Ethel was
convinced she had bombed: "Nobody screamed or jumped up and down,"
she recalled. "Nobody howled with joy." White Chicago, in fact, loved her.
"A new star [has] been discovered," proclaimed one critic. "Ethel Waters
is the greatest artist of her race and generation."

By the late 1920s, Ethel was recording for the mainstream Columbia label. Her repertoire had continued to grow, as had her theatrical characterizations, becoming increasingly more varied and stylistically complex.
Ethel could alternate effortlessly between light comedy and heartrending
pathos, writes Ann Douglas. She "could sing white or black and delighted
in doing both, sometimes in the confines of a single song." Sometimes she
half sang and half talked a song. Sometimes she slid into Louis Armstrong–
like scat. A brilliant caricaturist, she could do achingly funny parodies of
everyone from Ethel Barrymore to Mae West, complete with salty wise-
cracks dropped sotto voce from the side of her mouth. Ethel was doing
something that no singer before her had done: in her fusion of jazz and
blues, uptown and down, high and low, she had created a unique new
sound—pop-jazz.

Ethel's lifestyle was changing too. Mistrustful of whites, she had always
kept company exclusively with her own. But as the decade progressed, she
began taking work in downtown clubs, performing solo again. For the first
time she was making friends with whites, most of them artists and writers

who lived in the Village. A sculptor named Antonio Salemme regularly took her around: "Tony lived down in Greenwich Village, and he took me around to meet his friends and to Romany Marie's and the other Village places. Those bohemians were like my own people, and I liked them," she remembered. "Your color or your bank account made no difference to them. They liked you for yourself. They were doing work they loved, kept what hours they pleased, and didn't care what Mr. And Mrs. Buttinsky down the hall thought of them and their odd ways. That all made sense to me."

But of all Ethel's white friends, it was Carl Van Vechten she would come to know best. Carl had appeared backstage one evening when Ethel was playing at the Lafayette in Harlem. "He told me he'd been catching my act for years and he invited me to have dinner at his house," she remembered. At first she "didn't see any reason for going." But as Carl talked, she began to sense that "he was more like my Greenwich Village friends than the night-clubbing crowd I'd watched. He was rich, but that hadn't got him down. Carl had great life in him and enthusiasm."

Ethel accepted Carl's dinner invitation—the first, it turned out, of many. As a regular on Carl's guest list of Harlem notables, she would meet some of the most celebrated white writers of her time: Noël Coward; Cole Porter; the playwright Eugene O'Neill; the novelists Sinclair Lewis and Somerset Maugham; the columnist Alexander Woollcott—"prissy but brilliant" in Ethel's words—and the poets Edna St. Vincent Millay and Elinor Wylie.

The radicalism of Carl and his wife Fania's famous "integrated" parties—long, champagne-soused evenings where Paul Robeson might sing spirituals and celebrities like Tallulah Bankhead "let down their hair"—cannot be underestimated. As the Harlem journalist George Schuyler wrote:

> Such salons in the early twenties were rare to the point of being revolutionary. At the time it was most difficult for Negroes to purchase a ticket for an orchestra seat in a theater, even in Harlem, and it was with the greatest difficulty that a colored American in New York could get service in a downtown restaurant.

Most of the white people of Van Vechten's circle knew Negroes only

as domestics and had never had them as associates. It was extremely daring for a white person to dine publicly with a Negro, and certainly to dance with one.

Van Vechten would dine at Ethel's home in Harlem as well. "Carl loved that dinner and our informal way of living," she recalled. "My house, I guess, was a great novelty to him." Carl told her that she was the only Negro he'd ever met who was completely natural with him. Ethel felt something of the same about Carl: "Sometimes it seems to me that Carl is the only person in the world who ever has understood the shyness deep down in me."

In the late 1920s, Ethel met and married her second husband, Eddie Matthews. Soon after, Ethel adopted Algretta, the eighteen-month-old child of a friend, hoping, perhaps, to create the nuclear family she had never had.

In this spirit, and needing a break from work, Ethel, Eddie, and Algretta sailed first-class to France. They went to Paris, Cannes, and afterward to London, where Ethel accepted an engagement to perform at the elegant Café de Paris. Many nights, she recalled, she was playing to a room full of royals. One particular evening, she found Edward, Prince of Wales, sitting at the table that the management always reserved for her. When the prince was told that he was sitting at Ethel Waters's regular table, he came over and apologized. "I didn't like it later when he abdicated," she wryly wrote. "After all, he was the only king who had ever apologized to me for anything."

The Depression had just begun when Ethel returned to Harlem nine months later. Lew Leslie offered her a part in *Blackbirds,* a musical he was producing, and after that, a second revue, called *Rhapsody in Black,* which managed to support her through the darkest days of the Depression. But Ethel's private life had begun to unravel, and with it her spirit. Algretta had been stricken with poliomyelitis. Unable to provide her with the proper care, Ethel was forced to send her away for treatment. Her marriage was

Left: **Carl Van Vechten with wife, Fania Marinoff, 1922**

coming apart too; she and Eddie were bitterly estranged. "I felt like I was working my heart out and getting no happiness," she wrote.

In the spring of 1933, still in the doldrums, Ethel was invited to perform at the glamorous Cotton Club, the haunt of everyone from Lady Mountbatten to Greta Garbo and Al Capone. "The Cotton Club was a classy spot," recalled Duke Ellington. "Impeccable behavior was demanded. . . . Sunday night . . . was the *night.* All the big New York stars in town, no matter where they were playing, showed up . . . to take bows. . . . It was all done in pretty grand style." Shows at the Cotton Club were "Ziegfeldian in their gaudiness," writes the historian David Levering Lewis, "with feathers, fans, and legs flying in time to Ellington's tornado renditions. . . . 'Celebrity Nights' became panting, jumping spectaculars of costume and cacophony." Only the "tops of the tops in terms of names or influence could get a reservation," remembered Cab Calloway. "Even on an ordinary Sunday night it was difficult to get in." Not surprisingly, Ethel jumped at the job.

Arriving for her first rehearsal, Ethel was given a new song by Harold Arlen. Feeling the arrangement needed work, she asked if she could take it home. That night, as she began reworking the score, she didn't have far to look for inspiration. "Everything I had is gone / Stormy weather," the song began. "I was singing the story of my misery and confusion," she remembered, "the misunderstandings in my life I couldn't straighten out . . . the wrongs and outrages done to me by people I had loved and trusted.

"Your imagination can carry you just so far. Only those who have been hurt deeply can understand what pain is, or humiliation. I sang 'Stormy Weather' from the depths of the private hell in which I was being crushed and suffocated."

Word of Ethel's subtle interpretation of the song moved through the grapevine. Then one night the great songwriter Irving Berlin appeared at the Cotton Club to hear Ethel sing. The next morning he called to offer her a leading role in his new Broadway revue, *As Thousands Cheer.* As Ethel would later recall, the moment she saw Berlin's score, she knew she'd never had better material to work with. Of the four numbers she was given,

Ethel Waters on Broadway, 1935

Ethel Waters singing "Heat Wave" in Irving Berlin's
***As Thousands Cheer,* 1935**

the one that sparked her imagination most was a somber ballad titled "Supper Time." The lament of a colored woman whose husband has been lynched as she ponders how to break the news to her children, it told "the whole tragic history of a race," she felt. But the song was controversial. Several of the actors, judging it too tough for a musical revue, lobbied to have it dropped. It was decided the song would remain for the first few shows, to see how it played, before making the final decision.

On opening night, as Ethel walked onstage, she silently prayed. She had only to reach back to her memories of the lynched boy in Macon, Georgia, to touch the emotions she needed: the wrenching anguish of his family; the horror and defeat. As she began to sing "Supper Time," she gave it all she had. She knew that family's heartache as if it were her own. When at last the curtain fell, the applause was deafening; Ethel was called back to the stage again and again.

As Thousands Cheer was a smash hit on Broadway, and Ethel was proclaimed a star. That year she became the highest-paid female performer on Broadway, and when the show hit the road, she made history again as the first black actress ever to co-star with whites below the Mason-Dixon line. "Ethel Waters is having such a delightful present that she doesn't brood over her past," reported the stylish *New Yorker* in 1933.

But it wasn't altogether true. Despite her professional stature, her soaring salary, and steady work, Ethel felt increasingly empty. She had countless opportunities to do light song and dance shows, but she no longer wanted that work. She yearned for another pithy dramatic part, painfully aware of how few such roles existed for black actresses.

A chance encounter at a party one evening drew Ethel into conversation with a white woman who wondered what she had thought of *Porgy and Bess,* the black folk opera. Ethel ventured that the story hadn't seemed "quite true to life." There *was* a novel, she added—*Mamba's Daughter*—that had been so convincing when she read it, she had almost felt it was about her own family, especially the character of Hagar. "In Hagar was all my mother's shock, bewilderment and insane rage . . . and her fierce primitive religion," she explained. "But Hagar, fighting on in a world that had wounded her so deeply, was more than my mother to me. She was all Negro women lost and lonely in the white man's antagonistic world."

The woman Ethel had been speaking to turned out to be Dorothy Heyward, who with her husband, Dubose Heyward, had dramatized *Porgy and Bess.* Dubose was also, coincidentally, the author of *Mamba's Daughter.*

Some months later, a script of *Mamba* arrived in the mail. Ethel, of course, leapt at the chance to play the "lumbering, half-crazy" black woman Hagar. "All my life I'd burned to tell the story of my mother's despair and long defeat," she wrote, "of Momweeze being hurt so by a world that then paid her no mind."

Though another two years would elapse before a producer was found,

Mamba's Daughters finally opened on January 3, 1939. Ethel, the first black actress ever to star in a serious Broadway drama, took seventeen curtain calls that night.

Ethel had once again broken the color line. In a searching performance of astonishing depth, Ethel had refuted the notion that a black woman could perform only comedic song and dance parts, not significant dramatic roles.

The critics were effusive. "In her moments of tenderness, she is heart wrenching," wrote one, "in her moments of blind passion magnificent." For Ethel's white audiences, it was a new and stirring experience: a powerful glimpse into a black woman's heart. For Ethel, however, it was catharsis: the chance to rid herself of the "terrible inward pressure, the flood of tears I'd been storing up ever since childhood." In truth, Ethel had been "no actress that night," she said. "I had only been remembering. . . . I had shown them all what it is to be a colored woman, dumb, ignorant, all boxed up and feeling everything with such intenseness that she is half crazy."

Still, for all its emotional release, the play was physically draining. Night after night, Ethel became the character rather than playing it. Many weeks into the run, a journalist doing a dressing-room interview described her "shivering with fatigue" after the final curtain call. "It's made me feel cold and numb," Ethel told him. "We really fight onstage. I don't know how to play-fight . . . when my daughter has been hurt, it is a real Hagar and a real daughter." When it's over, she added, "There's nothing I can take for a bracer. I don't drink. I don't smoke. I'm just here. I'll go home. Tomorrow it will still be inside."

But in fact Ethel would find a bracer, as Susannah McCorkle writes: food. As a sultry cabaret singer, there had been reason to keep up her looks. Now, playing the part of a haggard older woman, Ethel had none. Her health began to deteriorate as she ate her way to obesity.

When *Mamba's Daughter* finally closed after fourteen successful months, Ethel announced that she had no interest in returning to musicals. She told a *New York Times* reporter that to go back to singing as she had before would be "destroying everything" she'd built up in *Mamba*. But in 1940, when another serious dramatic role still hadn't appeared, she had to back down and accept a part in the musical comedy *Cabin in the Sky.* Because of her weight gain, she was now unquestionably a matron, however, rather than the romantic lead. Two years later, when the hit musical was filmed, the sultry Lena Horne was brought in to give the movie sexual heat.

Ethel Waters singing "Stormy Weather" at a Cotton Club Revue, 1935

According to many writers, Ethel "outsang," "outdanced," and "outvamped" everyone in the picture. But her Hollywood experience went badly. She clashed with the studio and many in the cast, including Lena Horne, who Ethel felt was getting too much attention. After Ethel lashed out at Lena on the set one day, the two women never spoke again. Worse still, Ethel's reputation for being scrappy and intransigent was by then confirmed. For the next six years, she claimed, she was blacklisted from Hollywood.

Almost overnight, agents couldn't seem to get her anything but nightclub dates. Friends said she was washed up, that she'd never get another play or picture again. Barred from Hollywood, she was now, for the first time, also feeling shut out of the black street culture out of which she'd come. She had been living in a first-class hotel room in midtown Manhattan. Now she began spending more and more time in Harlem. "But I quickly learned there are great disadvantages when you are prominent and try to live in a humble place. . . . All I wanted was to be with the kind of people I 'd grown up with, but I discovered you can't go back . . . no matter how hard you try."

She stayed for a while with a Harlem friend, but the arrangement grew

The boxer Joe Lewis celebrates his birthday with Ethel Waters and Duke Ellington, 1938

awkward, so she moved on, this time to a basement room in a run-down building on 149th Street. Week after week, she sat alone with the shades drawn, listening to herself sing on old records. The months passed in a blur, her depression boring deeper down. A recluse now, she was afraid to go out, even to answer the door. She tried to cheer herself up by remembering all the fine breaks she had gotten, but it was no use. She felt that her brain was "breaking wide open," she wrote.

THEN IN 1949, Ward Bond, an old friend, recommended her for a role in an upcoming Hollywood picture called *Pinky*. Shortly after, she was asked to play the brooding, one-eyed cook in the Broadway production of Carson McCullers's *The Member of the Wedding*. Ethel threw herself into both roles. "*Pinky* was a timorous social-conscience movie," writes Giddins, "but there was nothing half-stated about Waters." Ethel's performances in *Pinky* and in the 1952 film version of McCuller's *The Member of the Wedding* blasted apart one of Hollywood's most enduring clichés: the soothing, asexual, cartoon-simple black mammy. Looking for inspiration to her own fiercely proud grandmother Sally Anderson, Ethel imbued the two black women she played with a gritty wisdom and a near mythic stoicism. Not only did she reveal the buried complexities behind the stereotype, she once again defied the color bar, proving that a black actress could bring gravitas to a screen role.

But America rarely treats its heroes well, and cultural memories are especially fleeting. Ethel Waters, the sexy "crossover" artist of the Jazz Age, who had moved black music into the white mainstream; Ethel, the droll comedienne and pop idol of the 1930s, who had starred in Broadway musical comedies; the strong-willed actress who had stunned Hollywood in the 1940s with her dramatic performances, was all but forgotten. Having repeatedly insisted that audiences take her on her own terms, Ethel would spend the next twenty-five years waiting for another substantial role. Though there was occasional theater work, even bit parts on television, her career slipped into decline. The fact was, Hollywood wrote no substantial roles for black women. To be black, middle-aged, and female meant being limited to playing cooks and maids.

When Ethel died in 1977 at age eighty, the picture that accompanied her obituary in *The New York Times* was that of an overweight, white-haired matriarch. No longer the bold and trailblazing musical star, the "radiant jewel of the Jazz Age," as Giddins dubbed her, she was remembered chiefly for her acting. Once she had been a glamorous cultural icon, now she was an artifact. Her dazzling accomplishments in music, theater, nightclubs, and film had made a crucial difference, however. Ethel Waters opened the door to white mainstream culture, a door through which countless other blacks — men as well as women—would pass. For them she remained the youthful gem of the Jazz Age, a paradigm of the promise and unparalleled inventiveness that was New York in the 1920s.

EPILOGUE

THE END OF THE PARTY

Few could have predicted how quickly the freedoms and opportunities claimed by women in the 1920s would be reversed by the Depression. When the stock market crashed in 1929, the economic devastation that followed put an end to the party, impacting the black community most severely, though women weren't far behind. While all industries were financially ravaged, the performing arts were among the first to feel the *cultural* fallout. Broadway theater was in ruins, as was the recording industry, both dependent on a public hungry for diversion yet unable to spend. The literary world was little better. New York publishing houses, faced with a withering market, scaled back acquisitions, with black authors the first to be excised from the lists and untraditional work (much of it by women) the next to be cut. But for Harlemites, already prey to five times the unemployment as the rest of the city, the most brutal blow came in 1933 with the repeal of Prohibition. Harlem's thriving nightclub scene, a lifeline for performers like Ethel Waters and Bessie Smith, went dark.

There was little light anywhere, in fact. Fascism was on the rise, both at home and abroad. Among writers, there was a deepening sense of gravity and political despair. Many drifted leftward in response to mass unemployment and what was perceived as a crisis in capitalism. Los Angeles was becoming the new capital of the entertainment industry, upstaging New York as the expressive channel for the impulses and preoccupations of the culture. In 1934, Hollywood's Production Code outlawed not only "immoral plots" but "indecent words" such as "floozy," "slut," "fairy," "sex," "hot mamma," and most profanities.

Even women's fashions, once the bellwether of the new woman, took a

Left: **Tempo of the City, Fifth Avenue and 44th Street. Photo by Berenice Abbott.**

step backward: hemlines dropped precipitously, hips and waists returned, short hair, once the symbol of radicalism and free love, disappeared. In the preceding two decades, women had dropped an average of ten yards of fabric per dress and ten pounds of flesh, only to put them on again as taste reversed.

The Great War had ruptured the culture's connections to the moral certainties of the Victorian era. But just as quickly, the liberalism that arose in its stead was undercut by the fear and disaffection produced by the Depression. Old hierarchies of class and race, and high and low art reappeared, undoing the pluralism that had driven the creative experiments of the period. Langston Hughes now openly decried the premise on which the Harlem Renaissance was predicated, that "art could break down color lines . . . and prevent lynching." The Harlem writer Dorothy West, in a moment of gross understatement, observed that the "promise [of the] New Negro . . . is enormously depleted."

It was perhaps inevitable, given the hardship and privation of the Depression years, that the cultural pendulum would swing backward, precipitating a regression to the forms and beliefs of more stable times. Religion crept back into the culture, regaining a measure of its former authority. Women, facing little hope of employment, withdrew into the certainties of motherhood and domesticity. The momentum of liberation slid away, eclipsed by narrower and more repressive values.

RADICAL TIMES GIVE rise to radical personalities, yet the opposite is also true. The bold and irreverent band of bohemian women who had flourished in Greenwich Village and Harlem in the years between 1913 and 1930 quietly dispersed. Mina Loy, Margaret Anderson, and Jane Heap moved to Paris. Edna St. Vincent Millay retreated to her house in upstate New York. Mabel Dodge reinvented her salon in Taos, New Mexico. Bessie Smith toured the Deep South. In their absence, the crusade they'd begun for sexual freedom and artistic independence went underground, lying dormant for several decades.

Yet their legacy survived, re-igniting in the 1960s, when the struggle for women's rights exploded with new militancy, culminating in a revolution that opened up opportunities for women not only in the arts and private life but in business, politics, finance, and the law—an equality unforeseen even by those pioneers of the 1920s, whose hard-won victories seem no less daunting today.

IT MIGHT REASONABLY be asked, Why revisit these women of 1913–1930 now? What is it about our own moment, almost a century later, that draws us back in time to theirs? Looking at photographs of these women's faces, there is a canniness to their expressions, an unapologetic worldliness and informality. These women look more like us than they do the generation just before them. They stand on *our* side of the cultural divide between the Victorian and the Modern. There is amusement, curiosity, skepticism—even self-doubt—in their gazes, an expressiveness and accessibility utterly unlike the prim decorum in their Victorian mothers' faces. This is our connection to them: these women were the first Moderns. They plundered what was previously imprisoned in the private realm and made it part of the public discourse through their work. In so doing, they shattered what had been the inviolable boundary between the outside world and the private sphere of the innermost self. These women were the first to dismantle the old codes of feminine behavior and cultural expectation, to insist that there was more than a single, pinched definition of womanhood.

Lionel Trilling defined modern literature as "shockingly personal," asking "every question forbidden in polite society." So it was with these cultural pioneers. The focus of their art was the shockingly personal. These women gave voice to subjects that were previously unspeakable: sex, lust, female orgasm, birth control, childbirth, the terror of back-alley abortions. They offered up explicit descriptions of carnal love and unsentimental meditations on the relations of the sexes. They poked holes in notions of conventional marriage and introduced a language of sexual desire from a strictly female point of view. They chafed against assigned definitions and oppressive sexual double standards, clear-eyed in their recognition that romanticized sexuality was one means of subjugating women. These women named the terms of the struggle. *Our* search for female identity began with *their* dissatisfaction and rebellion.

Filled with questions, these women had few answers, as their tangled stories so often testify. Emotionally, they grappled with the relativity of truth, the fungibility of any single perspective. Their solution was to describe the world from the inside out, to give voice and form to subjective experience, putting the untidy, unresolved complexities of their lives to the service of their work. Modernism, with its belief in art as an expression of the inner self, rather than a representation of the outer world, was the perfect vehicle for their aspirations.

Their choices began in negation: they knew what they didn't want—the example set by their mothers of invisibility, denial, and capitulation. Yet they also dared to imagine what might replace that paradigm, and they set out to create the alternatives. But, there is something more that connects us to these women. For this first generation of feminists, the idea of "female" summoned up certain oppositions that hadn't existed for prior generations: career versus motherhood, romantic love versus self-affirmation through work, beauty as a useful tool or an interference to get past, rebellious creativity versus feminine self-sacrifice—issues that even now, a century later, still divide and preoccupy us. Perhaps because the questions and inner divisions that these women faced confound any notions that there are simple, reductive answers to the paths they chose, their stories seem as resonant now as ever. These women—bold, provocative, irreverent, and compulsively creative—gave everything they had in the effort to make their lives new. For all their uncertainties, they blasted the door open to the rest of the century, leaving it to us to imagine future lives as stunningly original as theirs.

—Andrea Barnet

Right: **Court of the First Model Tenements in New York City. Photo by Berenice Abbott.**

NOTES

INTRODUCTION: WILD IN PURSUIT

1 ***"fell in love with New York":*** Ann Douglas, *Terrible Honesty: Mongrel Manhattan in the 1920s* (New York: Farrar, Straus & Giroux, 1995), p. 16.

"No one who has not lived": Carolyn Burke, *Becoming Modern: The Life of Mina Loy* (Berkeley: University of California Press, 1996), p. 212.

"How do I like New York?": Douglas, *Terrible Honesty,* p. 16.

"mythic status": Burke, *Becoming Modern,* p. 212.

"Going public with one's": Douglas, *Terrible Honesty,* p. 48.

Scratchin' the Gravel and Ballin' the Jack: Jervis Anderson, *This Was Harlem: 1900–1950* (New York: Farrar, Straus, 1982), p. 154.

3 ***Details about late-night hot spots:*** Anderson, Ibid., pp. 169–80.

"buffet flats" and ***"varied and often perverse sexual":*** David Levering Lewis, *When Harlem Was in Vogue* (New York: Penguin, 1997), p. 107.

Details about the new informality of manners: Frederick Lewis Allen, *Only Yesterday: An Informal History of the 1920s* (New York: John Wiley & Sons, 1931/reprint 1997), p. 70.

Details about Prohibition in Harlem: Anderson, *This Was Harlem,* pp. 145–48.

"a monstrous 32,000 and an unbelievable": Douglas, *Terrible Honesty,* p. 24.

4 ***"The Castles were not":*** Anderson, *This Was Harlem,* p. 75.

5 ***"The Negro race was dancing"*** and ***"extremely careless about":*** Ibid., p. 74.

Details about New York bohemia's cultural commingling: Steven Watson, *Strange Bedfellows: The First American Avant-Garde* (New York: Abbeville Press, 1991), p. 9.

6 ***"loved seven men she didn't marry":*** Roberta Smith, Beatrice Wood obituary, *The New York Times,* Saturday, March 14, 1998.

9 ***"It was a period when"*** and ***"Books by Negro authors":*** Carole Marks and Diane Edkins, *The Power of Pride* (New York: Crown, 1999), p. 11.

10 ***"What American literature":*** Lewis, *When Harlem Was in Vogue,* pp. 93–94.

"in the ascendancy": Anderson, *This Was Harlem,* p. 168.

"the colored [woman] is confronted": Marks and Edkins, *The Power of Pride,* p. 13.

11 ***Details about the new paradigm for black women:*** Daphne Duvall Harrison, *Black Pearls: Blues Queens of the 1920s* (New Brunswick, N.J.: Rutgers University Press, 1988), p. 219.

12 *"I have come to know by experience":* Claudia Roth Pierpont, *Passionate Minds: Women Rewriting the World* (New York: Alfred A. Knopf, 2000), p. 142.

1.
MINA LOY: A MODERN SELF-EXPERIMENT

I am indebted to Carolyn Burke's superb biography of Mina Loy for the scene at the passport office and others in the chapter. See Carolyn Burke, *Becoming Modern: The Life of Mina Loy* (Berkeley: University of California Press, 1996), pp.193–94.

16 *"I must run away from this [feeling]":* Ibid., p. 193.
   "that gripping panic that so long had worn on me": Ibid., p. 194.

17 *"I have only one idea in my mind":* Ibid., p. 190.
   "I don't believe men in England": Ibid., p. 192.
   "shuddered" and *"derided her elimination of":* Ibid., p. 196.
   "Isadora-like abandon": Ibid., p. 197.
   "eroticism gone to seed": Ibid., p. 195.
   "pure pornography": Ibid., p. 191.
   "something without a sex undercurrent" and *"nothing about anything"* and
      "that life can only evolve": Ibid., p. 191.

18 *"the coiled wisps"* and *"corn-colored hair":* Ibid., p. 194.

19 *"the self-constructing strategies":* Ibid., p. vi.

21 *"My conceptions of life evolved":* Gillian Hanscombe and Virginia L. Smyers, *Writing for Their Lives: The Modernist Women 1910–1940* (Boston: Northeastern University Press, 1986), p. 113.

22 *"the latest philosophy":* Burke, *Becoming Modern,* p. 122.
   "a great salvation": Ibid., p. 119.
   "caffeine of Europe": Ibid., p. 154.

23 *"Burn the museums"* and *"Let's murder the moonlight!"* Ibid., p. 151.
   "revolutionizing all forms": Ibid., p. 152.
   "her susceptibility to this" and *"she felt as if":* Ibid., p. 156.
   "bizarre rhythms of free imagination": Mina Loy, *The Lost Lunar Baedeker,* edited and with notes by Roger L. Conover (New York: Farrar, Straus & Giroux, 1996), p. 179.

24 *"Live in the Future"* and other aphorisms: Ibid., pp. 149–50.
   "I am in the throes of" and *"But I shall never":* Burke, *Becoming Modern,* p. 157.
   "twenty years . . . to my life": Ibid., p. 180.
   "destination did not matter": Ibid., p. 168.

"Everyone I know at present": Ibid., p. 158.

25 *"I cannot tell you anything about myself"*: Hanscombe and Smyers, *Writing for Their Lives*, p. 114.

26 *"dreadfully ill—in bed"* and *"& am so afraid of America"* and *"I don't describe to you"*: Hanscombe and Smyers, *Writing for Their Lives*, pp. 115, 116.

femme fatales or madonnas: Burke, *Becoming Modern*, p. 156.

"advanced nature" and **misogyny of his views:** Conover, notes to *Lost Lunar Baedeker*, p. 180.

"an absolute resystemization": Burke, *Becoming Modern*, p. 179.

"Leave off looking to men" and *"Woman must destroy"* and *"Do tell me what you"*: Hanscombe and Smyers, *Writing for Their Lives*, pp. 116–17.

27 *"What I feel now are feminine"*: Burke, *Becoming Modern*, p. 187.

"Marinettian vitality" and *"it* meant *years of"*: Ibid., p. 183.

28 *"I am rather blue"*: Ibid., p. 181.

"I can just hang on to my sanity" and *"Giovanni [Papini] came within"*: Hanscombe and Smyers, *Writing for Their Lives*, p. 118.

"if hatred is the truth and love" and *"Don't ever live to see"*: Burke, *Becoming Modern*, p. 182.

"I want to design" and *"I do hope that family"* Hanscombe and Smyers. *Writing for Their Lives*, p. 119.

"an architecture conceived" and *"with the glittering clamor"*: Burke, *Becoming Modern*, p. 211.

"cigarette of literature": Ibid., p. 185.

"nonchalance in revealing": Conover, notes from *Lost Lunar Baedeker*, p. 189.

29 *"Her poems would have puzzled"* and *"rare and exotic species"*: Conover, Introduction to *Lost Lunar Baedeker*, p. xiv.

30 *"This woman is halfway"*: Hanscombe and Smyers, *Writing for Their Lives*, p. 119.

"modern way meant not caring" and *"the most civilized"*: Burke, *Becoming Modern*, pp. 7, 8.

"a distracted academic": Steven Watson, *Strange Bedfellows: The First American Avant-Garde* (New York: Abbeville Press, 1991), p. 260.

31 *"No sooner had we arrived"*: Gabrielle Buffet-Picabia, "Some Memories of Pre-Dada" etc., in Robert Motherwell, ed., *The Dada Painters and Poets* (New York: George Wittenborn, Inc., 1951), p. 259.

32 *"fully at ease"* and *"as far as I could tell"*: William Carlos Williams, *The Autobiography of William Carlos Williams* (New York: Random House, 1951), p. 141.

33 *"organized fratricide"*: Allen Churchill, *The Improper Bohemians: The*

Recreation of Greenwich Village in Its Heyday (New York: E. P. Dutton, 1959), p. 168.

Description of the Baroness: Watson, *Strange Bedfellows*, p. 270, and Robert Reiss, "'My Baroness': Elsa von Freytag-Loringhoven," in Rudolf E. Kuenzli, ed., *New York Dada* (New York: Willis, Locker & Owens, 1986), p. 87.

34   **"to shock old maids":** Francis M. Naumann, *New York Dada 1915–23* (New York: Harry Abrams, 1994), p. 173.

35   **"chicken guts"** and **"She reminded me of my":** Williams, *The Autobiography*, pp. 164–66.

    "You must come with me" and **"She revolted me, frightened me":** Ibid., p. 169.

36   **"Marcel, Marcel I love you":** Watson, *Strange Bedfellows*, p. 271.

    measure by which one judged worldliness: Burke, *Becoming Modern*, p. 215.

    "slick as a" and **"he could insinuate":** Roger Conover, "Mina Loy's 'Colossus': Arthur Cravan Undressed," in Rudolf E. Kuenzli, ed., *New York Dada* (New York: Willis Locker & Owens, 1986), p. 107.

37   **"fugitive, forger and master":** Hanscombe and Smyers, *Writing for Their Lives*, p. 119.

    obscenities penned in red: Burke, *Becoming Modern*, p. 235.

    "hotel thief, muleteer": Watson, *Strange Bedfellows*, p. 246.

    "Do a lot of fucking": Hanscombe and Smyers, *Writing for Their Lives*, p. 120.

38   **"the sort common among":** Burke, *Becoming Modern*, p. 236.

    "half-imbecile savage": Conover, "Mina Loy's 'Colossus,'" p. 108.

    "The Blind Man must see the sun": Watson, *Strange Bedfellows*, p. 320.

39   **"Slouched in his chair"** and **"completely drunk"** and **"lurching among the mob":** Conover, "Mina Loy's 'Colossus,'" p. 106.

40   **"a bewildering uproar":** Burke, *Becoming Modern*, p. 246.

    "a giant who carried the circus": Watson, *Strange Bedfellows*, p. 269.

    "You had better come and live": Burke, *Becoming Modern*, p. 239.

    "semi-destitute ease": Conover, "Mina Loy's 'Colossus,'" p. 112.

41   **"push his entire consciousness":** Ibid., p. 111.

    "All your irony is assumed" and **"My one desire":** Ibid., pp. 107–8.

    "It occurred to me": Burke, *Becoming Modern*, p. 242.

    "put something across": Watson, *Strange Bedfellows*, p. 336.

    "primitive inversely to" and **"No longer did he invade"** and **"In public he was":** Burke, *Becoming Modern*, p. 242.

42   **"I had found the one man":** Ibid., p. 244.

    "It is a great thing to be living": Watson, *Strange Bedfellows*, p. 10.

    He was lost without her and **"Tell me that":** Hanscombe and Smyers, *Writing for Their Lives*, p. 120.

"Better yet, come with": Burke, *Becoming Modern,* p. 251.

"Tenderness in a strong man": Watson, *Strange Bedfellows,* p. 336.

"making love or respectfully eyeing . . . groceries"; "eating our tomatoes" and *"the source of enchantment":* Conover, in "Mina Loy's 'Colossus,'" *New York Dada,* p. 117.

43   *"Now that I have caught you":* Ibid., p. 120.

"How can we die": Burke, *Becoming Modern,* p. 259.

45   *"As 'sanity' increases in the world":* Hanscombe and Smyers, *Writing for Their Lives,* p. 183.

46   *"the color of the inside":* Churchill, *The Improper Bohemians,* p. 188.

"an oasis for creative minds": Ibid., p. 183.

49   *"They were stunning"* and *"made a fine":* Burke, *Becoming Modern,* p. 296.

"I often think": Hanscombe and Smyers, *Writing for Their Lives,* p. 126.

"supreme elegance of clothing": Burke, *Becoming Modern,* p. 295.

50   *"a mind cry"* and *"a poetry of ideas"* and *"dance of the intelligence":* Ibid., p. 292.

only poets in America who were writing anything of: Conover, Introduction to *Lost Lunar Baedeker,* p. xv.

"novelty, freedom, and a break": Burke, *Becoming Modern,* p. 291.

51   *"rakish"* and *"clever"* and *"a sound philosopher":* Ibid., p. 222.

hard and too analytical: Conover, Introduction to *Lost Lunar Baedeker,* p. xiv.

"soliloquies of a library": Burke, *Becoming Modern,* p. 295.

52   *"whether she cares about"* and *"My health is very smashed up":* Ibid., p. 296.

"I suppose this is a ridiculous" and *"When once I have got":* Hanscombe and Smyers, *Writing for Their Lives,* p. 122.

54   *"I've messed my life up"* and *"I don't think I":* Ibid., p. 126.

"Looking for love": Burke, *Becoming Modern,* p. 251.

55   *"Mina is in the last stages":* Hanscombe and Smyers, *Writing for Their Lives,* p. 103.

56   *"the most beautiful of":* Conover, Introduction to *Lost Lunar Baedeker,* p. xvi.

57   *"an insider"* Ibid., p. 208.

2.
MARGARET ANDERSON AND JANE HEAP:
LIFE FOR ART'S SAKE

59   *"I have never felt much"* and *"I am no man's":* Margaret Anderson, *My Thirty Years' War* (New York: Covici Friede, 1930), pp. 4–5.

"a dilettante": Hugh Ford, *Four Lives in Paris* (Berkeley, Calif.: North Point Press, 1987), p. 228.

60   *"It was Art":* Allen Churchill, *The Improper Bohemians: The Recreation of Greenwich Village in Its Heyday* (New York: E. P. Dutton, 1959), p. 181.

   "an insouciant little pagan paper": Steven Watson, *Strange Bedfellows: The First American Avant-Garde* (New York: Abbeville Press, 1991), p. 292.

   "ever felt need of": Ford, *Four Lives in Paris,* p. 285.

   "My greatest enemy is reality": Anderson, *My Thirty Years' War,* p. 4.

   "Hysteric" and *"Wild":* Ford, *Four Lives in Paris,* pp. 284–85.

61   *"perfectly nice but revolting":* Anderson, *My Thirty Years' War,* p. 12.

   "going to the dogs": Ibid., p. 24.

62   *"First precise thought":* Ibid., p. 35.

63   *"intelligent from the artist's point of view"* and *"triumph of wide-eyed and high-hearted ineptitude":* Ford, *Four Lives in Paris,* p. 235.

   "just in time to turn": Anderson, *My Thirty Years' War,* p. 54.

   Art and anarchy were in the world for the same reason: Watson, *Strange Bedfellows,* p. 294.

   "going anarchist": Anderson, *My Thirty Years' War,* p. 56.

64   *"beneficent if [one] insisted"* and *"pristine life of nomads"* and *"Roast corn over":* Ibid., pp. 86–88.

   "So this is nature!": Ibid., p. 90.

   "She was always exquisite": Watson, *Strange Bedfellows,* p. 293.

   "So unbelievably beautiful" and *"so vital, and so absurd":* Ford, *Four Lives in Paris,* p. 236.

65   *"like a disgruntled tragedy queen"* and *"You see, [Emma's] a city anarchist":* Langner, Lawrence, *The Magic Curtain* (New York: E. P. Dutton, 1951), pp. 84–85.

   "Nietzchean revolutionaries": Anderson, *My Thirty Years' War,* p. 91.

66   *"the most interesting thing":* Ibid., p. 102.

   Margaret's habit of wearing one glove: Ford, *Four Lives in Paris,* p. 229.

   "an epileptic without gumption": Ibid., p. 229.

   "wouldn't have recognized the Sphinx": Churchill, *The Improper Bohemians,* p. 190.

   "a hand on the exact octave": Anderson, *My Thirty Years' War,* p. 106.

   "life should be ecstasy" and *"Why limit me"* Ibid., p. 232.

   "a new, unexpected extra life": Watson, *Strange Bedfellows,* p. 296.

67   she *"disliked frivolity":* Anderson, *My Thirty Years' War,* p. 107.

68   *"staggering with it"* and *"unconscious but still"* and *"This was what I had been":* Ibid., p. 122.

"Jane was the earth to": Watson, *Strange Bedfellows,* p. 297.

69 *"Please cease sending me":* Albert Parry, *Garrets and Pretenders: A History of Bohemianism in America* (New York: Covici Frieder, 1933), pp.197–98.

"the created life": Ford, *Four Lives in Paris,* p. 285.

"Never forget what you wrote": Anderson, *My Thirty Years' War,* p. 187.

"It's an awkward role": Ibid., p. 108.

"Why labor to perpetuate the dull": Ford, *Four Lives in Paris,* p. 239.

"since no art was being": Anderson, *My Thirty Years' War,* p. 124.

"The Little Review *hopes":* Watson, *Strange Bedfellows,* p. 297.

70 *"a thousand dramatized reserves":* Anderson, *My Thirty Years' War,* p. 130.

71 *"a special, haunting" place:* Ibid., p. 152.

"arty indolence": Parry, *Garrets and Pretenders,* p. 199.

"psychological gossip": Anderson, *My Thirty Years' War,* p. 110.

72 *"when writing was beautiful"* and *"Mon dieu, I had":* Ford, *Four Lives in Paris,* p. 284.

"We often printed rot": Watson, *Strange Bedfellows,* p. 292.

"tears, prayers, hysterics" and *"But I didn't say it was good":* Churchill, *The Improper Bohemians,* p. 181.

73 *"We may have to come out":* Watson, *Strange Bedfellows,* p. 293.

a "superb" cook: Churchill, *The Improper Bohemians,* p. 182.

"I have money" and *"No clairvoyant was needed":* Anderson, *My Thirty Years' War,* p. 61.

74 *"Art" was the "person":* Anderson, *My Thirty Years' War,* p. 134.

"earnestness that would prevent" and *"Use a little lip rouge":* Ibid., p. 154.

"Money absolutely abstained": Churchill, *The Improper Bohemians,* p. 189.

"It is much easier to find": Anderson, *My Thirty Years' War,* p. 146.

"a good principle for the artist" and *"it's a little better":* Ibid., p. 44.

75 *"a debauch of art"* and *"Should it be art for money's sake?":* Ibid., p. 134.

"advanced intellectual smut": Churchill, *The Improper Bohemians,* p. 183.

"tightly written manuscript" and *"as it would involve":* Ibid., p. 184.

"This is the most beautiful thing": Anderson, *My Thirty Years' War,* p. 175.

76 *"where the man went off in his pants":* Carolyn Burke, *Becoming Modern: The Life of Mina Loy* (Berkeley: University of California Press, 1996), p. 289.

"He was the perfect enemy": Anderson, *My Thirty Years' War,* p. 218.

"the most beautiful woman ever to bite": Churchill, *The Improper Bohemians,* p. 28.

77 *"Men think thoughts":* Burke, *Becoming Modern,* p. 289.

"But she is the publisher": Anderson, *My Thirty Years' War,* p. 221.

78 **"a cake of very good soap":** Ford, *Four Lives in Paris,* p. 249.

"It is always a mistake": Anderson, *My Thirty Years' War,* p. 226.

"Shaving one's head is like" and **"It's better when":** Ibid., p. 211.

80 **"The only figure of our generation":** Ibid., p. 177.

"We're taking the poem" and **"the only magazine of art":** Ibid., pp. 178–79.

"might have been great had it not been": Ibid., p. 180.

"You two poor things" and **"You're both crazy"** and **"but to the more important luxuries":** Ibid., p. 181.

82 **"In her young years":** Andrew Field, *Djuna: The Life and Times of Djuna Barnes* (New York: G. P. Putnam's Sons, 1983), p. 98.

"outside that was often stunning" and **"to attempt a relationship":** Anderson, *My Thirty Years' War,* p. 181.

"I had dinner with Djuna" and **"shit":** Field, *Djuna,* p. 102.

"I cannot read your stories": Anderson, *My Thirty Years' War,* p. 182.

83 **"withering in the sordid materialism":** Watson, *Strange Bedfellows,* p. 338.

84 **"the saddest and the most beautiful":** Anderson, *My Thirty Years' War,* p. 182.

"I will probably—yes, yes, yes": Ibid., pp. 182–83.

"couldn't believe that anyone as vibrant": Robert Reiss, "'My Baroness': Elsa von Freytag-Loringhoven," in Rudolf E. Kuenzli, ed., *New York Dada* (New York: Willis Locker & Owens, 1986), p. 96.

85 **"It had begun"** and **"It should end logically":** Anderson, *My Thirty Years' War,* p. 230.

"I certainly can give it up": Ibid., p. 239.

"did a nervous breakdown": Ibid., p. 231.

86 **"had heralded a renaissance"** and **"an organ" of that renaissance:** Ibid., pp. 272–73.

87 **"I shall die as I have lived":** Ford, *Four Lives in Paris,* p. 286.

3.
EDNA ST. VINCENT MILLAY:
IMPRISONED IN THE PERSONAL

The story of Armistice night is from Jean Gould, *The Poet and Her Book: A Biography of Edna St. Vincent Millay* (New York: Dodd, Mead, 1969), p. 101.

89 **"wild, grey-green":** Max Eastman, *Great Companions: Critical Memoirs of Some Famous Friends* (New York: Farrar, Straus and Cudahy, 1942), p. 78.

90 **"And if I loved you":** Joan Dash, *A Life of One's Own: Three Gifted Women and the Men They Married* (New York: Harper & Row, 1973), p. 142.

"the fleeing and challenging Daphne": Edmund Wilson, *The Edmund Wilson Reader,* edited with an Introduction and Notes by Lewis M. Dabney. (New York: Da Capo Press, 1997), p. 108.

"like a nymph": Ibid.

"She was one of those women": Ibid., p. 69.

"almost inevitable consequence" and *"created the atmosphere"* and *"It was partly that she gave"* and *"something of awful drama":* Ibid., pp. 70–72.

92   *"She was sometimes rather a strain":* Ibid., p. 75.

"lonely and unreachable": Gould, *The Poet and Her Book,* p. 90.

"tossing off a quatrain": Dash, *A Life of One's Own,* p. 124.

"Edna had as clear": Eastman, *Great Companions,* p. 83.

"Her determination to be a poet": Ibid., p. 78.

"will and need": Dash, *A Life of One's Own,* p. 125.

93   *"down across the swamp":* Ibid., p. 118.

"freewheeling spirit" and *details of the household:* Ibid., pp. 123–24.

94   *"Earth-Passion"* Gould, *The Poet and Her Book,* p. 20.

Self-reliance and *details about Edna's independent childhood:* Dash, *A Life of One's Own,* pp.119–20.

95   *"She was a little old woman"* and *"she looked not unlike":* Wilson, *The Edmund Wilson Reader,* p. 80.

96   *"I know all about poets at college":* Gould, *The Poet and Her Book,* p. 53.

"the thin sweet sound of leaves": Ibid., p. 98.

"You wrote me a beautiful letter": Edna St. Vincent Millay, *Letters of Edna St. Vincent Millay,* edited by Allan Ross Macdougall (Westport, Conn.: Greenwood Press, 1972), p. 69.

97   *"Love me, please; I love you;"* and *"When you tell me":* Ibid., p. 71.

"a study of claustrophobia" and *"buried alive":* Dash, *A Life of One's Own,* p. 129.

98   *"the luxury of a fireplace":* Ibid., p. 138.

"the social centers of the village": Malcolm Cowley, *Exiles Return* (New York: Penguin Books, 1994), p. 69.

101   *"it was as if a new form of escape"* and *"from freedom to enclosure to freedom":* Dash, *A Life of One's Own,* pp. 141–42.

102   *"Don't you think that our virtues":* Miriam Gurko, *Restless Spirit: The Life of Edna St. Vincent Millay* (New York: Thomas Y. Crowell, 1962), p. 92.

"darkness which was mine alone": Gould, *The Poet and Her Book,* p. 145.

"fearful thing" and *"lost and ominous key":* Ibid., p. 90.

"There began for us a romance": Dash, *A Life of One's Own,* p. 142.

"I'm not the right girl to cook": Gurko, *Restless Spirit,* p. 92.

"nobody's own": Gould, *The Poet and Her Book,* p. 145.

103   *Details about Edna's romantic patterns:* Dash, *A Life of One's Own,* p. 143.

104   *"a full blooded female":* Gould, *The Poet and Her Book,* p. 45.

"hand to hand" and *"like a loving cup":* Ibid., p. 94.

"a promise in your eyes" and *"a little challenge of lies":* Dash, *A Life of One's Own,* p. 144.

"that I would be": Ibid., p. 145.

106   *"the first man [she] ever kissed":* Gould, *The Poet and Her Book,* p. 95.

"My time, in those awful": Dash, *A Life of One's Own,* p. 145.

"the pure white heat": Gould, *The Poet and Her Book,* p. 94.

107   *"I always know exactly":* Ibid., p. 96.

"My candle burns at both ends": Ibid., p. 123.

"One could see upon her face": Dash, *A Life of One's Own,* p. 147.

"swarms of young painters" and *"Those evenings":* Lawrence Langner, *The Magic Curtain* (New York: E. P. Dutton, 1951), p. 110.

108   *"Hal dear,—My heart":* Letters of Edna St. Vincent Millay, p. 95.

"harsh and somber restraint": Ibid., p. 96.

"We had lost our ideals": Cowley, *Exiles Return,* p. 72.

"I find myself suddenly": Dash, *A Life of One's Own,* p. 146.

110   *"She was dressed in some bright batik"* and *"She had a lovely":* Wilson, *The Edmund Wilson Reader,* p. 69.

"I was thrilled and troubled": Ibid., p. 68.

111   *"This high table"* and *"heroic fortitude"* and *"pathologically inhibited":* Eastman, *Great Companions,* p. 90.

"I wonder if it has ever occurred": Ibid., p. 91.

112   *Mention of Edna's affair with Thelma Wood* found in Andrew Field, *Djuna: The Life and Times of Djuna Barnes* (New York: G. P. Putnams Sons, 1983), p. 84.

"If I didn't keep calling you": Letters of Edna St. Vincent Millay, pp. 119–20.

"I hate women who do that" and *"sternly sharp with an admirer"* and *"the dignity of her genius":* Wilson, *The Edmund Wilson Reader,* p. 74.

"Those who fell in love": Ibid., p. 72.

113   *"Her relations with us"* and *"aside from her mother"* and *"seldom the people":* Ibid., p. 75.

"harsh conditions" and *"cramped"* and "*this life of art, by which she had triumphed":* Ibid., p. 77.

"It is a pity you are so": Letters of Edna St. Vincent Millay, p. 96.

"I'm having a sort of nervous breakdown": Ibid., p. 93.

"it was not the deaths": Dash, *A Life of One's Own,* p. 149.

114 *"rather vague about meals"* and *"But they never apologized"* and *"That might be the solution"*: Wilson, *The Edmund Wilson Reader*, p. 82.
"I'll be thirty in a minute!": Ibid., p. 83.
"might marry this man": Gould, *The Poet and Her Book*, p. 118.

115 *"No matter how confused"*: Wilson, *The Edmund Wilson Reader*, p. 85.
"When are you two boys": *Letters of Edna St. Vincent Millay*, p. 102.
"It doesn't matter at all": Ibid., p. 105.
"as a free woman" and *"nothing to do with any"* and *"another small nervous"* and *"needs fresh grass"*: Ibid., pp. 105–7.

116 *"Arthur, it is wicked & useless"*: Ibid., p. 133.
"Now I have two bruvvers!": Ibid., p. 137.
"when I start to write": Ibid., p. 132.
"It seems a long time": Ibid., p. 139.

117 *"Do you really want me to marry"*: Ibid., pp. 139–40.
"You will let me hear from you": Ibid., p. 140.
"For surely one must be": Ibid., p. 142.
"all about the girl": Ibid., pp. 143–44.

118 *"Pity me that the heart is slow"*: Gould, *The Poet and Her Book*, p. 144.
"I only know that summer": Ibid., p. 146.
"Isn't it funny about you and Gladys?": *Letters of Edna St. Vincent Millay*, p. 169.

120 *"high, bright gaiety"*: Gould, *The Poet and Her Book*, p. 155.
"light-hearted as a troubadour": Dash, *A Life of One's Own*, p. 174.
"We were having" and *"like a mother"*: Floyd Dell, *Homecoming: An Autobiography* (New York: Farrar & Rinehart, 1933), p. 308.

121 *Description of Eugen Boissevain*: Dash, *A Life of One's Own*, pp. 160–61.
a *"Gallic"* appetite for the pleasure *"both of the mind and of the flesh"*: Ibid., p. 161.
"a strain of something feminine": Wilson, *The Edmund Wilson Reader*, p. 88.
Analysis of Eugen's feminine traits: Dash, *A Life of One's Own*, p. 171.

123 *"the same imperious brows"*: Susan Edmiston and Linda D. Cirino, *Literary New York* (Boston: Houghton Mifflin, 1976), p. 85.
"a shy fire": Carl Van Doren, from "Three Worlds, Elinor Wylie," in *The Portable Care Van Doren*, (New York: Viking, 1945), p. 71.
"a lovely, amused formality" and *"Doubly driven, she was"* and *"profound"* and *"exquisitely superficial"*: Ibid., p. 85.
"Dear Elinor Wylie": *Letters of Edna St. Vincent Millay*, p. 138.

124 *"one of the loveliest places"*: Dash, *A Life of One's Own*, p. 169.

125 *"If I let her struggle with"* and *"She must not have"*: Ibid., p. 169.

"But I haven't made": Ibid., p. 188.

"There was only one of her.": Letters of Edna St. Vincent Millay, p. 230.

"It was you just as you": Ibid., p. 228.

126 *"protective attitude":* Wilson, The Edmund Wilson Reader, p. 89.

"She had now" and *"It brought her back":* Ibid., p. 93.

"But I'm not a pathetic" and *"While we were talking"* and *"Though I did not see much":* Ibid., p. 94.

128 *"She seemed to be mysteriously":* Eastman, Max, Great Companions, pp. 101–2.

"babied herself" and *"chemical stimulation":* Ibid., p. 103.

129 *"recurrent depression":* Nancy Mitford, Savage Beauty (New York: Random House, 2001), p. 486.

"a very handsome" and *"Anyway, I have them [the poems]":* Ibid., p. 487.

"As we drove through" and *"I'll go and get":* Wilson, The Edmund Wilson Reader, p. 99.

"The whole place seemed" and *"She had so changed":* Ibid., p. 100.

131 *"Very quietly he"* and *"of an almost unrelieved blackness"* and *"just emerging from":* Ibid., p. 101.

"deteriorating ghosts": Ibid., p. 103.

"as if she were a recently invalided": and *"fussed over her . . . wanting to be babied"* and *"As soon as he was gone . . . hearty way"* and *"gossiped like a pair of old cronies"* and *"Eugen entered carrying":* Gould, The Poet and Her Book, p. 272.

132 safe *"harbor":* Wilson, The Edmund Wilson Reader, p. 94.

"in perfect and beautiful order": Ibid., p. 105.

4.
ENTERTAINING BOHEMIA:
THE HOSTESSES AND THEIR SALONS

135 *"of never experiencing anything . . . first hand":* Christopher Lasch, "Mabel Dodge Luhan: Sex as Politics," in The New Radicalism in America: The Intellectual as a Social Type (New York: W. W. Norton, 1965), p. 116.

"It was always stimulating to go and listen": Mabel Dodge Luhan, Intimate Memories, edited by Lois Palken Rudnick (Albuquerque: University of New Mexico Press, 1999), pp. 120–21.

136 *"I became a Species"* and *"I wanted to know everybody":* Ibid., p. 124.

"I have always known how": Steven Watson, Strange Bedfellows: The First American Avant-Garde (New York: Abbeville Press, 1991), p. 129.

"most ample woman-personality": Carolyn Burke, *Becoming Modern: The Life of Mina Loy* (Berkeley: University of California Press, 1996), p. 119.

"a fleshy odalisque": Ibid., p. 120.

"While many salons": Max Eastman, *Enjoyment of Living* (New York: Harper & Brothers, 1948), p. 523.

137 *Details about Dodge's self-indulgent style:* Allen Churchill, *The Improper Bohemians: The Recreation of Greenwich Village in Its Heyday* (New York: E. P. Dutton, 1959), p. 16.

"a dynamo [with] a face": Watson, *Strange Bedfellows,* p. 131.

"think more fluently": Luhan, *Intimate Memories,* p. 122.

"a magnetic field": Churchill, *The Improper Bohemians,* p. 51.

138 *"Like yourself, Mabel Dodge":* Watson, *Strange Bedfellows,* p. 131.

139 *a cult of the orgasm:* Lasch, *The New Radicalism in America,* p. 118.

"He was a wet blanket": Luhan, *Intimate Memories,* p. 99.

"I so deep, so fatal": Ibid., p. xii.

"to wish him away": Ibid., p. 107.

"prodigious" and *". . . her body seemed to be":* Ibid., p. 89.

"laugh like a beefsteak" and *"a sort of kimono made"* and *"she was not at all repulsive":* Ibid., pp. 89–90.

140 *"Why are there not more real people":* Burke, *Becoming Modern,* p. 133.

the "dignified" air: Churchill, *The Improper Bohemians,* p. 20.

"slightly raffish look": Ibid., p. 21.

"flaneur-at-large": Ann Douglas, *Terrible Honesty: Mongrel Manhattan in the 1920s* (New York: Farrar, Straus and Giroux, 1995), p. 81.

"funny-looking" and *"large teeth with slits showing"* and *"looked quite domesticated":* Luhan, *Intimate Memories,* p. 108.

143 *Details about Van Vechten's entourage:* Watson, *Strange Bedfellows,* p. 134.

"You have a certain faculty" and *"You attract, stimulate":* Luhan, *Intimate Memories,* p. 122.

"Organize all this unplanned": Ibid., p. 124.

"Life in New York": Watson, *Strange Bedfellows,* p. 136.

"Socialist, Trade Unionists": Luhan, *Intimate Memories,* p. 124.

144 *"eat as many sandwiches as my suburban":* Andrew Field, *Djuna: The Life and Times of Djuna Barnes* (New York: G. P. Putnam's Sons, 1983), p. 48.

For more details about the appointments of Dodge's salon, see Churchill, *The Improper Bohemians,* p. 42, and Watson, *Strange Bedfellows,* p. 136.

"a sacred, all-pervasive and spiritualizing": Joan Dash, *A Life of One's Own: Three Gifted Women and the Men They Married* (New York: Harper & Row, 1973), p. 16.

"for unorthodox women": Luhan, *Intimate Memories,* p. 128.

145 *"It was [Sanger] who introduced":* Ibid., p. 119.

146 *"hausfrau"* and *"had endured so much pain":* Churchill, *The Improper Bohemians,* p. 24.

147 *"they also resented her":* Watson, *Strange Bedfellows,* p. 136.

"Everybody in the ferment": Eastman, *Enjoyment of Living,* p. 523.

"You should have known A'Lelia": Carole Marks and Diane Edkins, *The Power of Pride* (New York: Crown, 1999), p. 74.

148 *"a gorgeous dark Amazon"* and *"light-skinned ladies in waiting":* Ibid., p. 67.

The guests at A'Lelia's parties: David Levering Lewis, *When Harlem Was in Vogue* (New York: Alfred A. Knopf, 1997), p. 166.

"Xanadu of Harlem's artistic and intellectual": Ibid., p. 111.

150 *"One couldn't help being impressed":* Marks and Edkins, *The Power of Pride,* p. 74.

"no judge of character": Bruce Kellner, *Keep A Inchin' Along* (Westport, Conn.: Greenwood Press, 1979), p. 154.

"parasites, jesters and well-meaning courtiers": Lewis, *When Harlem Was in Vogue,* p. 166.

"a parvenu": Jervis Anderson, *This Was Harlem: 1900–1950* (New York: Farrar, Straus, 1982), p. 225.

"went precipitously downhill": Lewis, *When Harlem Was in Vogue,* p. 166.

"She made no pretense of being" and *"the art of reading headlines":* A'Lelia Bundles, *On Her Own Ground: The Life and Times of Madam C. J. Walker* (New York: Scribner, 2001), p. 282.

151 *she was especially fond of homosexuals:* Lewis, *When Harlem Was in Vogue,* p. 168.

"She made no effort to limit society": Marks and Edkins, *The Power of Pride,* p. 74.

"There are near-white cliques, mulatto": Anderson, *This Was Harlem,* p. 336.

152 *"was so spectacular that the singers":* Bundles, *On Her Own Ground,* p. 279.

"She looked like a queen" and *"She was tall and black and extremely handsome":* Bundles, *On Her Own Ground,* p. 282.

"sent word back that she saw": Ibid., p. 283.

"bathtub" gin: Lewis, *When Harlem Was in Vogue,* p. 166.

"A big black man appeared": Anderson, *This Was Harlem,* p. 98.

153 *"I want to say to every Negro woman":* Marks and Edkins, *The Power of Pride,* p. 69.

"I feel we have exploited": Bundles, *On Her Own Ground,* p. 281.

154 *"She wanted to miss nothing":* Ibid., p. 282.

"completely informal" and *"eat for prices":* Ibid., p. 286.

"a breed of chiselers": Lewis, *When Harlem Was in Vogue,* p. 169.

155 *"We dedicate this tower to the cultured":* Bundles, *On Her Own Ground,* p. 286.

    "was a seething picture of well-dressed people": Marks and Edkins, *The Power of Pride,* p. 75.

    "were at a premium": Bundles, *On Her Own Ground,* p. 286.

156 *"Dear Members and Friends":* Marks and Edkins, *The Power of Pride,* p. 75.

    "In love and in marriage": Bundles, *On Her Own Ground,* p. 290.

    "I have been holding on to this": Anderson. *This Was Harlem,* p. 229.

157 *"But, dear A'Lelia"* and *"White Buyers Strip":* Marks and Edkins, *The Power of Pride,* p. 76.

    "Sale of Villa Lewaro Nets": Bundles, *On Her Own Ground,* p. 288.

    "A few of us who had once enjoyed": Anderson, *This Was Harlem,* p. 229.

    "So all who love laughter": Bundles, *On Her Own Ground,* p. 291.

158 *"gaudiest spree in history":* Douglas, *Terrible Honesty,* p. 471.

    "was really the end of the gay times": Anderson, *This Was Harlem,* p. 231.

5.
BESSIE SMITH:
'TAIN'T NOBODY'S BUSINESS IF I DO!

I am indebted to Chris Albertson's dogged footwork in his groundbreaking biography of Bessie for the pig's foot party anecdote and others in the chapter. See Chris Albertson, *Bessie: Empress of the Blues* (London: Abacus Edition, 1975).

161 *"The funk is flyin'":* Ibid., p. 70.

162 *"C'mon, baby, let's dance"* and *"We don't want"* and *"Who in the hell"* and *"Did that fucker"* and *"This here sure"* and *"Baby, take this thing out":* Ibid., pp. 71–72.

163 *"Bessie cared remarkably little":* Ibid., p. 12.

    "That wasn't a voice": David Levering Lewis, *When Harlem Was in Vogue* (New York: Penguin, 1997), p. 172.

    "sadness . . . not softened with tears": Carole Marks and Diane Edkins, *The Power of Pride* (New York: Crown, 1999), p. 122.

    "within the tighter Negro": Daphne Duvall Harrison, *Black Pearls: Blues Queens of the 1920s* (New Brunswick, New Jersey: Rutgers University Press, 1988), p. 7.

    "Bessie Smith was the greatest": Marks and Edkins, *The Power of Pride,* p. 122.

"She was a natural singer" and *"She was just a teenager"*: Albertson, *Bessie,*
  p. 26.

164 *Mamie Smith and phenomenon of "race records"*: Ibid., pp. 30–32.
165 *"I just stood there and watched"*: Ibid., p. 37.
  "If I should get the feelin'": Marks and Edkins, *The Power of Pride,* p. 133.
166 *"We'd walk into a joint"*: Albertson, *Bessie,* p. 98.
  "Bessie was in a pretty good": Ethel Waters with Charles Samuels, *His Eye Is
  on the Sparrow: An Autobiography* (New York: Da Capo Press, 1992),
  p. 91.
  "Blues! Blues! Come on" and *"yelling things about"* and *remainder of
  anecdote:* Ibid., pp. 91–92.
167 *"I don't know what happened"*: Albertson, *Bessie,* p. 46.
  "Bessie liked to dress": Ibid., p. 50.
168 *"a voice that will never"*: Ibid., p. 54.
  "Bessie Smith is Queen": Ibid., p. 56.
  "straightened hair" and *"ugliest face"*: Ibid., p. 85.
  "the earliest link": Ibid., p. 25.
169 *"My uncle was a real cool dude"*: Ibid., p. 62.
170 *"mean man, a really"*: Marks and Edkins, *The Power of Pride,* p. 125.
  "but when she went on one": Albertson, *Bessie,* p. 67.
  "more literate" and *"ethnic"*: Ibid., p. 75.
171 *Details of Bessie's private railcar*: Ibid., pp. 78–79.
172 *Story of Bessie and Ku Klux Klan*: Ibid., pp. 115–16.
  "Some shit!" and *"What the fuck you think"*: Ibid., p. 116.
173 *"Tough On Black Asses"*: Ibid., p. 55.
  "It's me goddammit," and *"I don't give"*: Ibid., p. 84.
  "If you don't want my girls": Albertson, *Bessie,* p. 174.
174 *"You ain't so much"*: Ibid., p. 84.
  "never believed stories": Ibid., p. 87.
175 *"Jack was the fightingest"*: Ibid., p. 93.
176 *"You no good two-timing"* and *"alleged indiscretion"*: Albertson, *Bessie,*
  p. 100.
  "Buffet flats were small": Ibid., p. 104.
177 *"It was nothing but faggots"*: Ibid., p. 105.
  "C'mon, Marie, show your stuff" and *"If Jack knocks"* and *"Come out here"*:
  Ibid., p. 106.
179 *"Oh, the blues has got me"*: Harrison, *Black Pearls,* p. 79.
  "I cried and worried" and *"It's all about a man"* and *"I think [Bessie]
  wanted to break away"*: Albertson, *Bessie,* p. 132.

180 *"Ruby, I'm hurtin'"*: Ibid., p. 134.

"attained preeminence": Jervis Anderson, *This Was Harlem: 1900–1950* (New York: Farrar, Straus, 1982), p. 178.

"danced the Charleston": Ibid., p. 171.

"as many limousines from Park": Ibid., p. 178.

181 *"thrived on his affectations"*: Anderson, *This Was Harlem,* p. 214.

"did more to forward the Harlem": Ibid., p. 215.

"a voice full of shouting" and *"hysterical, semi-religious shrieks of sorrow"* and *"when Bessie proclaimed, 'It's true'"*: Albertson, *Bessie,* p. 89.

182 *"How about a lovely dry martini?"*: Ibid., p. 126.

"I am quite certain that anybody": Ibid., p. 123.

183 *"Miss Smith, You're not leaving"* and *"I don't care if she dies"*: Ibid., p. 127.

184 *"She wouldn't cry"*: Ibid., p. 152.

185 *"She was like a new person"*: Ibid., pp. 157–58.

"the essence of cool": Marks and Edkins, *The Power of Pride,* p. 126.

186 *"cold sober and in a quiet"*: Albertson, *Bessie,* p. 177.

187 *"Still Tops"*: Ibid., p. 181.

"I never saw so much life" and *"We were going to make"*: Ibid., p. 186.

188 *"Show folk on Beale Street"*: Ibid., p 189.

"pink two-tone velvet": Ibid., p. 20.

190 *"I never saw three cents"*: Ibid., p. 205.

"I've got the world in a jug": Ibid., p. 69.

"The Greatest Blues Singer in the World": Ibid., p. 208.

6.
ETHEL WATERS: AM I BLUE?

193 *"I never was a child."*: Ethel Waters with Charles Samuels, *His Eye Is on the Sparrow: An Autobiography* (New York: Da Capo, 1992), p. 1.

"dark brown in color": Ibid., p. 3.

"as a Negro and among Negro": Ibid., p. 4.

194 *"I'm Lydia Waters, your grandmother"*: Ibid., p. 67.

Ethel's psychological division: Carole Marks and Diane Edkins, *The Power of Pride* (New York: Crown, 1999), p. 92.

Ethel's role in popularizing the blues among white audiences: Gary Giddins, "The Mother of Us All," in *Riding on a Blue Note: Jazz and American Pop* (New York: Oxford University Press, 1981), p. 4.

"shouters" and *"with unladylike growls"*: Ibid., p. 6.

"By the time I was seven, I knew": Waters, *His Eye Is on the Sparrow,* p. 1.

For details on Waters's many changes, see Donald Bogle, Preface to Waters, *His Eye Is on the Sparrow,* p. vii.

"the mother of all popular singing": Giddins, *Riding on a Blue Note,* p. 4.

"was the mother of us all": Susannah McCorkle, "The Mother of Us All," *American Heritage,* vol. 95 (February–March 1994), p. 62.

195 **"captured the sensuous stance":** Giddins, *Riding on a Blue Note,* p. 8.

"I've always thought that I inherited": Waters, *His Eye Is on the Sparrow,* p. 68.

"She never wanted me": Ibid., p. 5.

196 **"a plague spot of vice and crime"** and **"I came to know well":** Ibid., p. 15.

"What did you bring me?": Ibid., p. 21.

"Blanche, poor soul": Ibid., p. 19.

197 **"I held Mom tight":** Waters, *His Eye Is on the Sparrow,* p. 59.

"I thought . . . she'd agreed only": Ibid., p. 58.

"I had about a half hour": McCorkle, "The Mother of Us All," p. 64.

198 **"What I dreamed of":** Waters, *His Eye Is on the Sparrow,* p. 66.

"I seldom depended on my voice": Ibid., p. 71.

199 **"Rugged individualists all"** and **"But they were also the most appreciative"** and **"my kind of low singing get by"** and **"You could have heard":** Ibid., p. 74.

"the money fell like rain on the stage": Ibid., p. 75.

"an old doughnut": Ibid., p. 81.

200 **"I still had no feeling"** and **"clean surroundings":** Ibid., p. 87.

Never made a career move without being pushed: McCorkle, "The Mother of Us All," p. 65.

"Harlem was anything but an exclusively Negro section": Waters, *His Eye Is on the Sparrow,* p. 123.

201 **"the last stop on the way down"** and **"After you worked there":** Ibid., p. 124.

"There was no set closing time": Ibid., p. 126.

"It's the story told in the songs": Ibid., p. 129.

"White society folks began to come": Ibid., p. 131.

"Deep South talents": Ann Douglas, *Terrible Honesty: Mongrel Manhattan in the 1920s* (New York: Farrar, Straus, & Giroux, 1995), p. 335.

For more on Ethel's ability to incorporate her contradictions in her work, see Giddins, *Riding on a Blue Note,* p. 7.

202 **"refined":** Hazel Carby, "'It Jus Be's Dat Way Sometime.': The Sexual Politics of Women's Blues," in *Unequal Sisters,* edited by Ellen Carol DuBois and Vicki Ruis (New York: Routledge, 1990), p. 246.

"the clarity of Ethel's diction" and **"relative whiteness of her style":** Giddins, *Riding on a Blue Note,* p. 7.

203 *"black velvet and pearls"* and *"I saw her from a distance":* McCorkle, "The Mother of Us All," p. 63.

"grim and forbidding": Waters, *His Eye Is on the Sparrow,* p. 159.

204 *"Did I hear you saying you can't go on?"* and *"And Georgia cracker":* Ibid., p. 166.

205 *"By the time I was seven":* Ibid., p. 19.

206 *"girlish reticence"* and *"wolves":* Ibid., p. 90.

"Tell him I don't drink nothing" and *"I'd never heard anyone talk like":* Ibid., pp. 112–13.

207 *"nastier or more unpleasant":* Ibid., p. 58.

Ethel's "notorious" behavior with her lovers: Frank C. Taylor, with Gerald Cook, *Alberta Hunter: A Celebration in Blues* (New York: McGraw Hill, 1987), p. 72.

"shouters" and *"grief-and-rage-struck":* Douglas, *Terrible Honesty,* p. 8.

208 *"the white time":* Waters, *His Eye Is on the Sparrow,* p. 173.

"off the beat most of the time" and *"they wouldn't understand":* Douglas, *Terrible Honesty,* p. 336.

"getting by on white time" and *"I ain't changing my style":* Waters, *His Eye Is on the Sparrow,* p. 174.

"Nobody screamed or jumped": Ibid., p. 175.

"A new star [has] been discovered": Ibid., p. 181.

"could sing white or black and delighted": Douglas, *Terrible Honesty,* p. 336.

209 *"Tony lived down in Greenwich Village"* and *"Your color or your bank account":* Waters, *His Eye Is on the Sparrow,* p. 193.

"He told me he'd been catching my act": Ibid., p. 194.

"integrated" and *"let down their hair":* David Levering Lewis, *When Harlem Was in Vogue* (New York: Penguin, 1997), p. 183.

"Such salons in the early twenties": Anderson, *This Was Harlem,* p. 216.

211 *"Carl loved that dinner":* Waters, *His Eye Is on the Sparrow,* p. 196.

"Sometimes it seems to me": Ibid., p. 195.

"I didn't like it later when he abdicated": Ibid., p. 211.

212 *"I felt like I was working my heart out":* Ibid., p. 220.

"The Cotton Club was a classy spot": Anderson, *This Was Harlem,* p. 174.

"Ziegfeldian in their gaudiness" and *"with feathers, fans, and legs flying":* Lewis, *When Harlem Was in Vogue,* p. 210.

"tops of the tops": Anderson, *This Was Harlem,* p. 175.

"I was singing the story of my misery" and *"Your imagination can carry you just so far":* Waters, *His Eye Is on the Sparrow,* p. 220.

214 *"the whole tragic history of a race":* Ibid., p. 222.

215 *"Ethel Waters is having such a delightful present":* Marks and Edkins, *The Power of Pride,* p. 102.

"quite true to life" and *"In Hagar was all my mother's shock":* Waters, *His Eye Is on the Sparrow,* p. 239.

"lumbering, half crazy" and *"All my life I'd burned to tell":* Ibid., p. 239.

216 *"In her moments of tenderness":* Ibid., p. 248.

"terrible inward pressure": Ibid., p. 250.

"no actress that night. I had only been remembering": Ibid., p. 248.

"shivering with fatique" and *"It's made me feel cold and numb":* McCorkle, "The Mother of Us All," p. 68.

"destroying everything": Ibid., p. 69.

217 *"outsang," "outdanced,"* and *"outvamped":* Giddins, *Riding on a Blue Note,* p. 11.

"But I quickly learned": Waters, *His Eye Is on the Sparrow,* p. 263.

218 *"breaking wide open":* Ibid., p. 264.

"Pinky was a timorous social-conscience": Giddins, *Riding on a Blue Note,* p. 12.

one of Hollywood's most enduring "clichés": Donald Bogle, Preface to *His Eye Is on the Sparrow,* p. xiv.

219 *no substantial roles for black women:* Giddins, *Riding on a Blue Note,* p. 10.

"the radiant jewel of the Jazz Age": Ibid., p. 3.

EPILOGUE:
THE END OF THE PARTY

221 *Hollywood's production code of 1934* and *"floozy," "slut," "fairy," "sex," "hot mamma":* Douglas, *Terrible Honesty,* p. 468.

222 *For fact about women's drop of dress fabric and pounds,* see Susan E. Dunn, "Mina Loy, Fashion and the Avant-garde," in Maeera Shreiber and Keigh Tuma, eds., *Mina Loy: Woman and Poet* (Orono, Maine: The National Poetry Foundation, University of Maine, 1998), pp. 447–48.

"art could break down color lines . . . and prevent": Douglas, *Terrible Honesty,* p. 466.

"promise [of the] New Negro . . . is enormously depleted": Ibid.

223 *"shockingly personal"* and *"every question forbidden":* Houston A. Baker Jr., *Modernism and the Harlem Renaissance* (Chicago: University of Chicago Press, 1967), p. 6.

BIBLIOGRAPHY

Albertson, Chris. *Bessie: Empress of the Blues.* London: Abacus Edition, 1975.

Allen, Frederick Lewis. *Only Yesterday: An Informal History of the 1920s.* New York: John Wiley & Sons. 1931; reprint 1997.

Anderson, Jervis. *This Was Harlem: 1900–1950.* New York: Farrar, Straus & Giroux, 1982.

Anderson, Margaret. *My Thirty Years' War.* New York: Covici Friede. 1930.

Baker, Houston A. Jr. *Modernism and the Harlem Renaissance.* Chicago: University of Chicago Press, 1967.

Barnes, Djuna. *New York.* Edited with commentary by Alyce Barry. Los Angeles: Sun and Moon Press, 1989.

Bundles, A'Lelia. *On Her Own Ground: The Life and Times of Madam C. J. Walker.* New York: Scribners, 2001.

Burke, Carolyn. *Becoming Modern: The Life of Mina Loy.* Berkeley: University of California Press, 1996.

Carby, Hazel. "'It Jus Be's Dat Way Sometime': The Sexual Politics of Women's Blues." In *Unequal Sisters,* edited by Ellen Carol DuBois and Vicki Ruiz. New York: Routledge, 1990.

Churchill, Allen. *The Improper Bohemians: The Recreation of Greenwich Village in its Heyday.* New York: E. P. Dutton, 1959.

Conover, Roger L. "Mina Loy's 'Colossus': Arthur Cravan Undressed. In Rudolf E. Kuenzli, ed. *New York Dada.* New York: Willis Locker & Owens, 1986.

Cowley, Malcolm. *Exiles Return.* New York: Penguin Books, 1994.

Dash, Joan. *A Life of One's Own: Three Gifted Women and the Men They Married.* New York: Harper & Row, 1973.

Dell, Floyd. *Homecoming: An Autobiography.* New York: Farrar & Rinehart, 1933.

———. *Love in Greenwich Village.* New York: George H. Doran, 1926.

Douglas, Ann. *Terrible Honesty: Mongrel Manhattan in the 1920s.* New York: Farrar, Straus & Giroux, 1995.

Eastman, Max. *Enjoyment of Living.* New York: Harper & Brothers, 1948.

Eastman, Max. *Great Companions: Critical Memoirs of Some Famous Friends.* New York: Farrar, Straus & Cudahy. 1942.

Edmiston, Susan, and Linda D. Cirino. *Literary New York.* Boston: Houghton Mifflin, 1976.

Field, Andrew. *Djuna: The Life and Times of Djuna Barnes.* New York: G. P. Putnam's Sons, 1983.

Fitzgerald, F. Scott. *The Jazz Age.* New York: New Directions Bibelots, 1996.

Ford, Hugh. *Four Lives in Paris.* Berkeley, Calif.: North Point Press, 1987.

Frank, Elizabeth. *Louise Bogan.* New York: Columbia University Press, 1986.

Giddins, Gary. "The Mother of Us All." In *Riding on a Blue Note: Jazz and American Pop.* New York: Oxford University Press, 1981.

Gould, Jean. *The Poet and Her Book: A Biography of Edna St. Vincent Millay.* New York: Dodd, Mead, 1969.

Green, Martin. *New York 1913: The Armory Show and the Paterson Strike Pageant.* New York: Charles Scribners & Sons, 1988.

Gurko, Miriam. *Restless Spirit: The Life of Edna St. Vincent Millay.* New York: Thomas Y. Crowell, 1962.

Gurstein, Rochelle. *The Repeal of Reticence.* New York: Hill and Wang, 1996.

Hanscombe, Gillian, and Virginia L. Smyers. *Writing for Their Lives: The Modernist Women 1910–1940.* Boston: Northeastern University Press, 1986.

Harrison, Daphne Duvall. *Black Pearls: Blues Queens of the 1920s.* New Brunswick, N.J.: Rutgers University Press, 1988.

Kellner, Bruce. *Keep A Inchin' Along.* Westport, Conn.: Greenwood Press, 1979.

Kuenzli, Rudolf E., ed. *New York Dada.* New York: Willis Locker & Owens, 1986.

Langner, Lawrence. *The Magic Curtain.* New York: E. P. Dutton, 1951.

Lasch, Christopher. *The New Radicalism in America: The Intellectual as a Social Type.* New York: W. W. Norton & Company, 1965.

Lewis, David Levering. *When Harlem Was in Vogue.* New York: Penguin, 1997.

Loy, Mina. *The Lost Lunar Baedeker.* Edited by Roger L. Conover. New York: Farrar, Straus & Giroux, 1996.

Luhan, Mabel Dodge. *Intimate Memories.* Edited by Lois Palken Rudnick. Albuquerque: University of New Mexico Press, 1999.

Marks, Carole, and Diane Edkins. *The Power of Pride.* New York: Crown, 1999.

May, Henry F. *The End of American Innocence: A Study of the First Years of Our Own Time, 1912–1917.* New York: Columbia University Press Morningside Edition, 1992.

McCorkle, Susannah. "The Mother of Us All." *American Heritage,* vol. 95 (Feb.–March 1994), pp. 60–73.

Mitford, Nancy. *Savage Beauty: The Life of Edna St. Vincent Millay.* New York: Random House, 2001.

Millay, Edna St. Vincent. *The Letters of Edna St. Vincent Millay.* Edited by Allan Ross Macdougall. Westport, Conn.: Greenwood Press, 1972.

Motherwell, Robert, ed. *The Dada Painters and Poets: An Anthology.* New York: George Wittenborn, 1951.

Naumann, Francis M. *New York Dada 1915–23.* New York: Harry Abrams, 1994.

Naumann, Francis M. *Making Mischief: Dada Invades New York.* Whitney
  Museum of American Art. New York: Harry Abrams, 1996.

Parry, Albert. *Garrets and Pretenders: A History of Bohemianism in America.*
  New York: Covici Friede, 1933.

Reiss, Robert. "'My Baroness': Elsa von Freytag-Loringhoven." In Kuenzli, Rudolf
  E., ed. *New York Dada.* New York: Willis Locker & Owens, 1986.

Rule, Jane. *Lesbian Images.* New York: Doubleday, 1975.

Shreiber, Maeera, and Keith Tuma, eds. *Mina Loy: Woman and Poet.* Orono,
  Maine: National Poetry Foundation, University of Maine, 1998.

Stansell, Christine. *American Moderns: Bohemian New York and the Creation of a
  New Century.* New York: Metropolitan Books, 2000.

Taylor, Frank C., with Gerald Cook. *Alberta Hunter: A Celebration in Blues.* New
  York: McGraw Hill, 1987.

Van Doren, Carl. "Three Worlds, Elinor Wylie." In *The Portable Carl Van Doren.*
  New York: Viking, 1945.

Van Vechten, Carl. *Generations in Black & White: Photographs by Carl Van
  Vechten.* Edited by Rudolph P. Byrd. Athens, Georgia: University of Georgia
  Press, 1993.

Wall, Cheryl A. *Women of the Harlem Renaissance.* Bloomington and
  Indianapolis: Indiana University Press, 1995.

Ware, Caroline F. *Greenwich Village, 1920–1930.* New York: Harper Colophon
  Books, 1965.

Waters, Ethel, with Charles Samuels. *His Eye Is on the Sparrow.* New York: Da
  Capo Press, 1992.

Waters, Ethel. *To Me It's Wonderful.* New York: Harper & Row, 1972.

Watson, Steven. *Strange Bedfellows: The First American Avant-Garde.* New York:
  Abbeville Press, 1991.

Whelan, Richard. *Alfred Stieglitz: A Biography.* New York: Little, Brown, 1995.

Williams, William Carlos. *The Autobiography of William Carlos Williams.* New
  York: Random House, 1951.

Wilson, Edmund. *The Edmund Wilson Reader.* Edited with an Introduction and
  Notes by Lewis M. Dabney. New York: Da Capo Press, 1997.

Wood, Beatrice. *I Shock Myself: The Autobiography of Beatrice Wood.*
  San Francisco: Chronicle Books, 1985.

ILLUSTRATION CREDITS

ABBREVIATIONS

Beinecke: Courtesy of Yale Collection of American Literature, Beinecke Rare Book and Manuscript Library

Golda Meir Library: Golda Meir Library, University Manuscript Collection, University of Wisconsin, Milwaukee (Little Review Papers, 1914–1964)

Princeton: Princeton University Library, Rare Books and Special Collections (Sylvia Beach Papers)

Schlesinger Library: The Schlesinger Library, Radcliffe Institute, Harvard University.

Schomburg: Courtesy of Schomburg Center for Research in Black Culture, Photographs and Print Division, the New York Public Library

University of Maryland: Special Collections, University of Maryland Libraries, Djuna Barnes Papers

Pages ii, x: Jessie Tarbox Beals, Schlesinger Library. **xiv:** Frank Driggs, Schomburg.

INTRODUCTION: WILD IN PURSUIT

Pages 2, 4, 7, 8: Berenice Abbott © Museum of the City of New York. **10:** E. Simms Campbell, courtesy of Elizabeth Campbell Rollins. **12:** Frank Driggs, Schomburg.

1.
MINA LOY: A MODERN SELF-EXPERIMENT

Pages 14, 19, 47: Stephen Haweis, courtesy of Rare Book and Manuscript Library, Columbia University (Stephen Haweis Papers). **16:** Courtesy of Carolyn Burke. **18, 23:** Beinecke. **21, 22:** Henri le Savoureux, courtesy of Carolyn Burke. **25:** Futurismo & Futurismi, Katalog der Ausstellung, Mailand, 1986. **26:** Edward Steichen, Metropolitan Museum of Art. **29, 41, 43:** Courtesy of Roger L. Conover. **30:** William Eric Williams and New Directions Publishing Corp. **31, 35, 36, 38, 39:** Courtesy of Francis M. Naumann. **32:** Charles Sheeler, Philadelphia Museum of Art (The Louise and Walter Arensberg Collection). **33:** Man Ray, ©

Man Ray Trust, Paris/VG BildKunst, Bonn (University of Maryland). **40:** Ed Eich, Stevens Memorial Library, North Andover, Mass. **48:** Man Ray, © Man Ray Trust, Paris/VG BildKunst, Bonn (Princeton). **49:** University of Maryland. **50:** Berenice Abbott, © Museum of the City of New York. **53:** Princeton. **55:** Library of Congress. **56:** Man Ray, © Man Ray Trust, Paris/VG BildKunst, Bonn (Menil Collection, Houston).

2.
MARGARET ANDERSON AND JANE HEAP: LIFE FOR ART'S SAKE

Pages 58, 65: Golda Meir Library. **60:** Man Ray, © Man Ray Trust, Paris/VG BildKunst, Bonn (Library of Congress). **67, 77, 85:** Library of Congress. **70, 74, 81:** Berenice Abbott, © Commerce Graphics Ltd, Inc. (81: University of Maryland). **72:** Berenice Abbott, © Museum of the City of New York. **76:** Beinecke. **79:** Man Ray, © Man Ray Trust, Paris/VG BildKunst, Bonn (University of Maryland). **83:** Jessie Tarbox Beals, Schlesinger Library. **84:** Gotham Book Mart.

3.
EDNA ST. VINCENT MILLAY: IMPRISONED IN THE PERSONAL

Page 88: Mishkin. **91:** Arnold Genthe. **94, 95, 97, 99, 109** (109: Berenice Abbott, © Commerce Graphics. Ltd, Inc.), **101:** Jessie Tarbox Beals, Schlesinger Library. **100:** The Newbury Library, Chicago (Floyd Dell Papers). **105, 106, 117:** Beinecke. **111, 119, 121, 125, 130:** Special Collections, Vassar College Libraries.

4.
ENTERTAINING BOHEMIA: THE HOSTESSES AND THEIR SALONS

Pages 134, 136, 137, 138, 139, 141, 142 (142: Nicholas Muray), **145, 147, 149, 154** (154: Berenice Abbott, © Commerce Graphics, Ltd., Inc.): Beinecke. **144:** Library of Congress. **150, 155** (155: James VanDerZee, © Donna M. VanDerZee): Schomburg.

5.
BESSIE SMITH: 'TAIN'T NOBODY'S BUSINESS IF I DO!

Pages 160, 169: Frank Driggs, Schomburg. **164:** Corbis Bettman. **166:** *The Chicago Defender,* 1923. **172, 178, 186:** Berenice Abbott, © Museum of the City of New York. **180:** Carl Van Vechten, permission by Carl Van Vechten Trust, Beinecke. **183:** Nicholas Muray, *Vanity Fair,* July 1922.

6.
ETHEL WATERS: AM I BLUE?

Pages 192, 195, 203, 210: Beinecke. **198:** Berenice Abbott, © Museum of the City of New York. **204:** Moll Dieter, Das Buch des Blues. **206:** Frank Driggs, Schomburg. **213:** Rudolph Hoffman, private collection. **214:** Private collection. **217:** Courtesy of Keith de Lellis. **218:** Schomburg.

EPILOGUE:
THE END OF THE PARTY

Pages 220, 225: Berenice Abbott, © Museum of the City of New York.

INDEX